JEWISH LIFE IN RENAISSANCE ITALY

Jewish Life in
Renaissance
Italy

—

ROBERT BONFIL

translated by Anthony Oldcorn

University of California Press

Berkeley   Los Angeles

London

First published in 1991 as *Gli Ebrei in Italia nell'epoca del Rinascimento*
by Sansoni, Florence

The Publisher wishes to thank
The Lucius N. Littauer Foundation
for their generous donation

University of California Press
Berkeley and Los Angeles, California

University of California Press
London, England

Library of Congress Cataloging-in-Publication Data

Bonfil, Roberto.
    [Gli Ebrei in Italia nell'epoca del Rinascimento. English]
    Jewish life in Renaissance Italy / Robert Bonfil ;
translated by Anthony Oldcorn.
        p.   cm.
    Includes bibliographical references and index.
    ISBN 0-520-07350-9
    1. Jews — Italy — History.   2. Italy — Ethnic relations.
I. Title.
DS135.I8B6613   1994
945'.004924 — dc20   93-11424
                                                         CIP

Printed in the United States of America
    1   2   3   4   5   6   7   8   9

The paper used in this publication meets the minimum
requirements of American National Standard for Information
Sciences — Permanence of Paper for Printed Library Materials,
ANSI Z39.48-1984

TO THE JEWS OF ITALY
*among whom I lived
some of the best years
of my life*

CONTENTS

PREFACE

A NYONE FAMILIAR with the extraordinary wealth of material published in recent decades on the history of Italian Jewry has every reason to ask: is this volume really necessary? As far as the author is concerned, the answer is obviously in the affirmative. Indeed, I would go so far as to say that, as more and more books are published, with a frequency well-nigh impossible to keep up with, the more compelling the need for a work like the present study becomes.

The main tendency discernible in the current historiography of the Jews of Italy during the period covered by this book is that represented by scholars who have devoted their professional skills and energies to archival and paleographic research, bringing to light an enormous quantity of hitherto unknown materials. This is without question a praiseworthy enterprise, destined in the long run to prove more fruitful than any other. Nevertheless, the usefulness of the source documents published almost invariably outweighs the value of the accompanying analyses, whatever real value those analyses may ultimately have. Theories and interpretative models come and go, whereas historical "documents" remain, to solicit ever new readings.

And yet one of the paradoxical effects of the extraordinary preponderance of studies of this kind seems frequently, indeed almost inevitably, to be to pump new blood into outmoded interpretative theories and superannuated historiographical models, to serve, as it were, as *pièces justificatives* for a historical account designed to produce the impression that "the more things change, the more they stay the same." However up-to-date they may be with the most recent trends in historical scholarship, these studies tend to present themselves as a kind of updated version of the old kind of local history, informed by the desire to show how the heroes of the particular narrative are as fitted as any others to provide an appropriate illustration of the received model advocated by the general trend. As for the component parts of this model, for a long time now they have been those proposed by the illustrious masters of an earlier generation: Heinrich Graetz, Simon Dubnow, Israel Zinberg, Salo W. Baron, Cecil Roth, Umberto Cassuto, Vittore Colorni, Moses Avigdor Shulvass, and Attilio Milano. Dissatisfied as I am by the overall perspectives of current historiography, for some time now I have been suggesting partial revisions. And, although my proposals have found favor with a number of colleagues, for the most part specialists in cultural history,[1] so far no attempt has been made to present a unified overview from this particular standpoint.

I am convinced—in spite of the fact that I owe practically everything I know about the history of the Jewish minority in Italy to the works of the aforementioned masters, as well as to a number of others not mentioned by name—that it is their overall approach that produces a sense of dissatisfaction and compels us to go back and reread the sources. That approach, in fact, seems to be fed by a sense of uneasiness regarding the difference, or better the fundamental opposition, between the world of the (Christian) majority and that of the (Jewish) minority. As a result, the interpreter's chief concern seems to be the need to come to terms with this sense of uneasiness. The ways of doing so are extremely varied of course, depending on the particular ideological stance favored by each author. This is not the place to analyze the many variations on the prevailing theme. The reader who is patient enough to follow me will find some animadversions on the subject in the first part of the introduction and in chapter 3 of this book. In any case, taken altogether, the many variations on the theme make up a fairly rigidly structured whole from which the present work would like to distance itself in point of principle. As I see it, in fact, there is nothing to choose between those historians who attempt to minimize the difference/opposition, at times going so far as to present a picture of idyllic symbiosis, and those who tend on the contrary to exaggerate it, insisting only on the clashes between the two worlds seen in the context of what Salo W. Baron once called "the lachrymose conception of Jewish History"—in which the culprit is in each and every case the difference/opposition to which a purely negative role is assigned. I find both positions unacceptable.

In the present work, the difference/opposition between the world of the majority and that of the minority is seen as a pure and simple fact. Indeed, I cannot even deny the possibility that, as a member of the Jewish minority myself, I may in fact attribute to that difference/opposition a positive role. In any event, taking the fact of difference as our point of departure, the picture presented here is meant to be different from that usually found in current historiography, even its most recent manifestations. By adopting the point of view of the minority, my purpose has been to present the history of the Jews of Italy in the Renaissance and Baroque periods from the inside, from the point of view, in other words, of a historical subject who, having consciously opted to affirm his own diversity, faced the problem of defending it and giving it a meaning from which all residual tension and alienation had been expunged. A history "seen from the inside" is obviously not a history of isolation. Rather, it is the history of a coming to awareness of the Self in the act of specular reflection in the Other, by which I mean a reflection of oneself in the Other as in a mirror. This book is therefore intended as a concise account of a new reading of the sources undertaken with a view to identifying some of the component elements of that reflection, through an examination of the concrete expressions of everyday life and sociocultural activity. I have therefore taken care not to talk in terms of influences, of people participating in the world of the Other with the more or less guilty conscience that came from denying their own existence, of violence submitted to as the unavoidable price of not being forced to accept the alternative of detachment from one's own biological roots, of compromises arrived at simply in order to dispel tensions and alienation. I have tried instead to point out the component elements of the subject's *different* culture and the implications of that *difference* for the complex process of the insertion of the Jew into the sociocultural fabric of the Italian cities of the period.

This declaration of intentions is also a definition of the book — in a positive sense, as far as what the readers can expect to find in it is concerned, and in a negative sense, as regards what they should not expect to find here. What they will find is the result of a fresh reading of the sources, first undertaken some thirty years ago and in part already published in a series of specialized articles. There is no new material here, no original documentary "discovery." Nor will readers find detailed accounts of particular cases. The latter absence will probably be the one most noticed. It was the price, reluctantly paid, of achieving some kind of overall completeness in the necessarily limited available space. I say "reluctantly," in the first place because most of the preliminary studies, in which I was at liberty to go into greater detail and to engage in detailed textual analyses, are inaccessible to those of my potential readers unfamiliar with Hebrew and cannot therefore be considered complementary to the book itself; and, in the second place, because the choice necessitated a considerable effort of self-restraint on my part, if the book were not to become a collection of specialized essays or an enormous volume few would have been tempted to pick up.

In any event, the book as it stands presupposes the many contributions of earlier scholars, to whom it owes not only a debt of a documentary nature but also one of ideas, some of which were accepted and incorporated, whereas others served as a stimulus for further thought. Following the example of authors far more illustrious than myself, I have not included here, given the nature of the work, an elaborate "scientific" apparatus of quotations and references. They would have added little or nothing for the specialized reader and would have been of no use at all to the layman. In the notes, I have confined myself to listing the texts cited and, on rare occasions, to discussing one or two very recent studies, mostly to point out disagreements. The nonspecialist reader interested in pursuing matters further can in any case make up for the lack of a documentary apparatus by consulting the bibliographical note at the end of the volume. As for the specialist, he will have no trouble recognizing not only my debts to my predecessors but also my original contributions. After all, in the words of a tried and true rabbinical maxim (Mishnah, Avoth V, 7), one of the marks of the wise man is the ability to recognize the new, distinguishing it from what he has learned previously from other sources.

In concluding this brief prefatory note, I welcome the opportunity to thank cordially all those who have assisted me in various ways through the successive stages of the preparation of the text. In the first place, I thank my colleagues and friends, with whom I have discussed many of the book's major and minor arguments, and to whom I owe the all-important encouragement to persevere. In the second place, I thank my students, who, with their questions and objections, compelled me to re-think and reformulate more than one hypothesis. A heartfelt thanks to Anthony Oldcorn, who as translator not only had to struggle with a difficult text, but also to suffer my continuous intrusion upon his labors. Thanks also to the anonymous readers of the manuscript for their comments and suggestions, many of them extremely telling. A particular thanks to my good friend Benjamin Ravid, who read the first draft of the English translation and made many suggestions for its improvement. Thanks, too, to Stanley Holwitz, who encouraged me from the very beginning of our acquaintance, even before we set eyes on each other. His acceptance of the book for publication by the University of California Press was a model of dynamic decision making. I hope he will not be disappointed with the results. And last, thanks to Margaret Mullen, Diana Feinberg, Carol Lloyd, Rebecca Frazier, and Paula Cizmar for their invaluable assistance in the most delicate phases of the book's production.

Robert Bonfil
Hebrew University of Jerusalem

INTRODUCTION

ACCOUNTS of the history of the Jewish people in the Diaspora, from the year C.E. 70 to the present, oscillate between what Salo W. Baron defined as *"the lachrymose conception of Jewish history"* and what, paraphrasing Baron, we might call *"the antilachrymose conception of Jewish history."* This oscillation seems rooted in the elementary fact that for two thousand years, the existence of the Jews, unlike that of the non-Jewish peoples — Christians or Moslems — among whom they lived, has never been accepted as self-evident or taken for granted. Jewish existence is perceived as an *anomaly*. As such, it arouses curiosity, attracts interest, occasionally promotes the raising of consciousness, cries out for an explanation, and insists on being formulated in a variety of contexts from which it is difficult for value judgments to be excluded. All in all, as Benedetto Croce would have said, all history is contemporary history, because history is an integral part of the conception of the Self and its relation to the Other.

It is impossible not to question the inevitability, the appropriateness, indeed the very legitimacy of the persistence of this anomaly. Consequently, it is difficult, almost impossible, not to formulate a value judgment on the historical reality examined, on both the ideological and the factual levels. In the present instance, one is led to consider the available options: the choice of preserving Jewish Otherness, albeit at the cost of discrimination, oppression, and sociocultural alienation, of a life, in other words, lived in that constant state of psychological trauma which accompanies any abnormal mode of existence, whether freely chosen or imposed from without; or, alternatively, the denial of the right of Jewish Otherness to exist, at the cost of the annihilation of one's own identity — an option that may also be either spontaneously chosen or externally imposed. The various ways these prices-to-pay have been assessed have their roots in the psychology of the judges, in their culture and their mentalities. To speak of the heroism of those who chose to preserve Otherness, or of the grave responsibilities of those who made the choice so difficult, even impossible — instead of insisting on the senselessness and stubbornness of the choice itself — amounts to nothing less than passing judgment on the dramatis personae of history.

The contemporary relevance of the history of the Jews of Italy seems to be a necessary consequence of these general considerations in that it seems to present in a particularly acute form the problem of the integration of a minority into a space dominated by the Other. What are the necessary and sufficient conditions for satisfactory integration to take place; what are the means by which it is brought about and the obstacles placed in its way? In a word, what do we mean by "satisfactory integration"? In our own time, this problem appears to have been vested with an enormous importance, as part of the more general series of problems pertaining to international institutions, imperialism (political, military, cultural, and ideological), interracial relations, and so on. As a specific case, which paradigmatically concerns the relationship with the Other, our topic seems indeed to call into question the usefulness of the distinction between integration and acculturation, if by the latter we imply the absorption of one group by another.

We tend instinctively to distinguish between the two: integration is seen as a *positive* phenomenon, the symbol of cooperation, equality, fraternity, and reciprocal enrichment; acculturation, however, is seen as a *negative* phenomenon, the symbol of oppression, of the imposition of the cultural values of the stronger party, and hence of reciprocal impoverishment — impoverishment of the weaker party, who is compelled to abandon his own cultural heritage, but also of the stronger, since he proved unable to take advantage of the encounter, concerned as he was only to impose himself on the other. But is it really possible to distinguish between reciprocal enrichment and the impoverishment of assimilation? Are we sure we are not relinquishing an essential part of our truth the moment we recognize the truth of the Other? Do we not believe that there is a Superior Truth to which all other truths are inferior and therefore destined to succumb? And, if this is indeed the case, have we really taken sides with the partisans of integration, or have we not passed almost imperceptibly into the negative camp of the partisans of acculturation? Does the term "assimilation" itself carry with it a positive or negative connotation? Whatever our answers, it is the awareness of their own identity on the part of the members of the minority as well as of the majority that is called into question. The history of the Jews of Italy in the Renaissance is the history of the encounter between a minority determined to perpetuate its own Otherness and a majority equally bent on its assimilation.

The prevailing interpretation of the history of the Jews in the Renaissance derives from, is indeed intimately bound up with, the idea historians have of the Renaissance itself. This is certainly not the place to reopen the old controversies, great and small, that surround this question. Historians' choice, their selection of topics and events, is nevertheless part and parcel of their point of view. What point of view is one to choose then, if one wishes to take in the panorama in the most effective way? It is probably true that today, more than a hundred years after the appearance of Jacob Burckhardt's *Die Kultur der Renaissance in Italien*, first published in Basel in 1860,[1] a good proportion of the interpretative categories Burckhardt proposed have managed to survive the destructive criticism to which the book has since been subjected. It seems equally true, however, that our reliance upon these categories is no longer the same as it once was. On the one hand, the modern tendency to shy away from large syntheses, preferring instead detailed descriptions of very limited segments of the overall picture, using techniques of analysis previously unthinkable, has led to a curious situation: everything that is not the immediate object of such meticulous analyses is left to the old syntheses. The result is a persistence of terms and concepts difficult to characterize unless we call them "inertial." On the other hand, the growing interest in the study of mental attitudes has led us to reevaluate the testimony of the people of the Renaissance and to discover in it points of contact with the old interpretative categories, which were based, more than those that came later, on that firsthand testimony.

The tendency for modern historians to give greater weight to the general features of society than to exceptional personalities has probably weakened the force of the arguments of those who attempted to demonstrate the existence of every kind of mentality in every historical period. A modern reading of the story of Abelard and Heloise could hardly minimize the fundamental differences between their time and the time that produced, say, Guarino Guarini, Marsilio Ficino, and Pico della Mirandola (which was also the time of Poggio Bracciolini, Lorenzo Valla, Coluccio Salutati, Giannozzo Manetti, Vespasiano da Bisticci, Flavio Biondo, and Francesco Datini, and of popes like Pius II, Leo X, and Clement VII, to cite a few of the more significant names). The culture of the Renaissance can certainly not be compared to that of the Middle Ages, particularly when one considers the awareness of a sense of a break with the preceding period to which the men of the Renaissance themselves are the first to bear witness. Wherever one looks, one sees the same change in mentality, a new breadth of horizons and interests. One need only think of Vespasiano da Bisticci, "the king of booksellers." In imitation of the classical model of Aristeas, King Ptolemy's librarian, da Bisticci accumulated, according to his own estimate, five thousand volumes. (Others speak, more modestly, of three thousand volumes; but even if there had been no more than one thousand, his would still have been an extraordinary collection of Greek and Latin books, to say nothing of those in the Italian vernacular.) But it is not the number of books that ought to be stressed so much as their contents. No subject was slighted: original works on grammar, poetry, history, rhetoric, dialectic, cosmography, architecture, mathematics, music, astrology, painting, sculpture, the art of war, agriculture, civil and canon law, and theology, to say nothing, of course, of the commentaries. With the new interests, tastes also changed. Niccolò Niccoli, on whom the Medici lavished the funds to create one of the most prestigious libraries of the day, liked to sit down to dinner surrounded by archeological finds and have himself served on artistic porcelain plates. The new mentality changed people's attitudes toward reality and the imagination, toward the world they had inherited and the world they wanted to build in order to live better at their ease.

The dialogue with the past led to the discovery of new points of view, taught new lessons, opened up new directions of enterprise and inquiry. When Flavio Biondo wrote his *History of Italy*, he built a bridge between his own time and classical antiquity, spanning what was for him a millennium of barbaric darkness, with which, as Voltaire was to put it more brutally later, it was not worth bothering. When Lorenzo Valla discovered the elegances of the Latin language, he also discovered the techniques of critical philology and what it was capable of when placed in the service of political thought. When Aeneas Sylvius Piccolomini ascended the papal throne as Pius II (a name chosen to match his Virgilian given name), he never forgot what he had learned in the course of his experience as a humanist: that it was preferable, for example, to imitate the wisdom of the people of Florence and nominate as papal chancellor a man versed in eloquence rather than one skilled in jurisprudence.

Although we are by now accustomed to distinguishing between the "modernity" of the Renaissance and that of our own day, nevertheless it is true that the so-called medievalness of many aspects of the fifteenth and sixteenth centuries is negligible compared with the profound differences between these centuries and those that preceded them. Among these were such characteristics as the individualism of the men of the Renaissance, their consciousness of being in revolt against the "barbarisms" inherited from their ancestors, their consciousness of living in a period of total renewal, and hence of the responsibility to cultivate an extremely acute critical sense. Nor, it seems, can there be any doubt concerning their rediscovery of the desire for fame, their cult of Classical Antiquity and its archeological monuments, their literary humanism, their passion for seeking out lost classical texts over which they would then pore without the mediation of the "barbarous" authors of the Middle Ages. This quest and this study led to innovations whose importance for Western civilization can hardly be overemphasized: the spirit of civic humanism (in the admirable phrase of Hans Baron, which I cannot bring myself to enclose in quotes); the reevaluation of rhetoric as a cultural ideal, which led to the exceptional blossoming of historiography; examples of social mobility unthinkable in the foregoing period; the discovery of the human body and its needs and of the pleasures of bourgeois life (an adjective, incidentally, which I use without any negative connotations)— sociability, good music, theater, sport, games and pastimes—everything, in short, that our modern sensibility sees as culturally positive.

But it is not our intention here to write the history of the Italian Renaissance. This is supposed to be a book of Jewish history. The perspective adopted will be that of a minority, the center of our attention that minority's budding self-awareness. The features characterizing the majority will be referred to only insofar as they are relevant to this perspective. Yet these features, which condition members of the minority through a process that is anything but straightforward, will always be there in the background. In point of fact, the coming to self-awareness of this tiny minority took place in this period, as is indeed everywhere and invariably the case, in terms of the Other, as a result of a process of two-way mirroring: the mirroring of the Self in the Other, as a pole of comparison acting as a catalyst for self-definition; and the mirroring of the Other in Oneself, as an element bearing the essential components of that very self-definition. In any case, what one has to deal with is a set of relationships of conjunction as well as of disjunction between the Self and the Other. Our account examines these relationships. What were the patterns of interaction between the history of the persons mentioned above in a wholly positive light and that of the Jewish minority?

In point of fact, a whole modern historiographic tradition, romantic as well as idealistic, which has its roots in the sense of unease felt by European Jewry in the period of the Emancipation—in the course, that is, of the restructuring of Jewish sociocultural identity in its relationship with the Other, for which it evinced a strong acculturational or assimilational attraction—has until now presented the history of the Jews in the Renaissance as a model of felicitous acculturation and assimilation. This *Weltanschauung* can be satisfactorily explained by bearing in mind two of its principal components, or better, two halves of the same proposition. The first assumption is that the participation of the Jews in the progress of mankind is conditioned by the willingness of the Other to tear down the barriers of isolation and segregation and, provided the Jews demonstrate the necessary virtues, accept them as equals. This assumption is coupled with the parallel assumption that the Jews' participation is also dependent on their willingness to collaborate in tearing down the barriers, to cease seeing them as a justifiable protection for their own backward isolationism. Such was the conviction of the enlightened Jewish minds of Central and Eastern Europe in the last century, people who had grown up in the Jewish cultural tradition of those regions and were in full reaction against their world, which they saw as paralyzed by the exclusive authority it attributed to a Talmudism inadequately studied and understood. Victims of an inferiority complex with regard to the culture of the Other, the best solution they could come up with was acculturation, largely conceived of in terms of assimilation. Naturally they were on the lookout for historical models that could serve as paradigms on which to base their own ideological arguments. In this sense, the histories of the Jews of Italy in the Renaissance or the Jews of Spain in the Golden Age were made to order as paradigms of the desired process of acculturation.

This was how the importance of the Jews in the various local economies came to be exaggerated, as was the cordiality shown them by the Christians, a cordiality that was alleged to have favored the social integration of the Jews, which in its turn supposedly exerted a salutary cultural influence. This explains their insistent idealizing of the character of the Renaissance, which was seen as the precursor of the modern period. The idea was to present a picture of Jewish society in the process of giving way to centrifugal forces and forsaking the distinguishing features of its Jewishness, in other words, a Jewish society in the grip of an impulse toward assimilation, touched off by the close contacts that were a consequence of the high degree of integration, as well as by the force of attraction exerted by Renaissance cultural values. These values by their very nature could lead only to the progressive erosion of the traditional body of specifically Jewish culture. The most famous representatives of this historiographic trend do not appear to have been troubled by the fear that a mechanism of this kind might eventually have led to the total disappearance of the cultivated Jewish minority. From their point of view, this danger probably seemed out of the question: their consciousness of being the bearers of a cultural and religious tradition worth saving seemed to afford them sufficient protection. The same can hardly be said for their present-day epigones, less saddled as a rule with religious convictions and far less concerned by the prospect of total assimilation. As things turned out, in the historical situation we are about to study, the opportunity for verification never materialized. From this viewpoint, the mechanism that might have led to the disappearance of the cultivated Jewish minority suffered a setback as a result of the particular historical moment, a setback for which the Jews themselves were in no way responsible. To define the historical moment, one has merely to mention the expulsion of the Jews from Spain, the repressive climate in Italy after the Council of Trent, and the great crisis of the sixteenth century.

The process has been described any number of times, more than once in enthusiastic terms, by Cecil Roth for one; in Roth's view, "in no part of the world did such a feeling of friendliness prevail between the people and the Jews as in Italy"[2] during the Renaissance, a period that, adopting the historical point of view of Jacob Burckhardt, Roth saw as already coming to flower back in the times of Emperor Frederick II. The general lines of Burckhardt's interpretation, construed along vaguely Hegelian lines and backed up with the erudition of historians like the great Heinrich Graetz, adapted itself very well in fact to the topic at hand, permitting even historians more sensitive than Roth to evidence that might have undermined the supposed idyll to adopt without a qualm the model of thesis-antithesis-synthesis, and to explain away the contradictions by the dialectical process, pointing out how they had been transcended.

But was the sky of Italy really so blue and so bright for the Renaissance Jew? Did he really hear in the air such joyful and seductive music, inviting him to enjoy "laughter and singing and perhaps drinking in the streets" in an atmosphere of extreme cordiality that, according to Cecil Roth, would have shocked only the most fanatic? And what about the Jews who stayed home cultivating a tendency to cover their eyes and plug their ears so as not to see the blue sky and not to hear the marvelous music, closing themselves off in their own conservative particularism?

The implications of these questions for today are immediately evident. Did the refusal to assimilate and self-destruct really call for a gesture of detachment similar to Ulysses' refusal to be lured by the song of the Sirens? And was a refusal of that kind really an act of commendable heroism, or was it instead the expression of unforgivable attachment to old-fashioned values that could only perpetuate the sense of a useless *martyrdom*? Why not see self-destruction as the climax of the lover's erotic ideal, and, consequently, why not do everything in one's power to ensure its realization? The history of the Italian Jews in the Renaissance provides a historical paradigm for all these questions. In the following pages, I would like to propose a reading of this history from a point of view somewhat different from that currently adopted. But first, a few words about the space-time coordinates.

One of the most difficult problems is how to organize the history of the Jews of Italy within the framework of the period that interests us, since the history of Italy itself presents problems of organization. The history of Italy in our period continues to be a source of perplexity for scholars because of the extremely fragmented and unstable political configuration of the region. The general trend has always been to reduce the fragmentation of the discourse, as far as possible, while at the same time avoiding gross oversimplifications. How far to push such a trend obviously depends on personal idiosyncracies, conditioned at times by factors of a banal nature, such as the space available to the author. What is true for historians of Italy is equally true, of course, for historians of the Jews in Italy.

Cecil Roth, for instance, compelled to condense the entire history of the Jews in the Middle Ages into thirty-two pages for the *Cambridge Medieval History*,[3] presents Italy, dividing it into *"three, or even four separate zones,"* closely related to the *"bewildering political conditions of the country."* The zones were the free communes and independent cities of the north, the territories of the Church, the kingdom of Naples, and Sicily. This division must have seemed to Roth to correspond to the functional needs of his narrative, since he was to use it again in his *History of the Jews in Italy*,[4] where he was not compelled to do so by considerations of space. Nevertheless it is hard to accept it as a satisfactory solution to the question of the fragmented political configuration. Though the last three of the zones mentioned by Roth do in fact correspond to three political entities, more or less clearly defined from a geographical point of view, the same cannot be said of the first, which puts into one basket all of the independent cities, each of which could rightfully lay claim to independent treatment. Where is the difference in fact, in such a schema, between the kingdom of Naples and the Venetian Republic?

Moses Avigdor Shulvass, in his *The Jews in the World of the Renaissance,*[5] to this day the only book devoted entirely to our topic, proposes a schema divided into ten areas: Venice, Lombardy, Piedmont, Monferrato, Mantua, the Territories of the House of Este (Ferrara, Modena, Reggio) and the Principality of Parma, the Territories of the Church, the Principality of Urbino, the Kingom of Naples, and the Islands (Sicily, Sardinia, and Malta). It is a hybrid schema, perhaps of Burckhardtian inspiration, in which considerations of a political nature are mixed with geographical considerations in a way that is far from self-evident. Even less self-evident is the schema adopted by Salo W. Baron in the chapter significantly entitled "Italian Potpourri" in his monumental *Social and Religious History of the Jews* (vol. 10). This schema comprises a division into five zones: Southern Italy (including the Islands), the Territories of the Church, Tuscany and the other regions linked to the Church, the Northwest, and Venice and her Territories.

Here I would like to adopt a simpler schema, employing a dichotomy that would perhaps have been obvious to contemporaries: on the one hand the Peninsula, on the other the Islands, Sardinia and especially Sicily. This is clearly a geographical division. I do not propose it, however, merely on account of the difficulties arising from the fluidity of the political situation, but rather because, as will be seen, this dichotomy corresponded to another fairly clear-cut socioeconomic division. It was this last-mentioned fact that struck me as particularly convincing. The Jews in fact were only indirectly involved in politics. Political events to be sure *conditioned* Jewish lives in many ways, but the events themselves were certainly not *influenced* by the presence of the Jews. In terms of the history of the Jewish people, Italian political events are an entirely external factor to which the Jews responded in a totally *passive* manner since Jews could not, did not expect to, indeed did not even aspire to take an organically active part beyond the attempts at "lobbying," which can well be imagined. The Jews were, however, for better or for worse, organically involved on the socioeconomic level, playing an active role, with a specific function to perform, either as the instruments of power, or more simply as defenders of particular vested interests. Jewish society itself seems to have been modeled by behaviors that adhered to mental categories not very different from those of their Christian neighbors. As far as the socioeconomic profile of Italy is concerned, the Jews appear, then, to have played an active role. As a result, a set of socieconomic parameters seems better suited to the attempt to give an account of Jewish history than a set of parameters of a political nature.

From the political point of view, the period that interests us extends from the end of the thirteenth century to the end of the sixteenth. It is the period known to historians as the period of the Lordships (Signorie) and Principalities (Principati). The semantic distinction between the two terms is intended to underscore the fact that the lords were on occasion also princes, in the sense that their noble titles and their power were formally (and sometimes more than formally) conferred upon them by the pope or the emperor. There were, however, also the Republics and the Kingdoms. Venice and Florence were the most important of the former, then came Genoa, Lucca, and Siena. The territories of Naples, Sicily, and Sardinia were ruled by monarchs. As for the lords, who ruled over the rest of the peninsula, the most important were the Lords of Milan and Savoy, in addition of course to the pope who, as a prince, ruled over the territories of the Church. Next came the Gonzagas, Lords of Mantua; the Este family, Lords of Ferrara; the Carraras, Lords of Padua; the Montefeltros, Lords of Urbino; and so on. Of course, the fact that the Lordships were more numerous than the Kingdoms and the Republics is not sufficient reason to justify defining the whole period as the period of the Lordships. The point of the definition is rather to underscore the fact that the characteristic modes of exercising power were everywhere the same: kings, popes, and doges governed and behaved like lords, even if the way they conquered power, or otherwise acquired it, differed from that of the dukes and the marquises. Perhaps it can be affirmed as a general principle that the Lordships came into existence practically everywhere as a result of the struggles for power between oligarchical groups and were based on the capacity, real or virtual, of the lords to guarantee public order, security, and the prosperity of their citizens. The lords conquered power in various ways, from nomination in regular elections down to violence pure and simple, transferring into their own hands the financial and juridical organization, and above all the military power (usually provided by mercenary soldiers, which naturally freed the citizens from military service). Military might ended up as a tool in the hands of the lord, who could use it, as he often did, to bolster his own power and satisfy his ambitions for conquest, rather than to guarantee the protection of the citizens. In practice, both petty and powerful tyrants were constantly busy expanding their territories at the expense of their neighbors. The two roles were not mutually exclusive; rather, they were complementary, since the tyrants could not have held onto the power if they had not given their citizens a sense of security and well-being.

Power found itself faced on every side with particularistic tendencies: on the one hand the feudal aspirations of the great houses or the ecclesiastical institutions; on the other, the aspirations of the communal institutions toward independence, which were the expression of the "bourgeoisie's" defense of its own self-interest. An economic factor was added to the relationships between the various forces, which made them more complex: a monarch, for example, might one day be driven by economic considerations (such as the need to secure ready cash) to recognize feudal rights, only to annul all such concessions the following day for considerations of the same kind. It follows that, in such a context, there were constant rivalries between the various aristocratic groups who surrounded the tyrant. The most vivid example of this kind of situation is probably Sicily, where the local Sicilian aristocracy was forever at daggers drawn with the aristocracy of Catalan origin. Over and above these generalizations, the particular physiognomy of each place was conditioned by an infinite variety of political, social, economic, and cultural situations. In this connection, it has rightly been said that *"to the one hundred Italian cities corresponded in the long run a thousand different oligarchies which mixed landed interests, mercantile, financial, feudal residues or solid bourgeois structures, political adventurers and parvenus."*[6]

The propensity toward territorial expansion, more typical of the more powerful states, such as Venice, Milan, or the kingdom of Naples, was naturally one factor making for the unification of an extremely fragmentary scene. Other contributing factors can also be cited: what remained, for example, of the Roman imperial spirit, a certain sense of Italian unity nourished by the common cultural tradition, and the reverential attitude professed toward the Roman Church. In any case, all these factors together failed to prevail over the centrifugal forces. The force for religious unity was neutralized by the temporal aspect of papal power, which not only stood in the way of the tendency to give a political expression to Catholic piety, but at times succeeded in creating hotbeds of anticlericalism. Jacob Burckhardt interpreted this mixture of Catholic devotion and anticlericalism, which can still be found in Italy today, in terms of individualism, in accord with his overall interpretation of the Renaissance. In any event, the tendency of the great to gobble up the small was certainly not a trait exclusive to the Renaissance! Italy was to achieve unity and definitive extension of its sovereignty to Rome only in 1871. Up until then no Italian state had sufficient strength to impose itself on the others and force them to give up their independence, though it should be said that toward the end of the sixteenth century the extreme fragmentation typical of the preceding period was somewhat reduced, and a small number of states achieved a kind of equilibrium within the framework of a more or less stable political structure.

A first set of characteristics of the period seems, then, to have been the result of the fragmentation and instability of the political scene, as a consequence of the ambition, competition, violence, opportunism, and cynicism of the powerful. The old rivalry between pope and emperor persisted in the background. Every Italian state contracted alliances, only to break them immediately according to the most time-honored rules of political cynicism and opportunism. Popes and emperors could only recognize de jure what had been conquered de facto by force. Political tension and wars were, as a result, endemic. A second set of characteristics of the period, given this context, appears to have been a more or less widespread sense of insecurity and general anxiety. No one would have dared predict the political future of any city. But, when all is said and done, can one really be sure that security and stability, so important for our modern mentality, were also the ideal for the mentality of the Renaissance lords and their contemporaries? Be that as it may, if one were to attempt to measure in some way the intensity of the political instability and fragmentation in the entire region, one would probably reach the very schematic conclusion that these features increased gradually as one moved from the South toward the North. In other words, in states with a monarchical form of government (Sicily, the Kingdom of Naples, and, in some sense, the State of the Church), conservative and centripetal forces seem to have had the upper hand over subversive and centrifugal forces. This statement is especially true for Sicily, which was an island in far more than the literal sense of the word: here the conservative bent was evident on several other levels, as will soon be seen. This is already a justification, however approximate, of the dichotomic division adopted between Sicily and the rest of the Peninsula.

The very nature of the process that led to the formation of the system of Lordships produced at the same time the socioeconomic features peculiar to the various regions. When the Lordships, emerging from the struggles for power between oligarchic groups, showed a tendency to become hereditary, those same groups began to consider the exercise of the governmental function as a kind of noble family prerogative. The aristocracy tended to disassociate itself from any kind of productive activity, a phenomenon that reached its height in the sixteenth century, but which was quite discernible during the course of the preceding century. The nobility remained attached to landed property, which ensured a good income with a minimum of risk and expense of energy. Landed property seemed preferable to mercantile or banking ventures, all the more so after the memorable bankruptcies of the fourteenth century. To be a rich landed proprietor was furthermore an ideal condition for those who wanted time to themselves to cultivate their political, cultural, or artistic ambitions. All of this presupposed a certain persistence of feudal structures in the world of the nobility, who preferred to live in the cities at the court of the lords rather than in the countryside and who did so by exploiting the labor of the peasants, whose rights remained inferior to those of city-dwellers. In this context, if one wishes to measure the intensity of the feudal-archaic aspect of the socioeconomic structures, one will find it stronger in the South than in the North, reaching its high point in Sicily. Medieval structures persisted very strongly and more than elsewhere in Sicily on the economic, social, institutional, and cultural levels. This is a further trait of the phenomenon which, as will be seen later in detail, had important consequences for the history of the Jews, in particular as regards their demographic distribution and the stratification of the trades and professions that determine the socioeconomic profile of the groups. But it is not our intention, we repeat, to write a history of Italy in the Renaissance period. The considerations so far advanced seem sufficient at this point to justify our division and allow us to proceed with our account.

PART ONE
STRUCTURES OF SETTLEMENT AND THE ECONOMY

I
THE LAWS OF ·
TOPODEMOGRAPHIC
DISTRIBUTION

First Phase:
Italy, Land of Immigration
The Dynamic Laws of Settlement

STATIC AND DYNAMIC FACTORS

THE DEMOGRAPHIC distribution of the Jewish presence in Italy, from the close of the thirteenth century throughout practically the whole of the fifteenth, came about as the result of a process that can be reconstructed with a fair degree of accuracy. In Sicily, from thirty to thirty-five thousand Jews, spread over twenty or so different localities, chiefly Palermo, Syracuse, and Messina, continued a presence that went back more than a thousand years, a presence that was substantially *static* in character. On the mainland, in contrast, the demographic distribution of the Jews was essentially *dynamic*: here the Jews seemed to be constantly on the move. Their constant mobility makes it impossible to determine their number, though one will not be too far off the mark in estimating them at another twenty-five to thirty thousand souls, out of a total peninsula population of between eight and ten million. With the exception of Rome, which, as will be seen later, constituted a point of departure rather than a point of arrival, the Italian peninsula was for the Jews, during this initial phase of our period, a land of immigration. This feature can be added to the dichotomy between Sicily and the mainland mentioned in the introduction.

There was an upward migratory flow, headed northward, of Jews of Italian origin, from Rome for the most part, and a twofold downward flow, toward the south, of Jews of French and German origin. The French Jews, for the most part refugees expelled from their country in 1394, arrived from the west, whereas the German Jews, victims of the persecutions that came in the wake of the terrible plague of 1348, came down from the north in a slow but continuous stream. Others came in small groups from Alsace, the Rhine regions, even Poland. A return migration, on a reduced scale, was also recorded into southern Italy, from which the Jews had been expelled in 1291. Those involved were, for the most part, Jews of Italian origin, who were joined, roughly speaking toward the end of the fifteenth century, by a number of German and Spanish Jews.

THE REASONS FOR THE MIGRATIONS

WHAT DROVE these people to move? In the first place, they moved because of conditions of absolutely ineluctable necessity—expulsions, such as those mentioned above, to which others were added. These included the expulsion, for instance, of the Jews from the northeastern cities of Treviso, Vicenza, Feltre, Cividale del Friuli, and Udine, which probably occurred in the second half of the fifteenth century, an account of which can be found in a brief published chronicle.[1] Next, a reason to move was a wide variety of ways of evaluating one's circumstances, in the light of which some places of residence might appear considerably less advantageous than others. In some instances, the motive may have been the pure and simple quest for adventure. The Jews, in any case, were not the only ones to display this behavior. Migrations made in the hope of finding better living conditions in the chosen destination than in one's place of origin were an everyday affair. The Italian cities north of Rome, which were experiencing a phase of expansion and economic development, naturally favored this general trend through a relatively liberal policy with regard to the granting of citizenship, of a share, that is, in the rights and protection enjoyed by their own citizens. This circumstance provides a possible key to the extraordinary capacity demonstrated by the Italian states at the end of the Middle Ages to make the most of their human resources and therefore expand. Setting aside the sense of civic commitment or other values typical of the Renaissance, the interest someone might have in becoming and remaining a citizen (cives) of another city was often so strong as to justify any manner of sacrifice that city might demand. Seen in this perspective, the migratory movements of the Jews are perhaps one of the most typical expressions of their participation in the spirit of the century. Their migrations must also have been regulated, like those of the Christians, perhaps even more so, by the elementary terms of the age-old law of supply and demand.

It is not difficult to imagine how the various socioeconomic structures affected this law, making it more difficult for Jews to be accepted in those places where trade and professional guilds or groups of merchants enjoyed strong influence and translated their fear of competition into genuine hostility toward the Jews. Any investigation into the elements of the law of supply and demand which governed the migratory movements of the Jews can certainly take its cue from this essentially economic factor. Where this factor was operative, it was capable of permanently preventing Jewish settlement. In fact, commercially and industrially developed cities were very reluctant to accept Jews during the period that concerns us. Some, like Genoa and Milan, refused outright to allow Jews to settle there. Others, like Florence and Venice, allowed them in relatively late and after considerable hesitation.

ANTI-JEWISH HATRED AND THE PROPAGANDA OF THE MENDICANT FRIARS

THE DYNAMICS of opposition to Jewish settlement were, however, far more complex than appears from considerations of a purely economic nature. If one is to understand the problem better, one must return to a number of commonplaces that recent historiography has occasionally tended to forget. First and foremost, it should be emphasized that the presence of the Jews was, theoretically speaking, a circumstance abnormal enough to trouble a good Christan conscience, and hence was in constant need of justification. A particularly intense sentiment of Christian orthodoxy among the rulers was more than sufficient to prevent Jewish settlement or to provoke their expulsion. At times, the appeal to orthodoxy was simply a transparent pretext camouflaging more simple and ingenuous calculations of political pragmatism, such, for example, as the desire to curry favor with the ecclesiastical authorities by making a show of strong opposition to the acceptance of Jews or by support for their expulsion. But, more often than not, it was a case of a sincere feeling of Christian orthodoxy on the part of those who believed that the day of divine judgment was at hand. Above all, one should not forget the friars of the mendicant orders, who preached vehement sermons to the crowds gathered in the churches and public squares, and whom the local municipal councils could ill afford to ignore. "In my opinion, we ought to make provision, either by ordinances or by whatever other means may prove more effective, to drive out and expel from within the city limits and from the surrounding *contado* [countryside] all of the Jews making usurious loans in our city, because, as Friar Bernardino repeated in his recent preachings, they devour our flesh and blood with their usury, without our being aware of it,"[2] exclaimed a counselor from Foligno shortly after the visit of a Franciscan preacher to his city. And, rather than being an exceptional case, this was the rule.

The mendicant friars sometimes had a decisive say in determining the fate of the Jews of the period. In the eyes of the Observants, animated as they were — in the words of Léon Poliakov, to whom the present outline is not a little indebted — by a psychological dynamic which lay in "an inextricable mixture of love for the Christian people and hatred for the Jews," the latter were seen above all as usurers and enemies of the poor, and therefore as doubly odious.[3] The truth is that the Jews, as will be seen, were not all usurers; but this did not prevent the stereotypes spread by the hostile propaganda of the itinerant friars, especially the Franciscans, from dwelling almost exclusively upon this one aspect of their activity. The tendency to identify the Jews as usurers had taken root so profoundly in the mentality of the period that it can easily be unearthed even in linguistic expressions still current in our day. Bernardino of Siena (1380–1444), Giacomo della Marca (1391–1476), Giovanni da Capistrano (1386–1456), Bernardino da Feltre (1439–1494) are only the best-known names among a profusion of Observants who spread terror amongh the Jews. Exploiting the most venomous associations of ideas whenever they mentioned the Jews, the monks insisted in their sermons above all on the ancient myths of ritual murder, the profanation of the sacred host, and most of all on the rhetorical image of the blood sucked by Jewish moneylenders, immediately associated with the blood of Christ and with ritual murder. "You are far worse than pagans," thundered Giovanni da Capistrano, "by reason of the crime committed by you against Christ; you should be slaves, not only of the Christians, but also of Saracens and pagans."[4] Even more explicit was the less famous bishop of Amelia, Ruggero Mandosi, when he compared the Jews to powerful and voracious bears, or to rabid dogs, who, jaws gaping horribly open, suck the blood of good Christians.[5] How often one encounters this comparison of the Jews with bloodsuckers! How often we are reminded that, wherever the Jews have been permitted to lend out money on interest, the almost inevitable result has been the impoverishment of Christians. "In Bassano, a town in Lombardy," preached Bernardino da Feltre in Florence, "there was a Jew who lent out money at interest for forty-two years, so depleting the city and its surrounding *contado* that there is no longer a penny to be found there."[6] It appears that this was one of the Observants' arguments that never failed to make an impression. The head prior of Foligno mentioned above was so struck by it that he added to his proposal to expel the Jews the following consideration: "You heard what a vast sum they are able to accumulate by lending out fifty ducats at thirty percent interest for fifty years!" And how could it have failed to make an impression on the minds of the common people in the far-off fourteenth century, if there have even been modern historians who, on the basis of the same arithmetic as Bernardino's, have seriously claimed that in 1495, little more than fifty years after they were admitted to the city, the Jewish moneylenders in Florence had accumulated nothing less than the fabulous sum of 49,792,556 florins?[7]

But the preachers were not always so explicit in their sermons. Frequently ambiguous, they were not above playing upon double entendres, thereby encouraging the climate of violence without openly preaching it. Fortunato da Perugia, for instance, insistently defended the founding of a Monte di Pietà (loan bank) in Amelia in words whose meaning was far from transparent: "This crime of usury, and the excommunication it brings with it, is a horrible and grievous sin visited upon the entire population of Amelia, as a result of the charter of agreement concluded with the Jews."[8] What did he imply in practice? That they should throw themselves upon the Jews? Carry out a pogrom? Drive them out of the city perhaps? Or would it be sufficient simply to annul the clauses relating to usury contained in the residence permit issued to the Jews? In Orvieto the agreement with the Jews was annulled after the visit of Bernardino da Siena, who in addition boasted openly of having caused the expulsion of the Jews from Vicenza.

However ambiguous they might be, the semantics of the terms "usury" and "usurer" were sufficiently clear as to leave no doubt as to their immediate target: the Jews. To whom was Bernardino da Siena referring when he promised his listeners a sermon on usury "which would make them go into a cold sweat even in mid-January"? In theory, of course, he was referring not necessarily to the Jews. Still, given that the term "usurer" was generally used as a synonym of "Jew," Bernardino was in fact referring only to the Jews. On other occasions he could be more explicit:

Money is the vital heat of a city. The Jews are leeches who ask for nothing better than the opportunity to devour an ailing member, whose blood they suck with insatiable ardor. When heat and blood abandon the extremities of the body to flow back to the heart, it is a sign that death is near. But the danger is even more imminent when the wealth of a city is in the hands of the Jews. Then the heat no longer flows, as it does normally, towards the heart. As it does in a plague-ridden body, it moves towards the ailing member of the body; for every Jew, especially if he is a moneylender, is a capital enemy of all Christians.[9]

The image of the Jew immediately called to mind the ideas of cheating, sin, and evil. "Oh!" exclaimed Bernardino da Feltre, "to speak of a good Jew is like speaking of a good scoundrel!"[10] What more was there to say? "The usurer is the evilest of men, he is a martyr to the devil's cause, a cancer to the state and to the poor. Usury is forbidden by natural law, by canon law, and by civil law." The usurer is a pig, a thief, he destroys the natural order of things. Usury "is called *tokos* in Greek, which means 'childbirth,' because it is contrary to nature."[11] The anomaly represented by the presence of the Jews among the Christians was thus associated in the last analysis with everything that is *contrary to nature*, as was, for example, that other great scourge, real or imaginary, of the period: homosexuality.

At bottom, all of this was not necessarily aimed at driving out the Jews, and still less at persecuting them. The chief purpose of every attitude taken with regard to the Jews was that of converting them to Christianity. Everyone wanted to see sufficient pressure brought to bear on the Jews to convince them to convert. Every Jewish conversion was transformed into an occasion for festive celebration and Christian pride. Nobles and high-ranking ecclesiastics considered it a great honor to act as sponsors at the baptism of the neophytes, who for this reason frequently entered Christian society with aristocratic names. The better Christian a man was, the more ardent his desire to contribute to this holy cause. All the mendicant friars did was to give expression to the current mentality. Giovanni da Capistrano, for example, never ceased repeating, for the benefit of the Jews compelled to attend his sermons: "If I did not love the Jews, I would not be a good Christian. Were not Jesus and the Blessed Virgin both Jews? Were not the Apostles also Jews?"[12] This was the reason why "he would have done as much for converted Jews as he would have for his closest relatives."[13] Relatives like this could be dangerous!

Be that as it may, the common people were certainly not attuned to these subtle nuances. In fact many sermons ended in pogroms, like the one that took place in Florence in 1488, after an inflammatory sermon by Bernardino da Feltre, which took Manuelino da Camerino as its victim. Bernardino had addressed his sermon to the young, inviting them to organize militarily into armed prayer companies in a crusade for the reform of moral behavior; but, despite the fact that the monk had not explicitly incited them to assault the Jews, as the chronicler reports, "they were far from interpreting the call to arms in a spiritual sense."[14] The spiritual rite became quite naturally transformed into a rite of violence against Jews, and it was no less to be expected that the ones in the front rank should be the adolescents. This Florentine example was in no way exceptional. There are many witnesses to confirm the fact that popular uprisings and attacks on Jews frequently followed in the wake of Franciscan sermons. These disturbances clearly functioned as a catalyst for the anti-Jewish measures promulgated by those in power.

The majority of the religious, who were certainly not on a par with their more famous brethren, did not even bother with the appeal to ambiguity and simply incited their hearers to persecution and expulsion. In his famous diary, the Venetian Marino Sanudo describes how, on Good Friday of 1509, a certain Father Ruffino preached in Santa Maria dell'Orto "that it was lawful to strip the Jews of all their money and not permit them to live."

From statements like this to accusations of ritual murder was not after all such a far cry. This kind of accusation was perhaps relatively uncommon beneath the blue skies of Italy (a systematic statistical survey would be needed, however, to affirm this with certainty), but they were certainly not lacking, and they turned out to be fraught with tragic consequences. The accusation of having murdered little Simon, made against the Jews of Trent in 1475, is paradigmatic in this regard. On the basis of the accusation, on which the last word is still to be heard, the entire local Jewish community—some thirty persons—was exterminated. The description of the tortures inflicted upon these poor people to make them confess to a crime they had not committed is enough to make one's flesh creep even today, centuries after the event. Only a few women succeeded in resisting the pain and continuing to protest their innocence. (The steadfastness of the women is an interesting phenomenon, of which Jewish history offers a number of instances, such as the persecutions at the time of the Crusades.) According to medieval practice, the bodies of the confessed "culprits" were exposed to public mockery in order to reinforce in the popular mentality the idea that truth had triumphed and justice had been served. The Holy See itself, traditionally opposed to this

"Ritual murder" of Simon of Trent, as depicted in Hartmann Schedel's Book of Chronicles from the Beginning of the World [Liber chronicarum cum figuris et imaginibus ab initio mundi], *Nüremberg, 1493. It was published by Germany's largest printer (Anton Koberger) and contained over 2,000 woodcuts. Some 1,500 Latin and 1,000 German copies were printed.*

kind of anti-Jewish myth, later canonized little Simon, demonstrating its support for the accusation, which was not retracted until 1965.

The Trent affair deserves particular attention, not simply because of the unusual position taken by the Holy See, but more particularly because this was the first time the recent invention of printing was employed in the service of a hate campaign. The broadsides with the martyr's picture, and the pamphlets which described his martyrdom paying morbid attention to the gruesome details, proved capable of making a much stronger impression on public opinion than a mere rumor passed by word of mouth. A recent iconographic study has pointed out the influence exerted by the events at Trent on a whole series of figurative works painted in the churches of Lombardy, clear proof of the fact that what might have remained a passing incident ended up assuming a very different role in the formation of Christian fantasies with regard to Jews. A by no means negligible number of these churches belonged to the Franciscan order. This same accusation of ritual murder can no doubt be traced to the sermons of Bernardino da Feltre who, that very same year, had mentioned in passing in Trent, in his Lenten sermon, how "he had sometimes heard tell that the Jews drink Christian blood during their Easter celebrations."[15]

Surviving documents mention more than a dozen cases similar to the one in Trent during the second half of the fifteenth century, most of which have been brought to light only recently—which shows how incomplete our knowledge in this area continues to be. Over and above the individual circumstances, on the level of typology, every case boils down to the same thing. The accusations of ritual murder occurring in Italy are no different than similar accusations made elsewhere, which go back as far as William of Norwich (1144), the prototype of this kind of accusation in Europe. This would be sufficient in and of itself to cast doubt on the widespread conviction that Italian Christians had an extraordinarily favorable attitude toward Jews, spoiled only by the negative attitude of the Franciscans. We should certainly not make these itinerant propagandists, dispensers of the soul's salvation, the chief instigators of every misfortune that fell to the lot of the Jews. In order to be efficacious, even the most fiery preaching needs ears ready to be convinced. If the Franciscans and their institutions did indeed play an especially important role in the dynamics of the rites of violence against the Jews, this is because they were particularly in tune with the music of their times, to the strains of which Jews and Christians neither sang nor danced nor drank together, not even in Italy, whatever Cecil Roth may have thought to the contrary.[16] Of course, it is not impossible that such peaceful coexistence may exceptionally have occurred. But the general tenor of public opinion with regard to the Jews was certainly negative, and the Franciscans had no trouble stirring it up. It is legitimate to ask why the Franciscans had the principal role in almost all the Jewish tragedies of the period. We might reply with a hypothesis that has yet to be verified. The Franciscans were recruited from among the merchant classes, rather than from among the landed aristocracy, and, on account of their social origins, were therefore more sensitive than their brethren in other religious orders to the socio-economic needs of the times. Perhaps this is the reason why the "Jewish question" was bound up in their eyes with the problem of usury and took on so urgent an aspect.

THE "NEED" FOR THE JEWS

WE HAVE INSISTED at such length on this anti-Jewish prejudice in order to emphasize a consideration of prime importance to the understanding of the dynamics of Jewish settlement in the cities of Italy. In order to counter the essentially anti-Jewish tendency of public opinion, or at least neutralize it, cogent arguments were always needed. In the absence of a time-honored tradition of residence — which the Jews could appeal to in the case of Sicily or Rome, but not too easily elsewhere — it was usually necessary to come up with some justification for deciding to allow them to live among Christians. The arguments were usually of a utilitarian nature and stressed those practical needs that, in the opinion of the rulers, could best be met by recourse to the Jews. These arguments, however, are not without their ambiguous side.

The argument most frequently used was that the Jews were "necessary." What was the specific "need"? Bearing in mind the Franciscan campaign against usurers, one immediately tends to think of moneylending; but, as has already been pointed out, the Jews were not always money-lenders. One has only to recall, for example, the medical doctors. Jewish doctors were professionally trained, sometimes better trained than the majority of their Christian colleagues. Even the popes preferred them to Christians, in spite of ecclesiastical regulations forbidding them to avail themselves of the services of the Jews, on account of the supposed danger of assassination. Jewish doctors were less expensive than their Christian counterparts, for reasons there is no need to dwell on. In the case of the doctors, then, it would be reasonable to appeal to the concept of "necessity" in order to justify the invitation to take up residence among Christians. The chief justification offered by the documents, however, was in fact moneylending, a practice for which the Jews were considered essential. The issue deserves closer study. Did there really exist an economic need capable of setting in motion mechanisms of an automatic or practically automatic nature? There is every reason to doubt this impression, however firmly ensconced it may be in the interpretation (or misinterpretation) of the period.

The economic mechanisms sometimes referred to in historical interpretations of the period are often insufficient to explain why the "Jewish solution" was preferred in some places, whereas in others, where socioeconomic conditions were identical, different solutions were adopted. One has the impression that, by adhering to the letter of the documents that speak of the "need" for the Jews, and using this kind of expression as a basis for generalization, without taking into account the context in which it is found, one runs the risk of falling into the same error of method denounced by Marxist historiography — the error, in other words, of underrating the importance of the structures presupposed by such categories of thought and of then considering their verbal expression as constituting history. This is the case of the historians who saw in the allusions to the "need" for the Jews proof that this need went well beyond mere moneylending. At times historians have posited the existence of far-reaching economic mechanisms, which the available documents, even if one were to take them at their face value, would have difficulty justifying. A gifted scholar recently proposed that one should interpret the settlement of the Jewish moneylenders north of Rome in the fourteenth century in light of the financial policy of the Holy See, considering them as *mercatores romanam curiam sequentes*, that is to say, merchant-bankers upon whom the popes relied to carry out their financial transactions, in particular their transferrals of capital, which consisted for the most part of transferrals of the remittances paid to the Apostolic Chamber. Today we are quite well informed about the ways in which the popes used the *mercatores romanam curiam sequentes* to consolidate their power and extend their influence in the context of an expansionist policy. We have also been familiar for some time with the particular pontifical privileges granted to certain Jews known in the documents as *mercatores curiam nostram sequentes*. This is the case, for instance, of the document issued on 1 February 1255 to Angelo, Sabbatino, Musetto, Salamone, and another Angelo.[17] Nevertheless, the documentation adduced does not seem sufficient to convince us to abandon the usual view, which denies the Jews a prominent position in the papal economy. One cannot see in every Angelo, Sabbatino, or Musetto, with a capital of a few hundred or even a few thousand florins, an equal of the Florentine *mercatores romanam curiam sequentes*, such as the Medici, the Strozzi, the Acciaiuoli, or the Peruzzi, in whom papal political executives could place their absolute trust. Moreover, not a shred of evidence exists to suggest that any Jewish moneylender ever in practice played a role similar to bankers of this kind. This does not mean of course that the popes were loath to take advantage of the services of the Jews whenever the occasion arose.

The Jews in any case did not possess capital comparable to those of the great Christian bankers. Granted, no one has yet undertaken, for any Italian city, an overall quantitative analysis of the real contribution of Jewish capital to the local economy. We can nevertheless affirm, without fear of contradiction, that, except in a few rare instances, that contribution was not particularly high, especially when compared to the total budgets of the Italian states, about which we are in some cases quite accurately informed. One example: from 1320 to 1321 the expenditure of the Apostolic Chamber increased from 112,490 to 528,857 florins, and, in the years 1325–1326, 336,000 florins were budgeted for the war in Lombardy.[18] Another example: in the thirty-year period between 1402 and 1433, the budget of Florence showed annual deficits of the order of half a million florins. In 1426 the deficit was slightly higher, reaching a peak of 628,622 florins. In the same year, expenditures for the hiring of mercenaries reached a sum total of 550,499 florins, which was anything but a record: this figure was exceeded several times in the course of the ten-year period 1390–1402.[19] Now, in the year 1437, the Jews in Florence invested, in the banks they were authorized to open, 14,000 florins. And the Jewish banks were four in number, compared with an overall total of almost a hundred. More than a little imagination is needed if one is to be persuaded that these Jews made a substantial, indeed fundamental, contribution to the Florentine economy![20] Quite to the contrary, one is left with the impression that whenever considerable sums were called for, the best thing to do was to seek loans from the Christian banks. Another example: when in 1290 the Commune of Perugia found itself in urgent need of 30,000 florins, they turned to six Florentine banks.[21] That same year, there were Jews in Perugia who placed at the disposal of the Commune such sums as they were in a position to lend. They were sums of a quite different order of magnitude.[22] So, although the imposition of taxes on the Jews was never a negligible affair, and although at times the hundreds of ducats paid by the Jews provided relief to drained economies, it was always relatively little compared with the overall dimensions of the local economies. In other words, contrary to some assertions, the Jews never took the place of the Christian financiers, who were allegedly compelled to give them a free hand in the field of medium and small credit. Rather, they filled the small vacuums left by the Christian financiers, who were forbidden by local authorities, with increasing zeal as the fifteenth century progressed, to number among their economic activities small consumer loans. The insistence with which this ban, with respect to which late thirteenth- and fourteenth-century practice had shown itself to all intents and purposes indifferent, was pursued, must be explained in light of the more general changes in the religious attitudes of Italian society during this period, changes that must be attributed at least in part to the preaching of the mendicant orders. As proof, one may cite the fact, not yet studied from a diachronic point of view, that whereas in the last few decades of the thirteenth century usurious loans by Jews are documented alongside similar activities on the part of Christians, and sometimes even in partnership with them, as time goes by this activity tends to become more and more the exclusive prerogative of Jews. This additional note of ambivalence seems in any case worthy of note: the selfsame mendicant orders that, as has been shown, were responsible for the hostility toward Jews were also instrumental in the spread of a mental climate favorable to the attribution of the role of usurious moneylenders exclusively to Jews.

This ambivalence, however, never found a doctrinal, still less an ideological, justification. At this point, it is important to put in its proper light a kind of syllogism occasionally encountered in the documents, in which one is too often tempted to see a linear explanation of the true state of affairs. Given that usury is prohibited by law, and given that individual consumer loans are nonetheless necessary, it follows that Jews must be tolerated. What does this mean? Léon Poliakov has already pointed out that, from the standpoint of Christian doctrine, the usurious loans practiced by the Jews could not be viewed as purely and simply permitted. Many canon lawyers would have considered them forbidden in the same way that loans practiced by Christians were forbidden. In their eyes, the introduction of the Jewish moneylender presented problems of a rather complicated nature, even more complicated, paradoxically, than those regarding the tolerance of the Christian usurer. For the Jews had two strikes against them: not only were they usurers, they were also Jews. As one Franciscan monk said, "The Christian usurer, though his sin may be graver than the Jew's, is nevertheless preferable to the Jew in one sense, because he quite often makes restitution; whereas the Jews, who over and above usury, bear hatred for the Christians, after they have grown rich at Christian expense, frequently strain their ingenuity to expatriate their profits."[23] In other words, though usurious loans might be necessary, it was by no means a logical consequence that the activities of Jewish moneylenders were therefore to be tolerated. For the Christians who wielded power, solving the problem by recourse to the Jews was a choice fraught with serious questions; and in general it was the Franciscan preachers who formulated them. How many problems could have been avoided if only they had come up with a "Christian solution"! Why not attempt to tackle the situation without recourse to the Jews? Wouldn't simple Christian charity have done the trick, if only they had taken the trouble to cultivate it? The preachings of the Franciscans in favor of the founding of Monti di Pietà, of institutions, that is, designed to fulfill certain roles and to eliminate the "need" for the Jews, amounted to nothing more than variations on the theme of "do it yourself!"

THE MONTI DI PIETÀ

HALFWAY BETWEEN modern credit banks and charitable institutions, the Monti di Pietà were a definite failure throughout the entire Renaissance period, at least until the second half of the sixteenth century. Why? Taking into account their hybrid nature, it is perhaps possible to hazard a reply. The Monti di Pietà, insofar as they were credit institutions, were intended to resemble real private banks, both in their internal organization, as well as in the way they amassed and administered their capital. Nevertheless, the very facts that they were created with a charitable purpose in mind, that deposits were nonproductive and could be encouraged only by the promise of eventual rewards in heaven, that the attitude of their administrators was more "governmental" than private, with the resulting proliferation of officers, sinecures, fiscal irresponsibility, embezzlements, and financial scandals, obviously placed obstacles in the way of the development of a true banking ethos. The charitable character of the Monti di Pietà put further difficulties in the way of their development. By placing an arbitrary ceiling on the amounts that could be loaned, by compelling borrowers to declare, under oath and under pain of arrest, that they were taking out the loan strictly for their own personal needs and not for commercial purposes, or, worse still, to satisfy their appetites for vice and vanity, all that was achieved was to drive away potential customers, whose only recourse then was to Jewish usurers or to "Judaizing" Christians.

The Franciscan solution did not become truly practicable until all these obstacles had been overcome, until the Holy See, that is, authorized the payment of interest to those who made cash deposists (1542) and the Council of Trent approved the procedure, though still with the proviso that the money be deposited for charitable purposes and not for profit. Now that the Monti di Pietà had to guarantee their depositors a

City walls of Montagnana near Venice, where German Jews established a colony of moneylenders in 1383. Courtesy of Azienda di Promozione Turistica, Padova.

rate of interest, they were compelled to invest their capital on the sly, becoming transformed in the process into commercial banks. This evolution was inevitable. Loans to the poor took second place, becoming a mere pretext, whereas the institutions' various activities became more and more purely financial in character. The reversal of the trend, and of economic structures, could not be more evident. If, in the first phase, the pretext of loans to the poor served to legitimize the introduction of Jews and their insertion into the economic activities of the Italian cities, the selfsame pretext would later serve to legitimize the banking activities of the Christians and to render the presence of the Jews absolutely superfluous. The result was the economic suffocation of the latter, a problem to be returned to later. For the moment, suffice it to say that the greater part of the history of the Jews in Renaissance Italy takes place between these two extreme phases, in a period in which it proved easier to overcome the problems posed by the toleration of Jewish moneylenders than the problem of making Christian banking institutions responsive to the needs of the Christian poor.

HOW THE JEWISH PRESENCE WAS JUSTIFIED

THE STRATEGEM that was to enable the Italian cities to welcome Jewish moneylenders and doctors without pangs of conscience was the papal dispensation. Jewish sources amply confirm that this formed the basis of the permission granted to Jews to practice usury, a practice otherwise considered contrary to canon law. As Leone Modena acutely remarked: "Permission to make interest-bearing loans is conceded by the Pope as a mark of tolerance, and the explanation given is the following: 'according to strict doctrine, Jews ought not to be permitted to lend money to Gentiles; this circumstance notwithstanding, We are nonetheless prepared to make an exception in favor of so-and-so, and to allow him to practice moneylending. We have no intention that this should become the general rule; but, if the suit is insistent, We reserve to Ourselves the right, after due examination of each case, to grant permission or to refuse it.' "[24] There is plenty of evidence to confirm that the papal dispensation was at times considered by the communal bodies a necessary prerequisite to the granting of a residence permit. In such cases, the Jews involved were compelled to procure at their own expense from the papal chancery a pontifical brief of authorization.

Generally speaking, however, the existence of precedents and a sense of independence vis-à-vis the pope on the part of the local secular authorities was enough to exempt them from the duty of appealing to the pope before granting residence permits to Jews. Thus, in 1533, the Duke of Milan asserted: "Inasmuch as the Jewish nation is tolerated by the Most Holy Church and by Christian Potentates and allowed to reside in their places, states and cities, in order to protect Christians from the occasion of sin, in the form of usurious depravity, as well as to provide as-

San Marino, where Jewish loan banks appeared as early as 1369. It was a well-established community by 1442. Courtesy of photo studio MW.

sistance to their poor and needful subjects; in keeping with the example of our Illustrious predecessors, we have been moved to concede to the aforesaid Jewish nation the right to reside in our State."[25]

There can be no doubt that, once this preliminary obstacle had been overcome, the "Jewish solution" was for Christian rulers the most convenient, effective, and advantageous course, from both the fiscal and the sociopolitical point of view. The Jews were always handy, forever on the lookout for hospitable shores on which to disembark, and no doubt more willing than anyone else to accept the restrictive conditions imposed on them with regard to interest rates and the like; furthermore, they made far more profitable taxable subjects than most; and, finally, they did not represent a source of potential political danger to the ruling forces as might have been the case with other Christians. As the Dominican Sisto dei Medici remarked toward 1550, the raison d'être for the presence of the Jews could be put quite simply: "*quia magis timidi, quia profugi, quia servi, quia sine favoribus, quia foris sunt* (because they are more timid, because they are refugees, because they are servants, because they are without protection, because they are outsiders)."[26]

Nevertheless, none of this proved sufficient to avoid recourse to the solution of the Monti di Pietà. The Monti di Pietà won out in the end. The real problem, then, is to understand why their victory took so long, leaving the field open to the Jewish moneylenders throughout the entire first phase of the period. A quantitative detail, which has so far gone relatively unobserved, may perhaps help us find the answer. The low rates of interest, imposed as a condition on the Jews by the Christian authorities, had an evident fiscal component. The most explicit example is provided by Venice, which in 1387 gave moneylenders the alternative of lending at a high rate of interest and paying an annual tax of 4,000 ducats, or of reducing the interest rate by 2 percent and eliminating the tax.[27] We may therefore estimate the sum of 4,000 ducats to be the equivalent of 2 percent of the total interest that the Jews could presumably have earned. As it was, the Jews preferred to lend at lower interest rates rather than pay the annual tax and try to earn more, which demonstrates that the estimate was still somewhat high. Of course, it was wartime, and they certainly were not above adding a few coppers to the empty coffers of the state: this, however, does not prevent the sum involved from being, in the eyes of the Senate of the Most Serene Republic, a derisory one. In order to have an idea of just how derisory it was, all one has to do is to read the text of the speech made by the Doge Tommaso Mocenigo to the Signoria in April 1423, in which he estimated the gross product of Venetian commerce at no less than 20 million ducats, a figure that included 4 million ducats in annual profits for the merchants of Venice.[28] Had they been so inclined, the governments could have easily reduced interest rates to zero and taken upon themselves the responsibility of assisting their poor. What would 20,000 or 30,000 ducats more or less have signified in the annual budget of the wealthy Venetian republic? Less, certainly, than the Most Serene Republic saw fit to distribute to the numerous members of the impoverished nobility. The problem of the "Jewish question" is fairly well reflected in the debate that took place in Venice in November 1519 among the Savii of the Great Council concerning the proposal to renew the statutes of agreement with the Jews. The debate was summed up in the shorthand notes of his diary by Marin Sanudo, who also added his own opinion, not without a hint of regret at not having been able to express it in the Senate as a member of the ruling body. The lengthy and emblematic passage, not easy to follow because of its colloquial syntax, is nonetheless worth quoting here almost in its entirety:

The first speaker was Sier Antonio Condulmer, a former Savio di Terra Ferma. At first the Council was reluctant to hear him out, because he said they could not and should not make any agreement with the Jews and allow them to practice usury in this city. Once order had been restored to the Consiglio, he began to speak out against the Jews and to say that he did not want them in this city on any account, demonstrating by appeal to the sacred canons that Jews should not be permitted to lend out money in this most Christian city, and, citing saintly texts, he caused to be read out loud many former decisions to the effect that they should not be allowed to remain in the city, though during the present war they had stayed in the heart of Venice, and everything had been permitted. Sier Zacaria Dolfin also, being one of the Savii of the Consiglio, said they should go to the Ghetto so that they would not stay among us, adding that they have been given a castle and could not be better provided for, and he encouraged the Council, showing great hypocrisy in not wanting them and not wanting the agreement drawn up by the Savii to permit them to set up secondhand dealerships and take the bread out of the mouths of Christian secondhand dealers. And then he said that if they really wanted them, then make them live in Mestre where they lived before the war, and make them pay 10,000 ducats and not 6,000. And if they were kept, we should beware of the wrath of God, for in France and in Spain there are no Jews, and God makes those monarchs prosper, and so on. And he called for Francesco Bragadin, one of the Savii who had sponsored the motion, to come and answer his arguments. Bragadin spoke at considerable length, and he spoke out well against the Jews, but not on the subject at issue, saying that once it was necessary to have Jews for the sake of the poor—there being no Monte di Pietà as in other cities; whether to house them in Venice or in Mestre was something that could be discussed later, as well as whether the terms of the agreement were good or not; but he cautioned about arguing against the Jews, for even the Pope keeps them in Rome, though they are not allowed to engage in moneylending.

When he had stepped down, Sier Antonio Grimani, Procurator and Savio of the Consiglio for the week, got up and went to the stand and answered him, and he spoke well for an eighty-six-year-old man, saying that Jews are necessary to assist the poor, and that it makes no difference whether they live in the Ghetto or go to live in Mestre, but the statutes must be confirmed . . . and the Jews allowed to lend at interest, because they have no other livelihood, but the statutes should be carefully amended as they have been by the College, and that during the time they lived in Mestre, Mestre was burned by our enemies, and then, when they came to live in the city, we recovered our dominions. And that in this war they assisted us with large sums of money . . . and with other words befitting of a virtuous old man, he urged the Consiglio to vote in favor of confirming the statutes and continuing to behave as this State has behaved for many years, deciding in favor of having Jews; and already in the year . . . , it was proposed and voted that Christians could pay 10 percent interest on objects pawned and 12 percent on paper guarantees, and he had them read. Furthermore, when Cardinal of Nicea [Johannes, or Basilius, Bessarion] was Legate in this city in the year . . . , with great authority, he permitted Jews to be kept in this Dominion and to lend at usury; and he had the said brief read out loud, and so forth.

Next Sier Gabriel Moro, knight and Provveditore al Sale, got up and spoke out against the Jews, saying they should not be kept, and that Spain drove them from her lands, then they came to Naples, and King Alfonso lost his kingdom. The Duke of Milan was driven from power because he had favored and protected the Jews; and now we were going to do the same thing and stir up the wrath of God against us. And he added other things, saying he could prove that it was not good to harbor the Jews, and it is not in the Pope's power to give them permission to practice usury. Along with other considerations, and so on and so forth.

And many members of the Consiglio, who were concerned for the well-being of the poor, said that when the Jews were driven out of Spain they brought with them a great quantity of gold. They went to Constantinople, and Selim conquered Syria and Egypt. Others did not want the Jews to remain in the city and not even in the mainland Dominion, some for reasons of piety, others because they wanted to be the ones lending money out, not just at 20 percent interest but at 40 percent or 50 percent or more, as they do on the Rialto. With the result that the Consiglio was undecided: some against and some in favor; but nobody dared speak in favor of the statutes, for fear it be said that the Jews had put them up to supporting their cause.

And had I, Marin Sanudo, been a member of the Senate, as I was last year, I would have spoken out, but not to speak for the Jews because I would have described the tricks they get up to when loaning money, but to speak about the provisions that concern them, so as to have them amended, demonstrating that a city needs plenty of Jews and bakers, and especially ours, for the common good, citing laws and the way our forefathers have always behaved, and the opinions of the learned doctors Alessandro de Imola, Pietro de Ancorano, Baldus, and others, who conclude that Jews can be kept to lend money at interest, and I would have spoken to the point. True, I wouldn't have been in favor of them keeping secondhand shops, so as not to deprive Christians of their livelihood, although keeping them would be a great benefit for those who have things to sell. But at no time have our elders approved of the Jews having commercial shops in this city; rather, they are to buy and sell and then go their way. Nor do we need such tomfoolery in our State, like driving out the Jews, when there is no Monte di Pietà. The coffers of the Monte Vecchio and the Monte Nuovo are unable to pay interest, and the Monte Novissimo has trouble paying; the city has very little trade; the shopkeepers complain that they can't sell their goods; and they won't allow somebody to take out a loan at 15 percent interest from the Jews with his own property as security, for his own needs and in order to maintain and support his family. And on this point I would have really insisted, but unfortunately it was not to be. Excluded from the Giunta [Addition to the Consiglio] by a few votes, I came in thirtieth, and since then I have not been elected either to the Senate or the Consiglio. . . .

Sier Sebastian Foscarini, a doctor and teacher of philosophy and a member of the Senate, went to the podium. He spoke briefly, and he said that the Pope *de iure divino* could not permit the Jews to lend at usury, since it was against God's commandments, which say *non sinerabis fratrem tuum*, and so forth, citing in addition other passages from Holy Scripture; but he is right to permit the harboring of Jews, as long as they do not lend at usury. It is true that, if a sin or an evil is committed, the Pope can absolve it, therefore the Cardinal of Nicea could not make this concession. In conclusion, it is not advisable to keep Jews in this Christian city, but to send them away to their damnation, and so on. The vote was called: 10 abstentions, 64 in favor, 66 opposed, and those opposed prevailed, that is, the statutes proposed by the Savii were not approved.[29]

This is not the place for the detailed analysis that this balanced passage, suggestive as it is and full of typical local color, would rightfully deserve. But there is no one, even after the most superficial reading, who will fail to be struck by the author's powerful individual personality, as well as by the axiomatic nature of the negative image of the Jew — a negative charge that strong utilitarian self-interest might attenuate, but never eliminate. However irritating and stereotyped the case against the Jews may seem, even to the taste of Sanudo's contemporaries, who in their own defense appealed to the notion of the health of the state, and so forth, the fact remains that in the present instance it proved more successful than the opposing arguments. The main thing to observe from our point of view is that it never occurred to anyone to suggest that the State should take care of the poor. This fact is brought out even more clearly, in a subsequent session, by the way the opposition was overcome and the statutes signed. The description, taken once again from Sanudo, shows no change in basic assumptions, which cast the Jews in an essentially instrumental role, at the mercy of aleatory criteria of expediency not referable to a general model. It nevertheless demonstrates with extreme precision the importance of the role played by the chance of the moment, as well as the logic that informed the change of heart of the decision makers determining the reversal of policy. The occasion was offered by the report on the deficit balance of the Arsenal.

Then . . . Sier Alvise di Prioli, Provveditore for the Arsenal, took the stand, and reported on the state of the Arsenal, saying that the construction of a number of ships had still to be completed, but there were no funds available unless the Consiglio decided to make some provision. And he and Councilor Sier Hieronimo da Pesaro, both Provveditori for the Arsenal, proposed a half tithe for the needs of the Arsenal; and the Procurator Antonio Trun, one of the Savii of the Consiglio, proposed a full tithe. Whereupon, Sier Andrea Trivisan, the Cavalier Savio of the Consiglio for the week, said he was against any kind of tithe, and that the Arsenal had received 20,000 ducats and had spent the money building warehouse space, and so forth. As a result, the full tithe was not granted, nor was the half tithe. But it was said by some that the Jewish issue should be dealt with, and their money used for the Arsenal. Whereupon, the Procurator Sier Antonio Grimani, Sier Piero Capello, Sier Lunardo Mocenigo, Sier Andrea Trivisan, the Cavalier Savio of the Consiglio, Sier Pandolfo Moresini, Savio of Terraferma, proposed confirming the agreements with the Jews as they were for another five years (and here they were read), and that they should pay 10,000 ducats per year, with 4,000 ducats to be paid immediately [de praesenti], to be discounted from the annual payments at the rate of 1,000 per year, ut in parte. Sier Hieronimo Barbaro, doctor and knight, a member of the Senate, went to the stand to argue against the measure, saying they were excommunicates. The Consiglio would not listen to him, and the question was called. The vote was 93 in favor, 65 against, 15 abstentions, and the motion was victorious. And this is how the Jewish issue was dispatched, for fear of having a tithe.[30]

The number of votes against the renewal of the charter had not changed. The "fear of having a tithe," coupled with a greater diligence on the part of the Jews, no doubt caused the supporters of the renewal to do more lobbying than on the previous occasion, thereby ensuring themselves of a decent majority. It would no doubt have been easy to cover the momentary deficit of the Arsenal by imposing a "half tithe," as the Provveditore had proposed. It is also clear that, in addition to the current deficit, the administrative program of the Arsenal was also at stake (whether to continue to "build warehouse space" or not), and that the latter point had made it easier to influence the voting members. And finally, there can be no doubt that the supporters of the renewal of the charter were clearly influenced by their personal interest and their desire to economize — the "fear of having a tithe" that Sanudo cites with a touch of irony. But it was certainly not an "extraordinarily urgent" situation of necessity, as Cecil Roth once defined it, as, in perfect keeping with his own point of view, he went so far as to imagine how the senators "looked at each other with terrified expressions."[31] The first to realize it was the Jew Anselmo del Banco, who, when he was invited to sign the agreement, thought there was still room for negotiation. Instead, he was presented with an *aut aut*, take it or leave it, so that, and again our source is Marin Sanudo, he gave the reply destined to become famous: "When desire fights with power, power always has the upper hand."[32] But the thing most noteworthy is the fact that the Council's first reaction was to saddle the government with the economic responsibility, bringing into play the usual mechanism of ad hoc taxation. The argument goes like this: The Jews are always an evil. But, whenever it looks like they may not be the worst of evils, then it becomes possible to keep open a breach in the wall of Christian hostility.

It is legitimate to conclude, then, that the strongest argument for the settlement of Jewish moneylenders was the fact that the authorities were never willing to deal with the problem of poverty at the administrative level. Whenever the current political situation made it desirable to avoid recourse to taxation that would have been a burden on their own shoulders, their preexisting mental tendency was corroborated by considerations of self-interest, which were capable of overcoming all other reservations. Perhaps this provides a clue to why the Franciscan solution of the Monti di Pietà would only begin to work toward the end of the sixteenth century, in a period, that is, when the medieval mentality was going through a phase of rapid change.

THE POOR, THE JEWS, AND THE PROSTITUTES: "NECESSARY" ELEMENTS OF SOCIETY

TO THE MENTALITY of the period leading up to the end of the sixteenth century, the poor were never a problem in search of a solution: they were too necessary to the spiritual economy of the period. The rich needed the poor: by distributing alms, they were assured of the absolution of their sins. The have-nots were also necessary to throw into relief, by contrast, the wealth of the haves. They were necessary to provide labor for those whose ideal it was to live as gentlemen and who scorned "mechanical labor." They were necessary, in a word, if the rich were to play their ideal role as patrons, for which they felt themselves predestined by Divine Providence. Perhaps no one would have formulated this list of "necessities" as was done above, but they can all be amply confirmed in the literature and institutions of the period. This "need" for poverty carried with it, as a corollary, the necessity for the state not to concern itself with poverty directly: had the state done so, it would have brought down upon itself the hatred and hostility usually directed against the Jews. One is therefore entitled to interpret in this sense the stereotypical formulas used by those in power in which they justified the permits granted to Jews "for the good of the poor." These authorities, and with them all of Christian society, purged themselves of the accusation of perpetuating poverty by offering the palliative of Jewish moneylenders. At the same time they exonerated themselves from the consequences of their decision to exclude the poor from society, in the name of the general health of the social and spiritual body, by associating the poor with the Jews, or more accurately, by placing the latter at the service of the former.

These two functions were structurally consistent. Did not the continued presence of the Jews in the bosom of the Christian world present itself as necessary to the spiritual economy of Christianity? The centuries of Christian meditation, preaching, and legislation, modeled on the Augustinian notion of the need for the Jews as witnesses to the Truth, were there to suggest this consistency. From this point of view, the Jews were necessary to the Christians in order to provide, through their ultimate conversion, the psychological certainty of the truth, the realization of the triumph of *Ecclesia* over *Synagoga*, Good over Evil, God over Satan. Like the poor, the Jews were, then, necessary to the Christian world, for the help they provided in ensuring the salvation of the world, the final Redemption. Like the poor, the Jews were necessary to provide a foil to Christian wealth — spiritual wealth of course, but also material wealth, since Christian legislation had by this time institutionalized the inferiority of the Jews at a number of levels (the status of Jews before the law was not comparable with that of Christians, they could not serve on juries or act as witnesses in trials in which Christians were involved, and so forth). Like the poor, the Jews were considered potentially dangerous, and therefore to be avoided, though not eliminated.

Nonetheless, the very real service that Jews rendered to Christian society caused them to be associated in the mentality of the time with another category of persons who were considered necessary, however undesirable they might be on account of the many negative consequences that might result from contact with them: prostitutes. The association of ideas was so obvious and entrenched that there were even petitions, however odd it may seem to our modern eyes, in which Jews and prostitutes figured side by side. One such example is provided by the epistle sent on 13 July 1566 to Pope Pius V, "in which His Holiness is exhorted to tolerate in Rome Jews and Courtesans." In this epistle, the writer defends the usefulness of allowing a limited number of "unhealthy" elements into the social body, elements to which he attributes the role of emphasizing and reinforcing the healthy elements: a kind of inoculation of germs that would act as a vaccination, to put it in modern terms. According to the writer, if vice were to be extirpated, even the salutary coming of Christ would have been to no avail: "If the Lord God had wished to extirpate the vices of the world, it would have been in His power to do so. But human nature and the law would have suffered, and, had He taken away grace and the gift, as it was in His hands to do, the chief good would have been lacking, and the coming of His Divine Majesty would no longer have been necessary for our salvation, which however was done out of necessity with supreme magistery, as Your Holiness knows, you who, in imitation of the Lord, tolerate in the world Jews, adulterers, and prostitutes; some as witnesses to His sacred law, others so that there may be wicked people in the world for the exaltation of the righteous, and other wicked for the conversion of the righteous." The allusion to the adulterers was brilliantly inserted into the text so as to evoke the analogy between Christ's gesture in favor of the adulteress in the gospels and the desired behavior of the Vicar of Christ toward prostitutes. The writer, then, was prepared to extend the idea of the role of witnesses to the Truth, assigned by the Augustinian ideology to the Jews, and, openly expressing what all his readers had known in their heart of hearts since time immemorial, went right ahead and associated the Jews and the prostitutes. So that it was perfectly logical for him to continue: "So you too in your grace and goodness will tolerate all and sundry with the law of nature granted by the Lord Peter in Christ and with the Blessed example of Catholic living that Your Holiness pursues, and in this way you will win over with your tolerance many Jewish souls, as you have already done, and you will convert them by choice and not by violence, not to speak of many evil women, guiding their lives toward a better end."[33]

The author of this curious epistle to the pope was attempting to cast in a positive light an idea that had long been present with a negative connotation in the mentality of the period. It had found expression on more than one occasion in specific municipal ordinances. A number of the latter, such as those promulgated in 1439 in Perugia, went so far as to specify that Jews, like prostitutes, were forbidden to touch fruit that they had not previously paid for.[34] In more general terms, just as prostitutes were supposed to wear a conspicuous identifying sign designed to make them easily recognizable, so the Jews were compelled to wear a red or yellow badge of identity, usually a circle on their coats or a special cap, an obligation they could only escape through the concession of a special privilege. A privilege of this kind, then, by definition an exception to the rule, was tantamount to a declaration that the Jew who was the beneficiary was *different* from other Jews. The same was true for prostitutes, who could transform themselves along similar lines from common whores to privileged courtesans. In other words, both Jews (equated with usurious moneylenders) and prostitutes had, in premodern times, analogous roles to play: they provided a useful but despised service, just as the manual labor of those not in a position to have others serve them was also despised.

Furthermore, one should not forget that the condition of the Jew was supposed in theory to be that of *servitus*. This was how the theologians would have it, this is how it was institutionalized by kings, emperors, dukes, and marquises, as well as by the governing bodies of the communes. From this point of view, the attitude toward the Jews seems to develop as a necessity of a mental and psychological rather than an economic order. In a sense, this is what the Franciscans were preaching, and, looking at it from their point of view, it would be hard to fault their logic. For them the way toward love for poor Christians led through hatred for the Jews. When all was said and done, the end result was still love for the poor! Moreover, by insisting on the economic solution, that is, on the side of the problem that brought charity into play, the Franciscans were touching a sore point. The problem of the poor could not be solved until they were admitted into the society from which they had been excluded. This may have been why the Franciscans never condemned the 5 percent to 10 percent interest rates that, in their interpretation of canon law, were necessary to cover the running expenses of the Monti di Pietà. Had they done so, they would have saved themselves the doctrinal squabbles with which their Augustinian and especially Dominican brethren continued to afflict them. But the Franciscans pursued a sociopolitical policy consistent with that adopted in the fourteenth century when, against the opinions of the Augustinians and the Dominicans, they gave their seal of approval to an interest rate of 15 percent on loans enforced by the communes. This is another problem of the mentality of the time which calls for further investigation.

Proof of this interpretation is once again provided by Venice, where the prevalent spirit, at once pragmatic and conservative, led the authorities to approach the problem of poverty from above, without overturning the preexisting structures, which made the poor and the Jews together the objects of the same exclusion. Venice had been late recognizing the usefulness of the services offered by the Jews and had done so only when, toward the end of the period, it had discovered that its vocation was more financial than commercial. Venice was the first to face, in a somewhat more efficient manner than had previously been the case, the problem of the poor, without, however, clearly separating it from the problem of the Jews. In Venice, toward the end of the sixteenth century, the existing Jewish banks were simply transformed into Monti di Pietà, "Banks for the Poor," thus preserving the charitable character of the Monti, but at the same time avoiding their attendant drawbacks. An inspector sent from Paris to study the workings of the Italian Monti di Pietà noted significantly, "The Republic of Venice, like the other sovereign states of Italy, has understood that it would be very useful to the poor to find a place where they could receive on their personal belongings the wherewithal to relieve their pressing poverty, but the Republic has made strange use of this reflection and I believe it is only at Venice that the Monti di Pietà is run by Jews."[35]

The Jews would have been better advised to try and avoid becoming the instruments of a social order based on the oppression of the poor. But this was too much to ask, too remote indeed from their mentality. With the benefit of hindsight, it is not an exaggeration to say that their choice, dictated by myopia and considerations of immediate advantage, was in a way responsible for part at least of their misfortunes. Centuries-old practices fell in too easily with the opportunity of the moment for them to remember the old *loci talmudici* condemning moneylending to the gentiles from the standpoint of Jewish morality and recommending that whoever practiced it be persuaded to look for another way of earning a living. Even an enlightened spirit like Rabbi Joseph Colon makes only a passing allusion to the problem. Nevertheless, the allusion could be viewed as quite significant, since it was made in 1468, when the monks' preachings placed the Jewish community of Mantua in serious danger.[36] More than a century later, when the about-face had become a fait accompli, people's eyesight had gotten sharper. Leone Modena could still discuss the problem in apologetic terms. Since the Jews were forbidden "to possess land practically everywhere, as well as to exercise many other forms of commerce, and other useful and reputable pursuits, they have lost heart: and that is why they have made it permissible to lend out money at usury."[37] That this was not merely an apology for Christian consumption can easily be deduced from the fact that various other witnesses confirm the change in attitude that took place in the course of the seventeenth century. In this connection Léon Poliakov cites the violent words of an anonymous chronicler: "I have already repeated on several occasions that the expulsions of the Jews were chiefly due to the extraordinary usurious interest they demanded of the townspeople, as they robbed them of their very substance." Or elsewhere: "The children of Israel chose this profession in preference to all others, because from it they obtained peace and prosperity. Perched on their plump cushions, they earned their livings, with neither pain nor effort, knowing they would never lack for anything. This is why they all chose this profession. And they neither knew or understood that this was the cause of the envy and hatred directed against them; experience never taught them that this was the cause of their misfortunes."[38] Better late than never!

It may be concluded that there was no apparent utilitarian motive on the part of the Christians for maintaining that the Jews were necessary, apart from the mentality and psychology of the time. This does not, however, imply that such a "necessity" did not exist. Once it had been identified, official Christian theology, from Augustine on, was naturally able to provide doctrinal justification for the presence of the Jews among the Christians. The Jews were after all witnesses to the truth of the Gospels. In theory, however, the Christians were under no obligation to welcome them. On the contrary, it was always possible to find reasonable objections to the practical arguments, maintaining the conviction, dear to the hearts of the Franciscans, that the Christian world could solve its problems perfectly well without recourse to the Jews. Throughout the first phase of the settlement of Jewish moneylenders in the cities of Italy, no such settlement took place in any locality where the determination to do without them was sufficiently strong. For the hundreds of localities in which the presence of Jews is recorded, there are just as many where they were never authorized to set foot. One may therefore conclude these general considerations by establishing an elementary law that determined Jewish migration in the period: the Jews settled where they were given permission to settle and where life was not rendered unbearable by Christian hostility.

SOME FACTORS AFFECTING CHOICE OF RESIDENCE: SECURITY AND THE NATURE OF THE POLITICAL-JURIDICAL REGIME

THE GENERAL TENDENCY was of course to choose among the various places where it was easy to obtain a residence permit. What were the factors that influenced this choice? In the first place, localities where the guarantees of physical safety seemed insufficient were avoided. Preference was given to a locality defended by solid walls, whether it be a city, a small town, or a castle. Wars were anything but infrequent, and everyone knew from experience that the combatant troops, made up of mercenaries, considered it their right to put conquered cities to the sack. The *condottieri*, especially when they were Italians at the head of German or Swiss mercenaries, might try to mitigate the fury of their soldiers, but it was unreasonable to imagine that they could persuade troops to throw themselves into battle without luring them on with the promise of a good day's free looting in the case of victory. In these circumstances, no one was invulnerable, but the Jews were even more vulnerable than the Christians: first of all because they were moneylenders and had ready cash on hand, which was the main thing the plunderers were looking for; and also because, when the time came to stipulate conditions of surrender and consequent priorities for the protection of the various categories of citizens, the rulers of vanquished cities were certainly not likely to give special consideration to the Jews. One finds, for example, a chronicler who records how the inhabitants of Castel San Pietro (near Bologna), having surrendered to Niccolò Piccinino in 1434, promised to pay over 12,000 ducats and to give free rein to Niccolò's soldiers to "plunder the Jew who lent money in the castle precincts."[39] The same chronicler later reports how, in another negotiation, one of the conditions imposed by the victors was that they first be allowed to plunder the Jews and then drive them out of the city and the surrounding countryside. Despite these dangers, solid walls could still offer a relative guarantee of protection against dangers of this kind, and it was therefore perfectly natural that the Jews should seek a locality surrounded by walls rather than one without them.

It would be superfluous to insist that considerations of safety naturally included the nature of the political regime, the idiosyncratic attitudes of the governing classes toward the Jews, the stability of the government and of public institutions, starting with juridical institutions, and the like. If the choice were to present itself between a stable regime of the Lordship type, though nominally republican, as was the case of Florence and Venice, and a communal regime, in which political equilibrium and stability might appear more problematic, it went without saying that the former would be chosen. The Lordships were much more malleable on a day-to-day basis than the Communal Councils; the bigoted influence of the religious was probably less powerful on the more cosmopolitan princes than on the bourgeois gentlemen belonging to the citizen Councils; it was easier to satisfy a prince, always short of money, than to placate an entire municipal Consiglio; and in any case it was easier to deal with a single individual than with many, possibly in disagreement amongst themselves; and lastly, in the case of republics, it was in their interest to have strong men to deal with. From this point of view, the myth that had grown up around the regimes of Venice and Florence no doubt played a catalyzing role. In every myth there is a core of truth.

There is a great deal of evidence to confirm the general impression that the decision of the individuals in power was the determining factor in favor of the Jews, whenever things threatened to turn out badly as a result of some dangerous initiative like that of the itinerant friars. In 1484, the Marquis of Mantova, Francesco Gonzaga, for instance, ordered the city authorities to instruct Bernardino not to preach any more in the town square but rather in the church of San Francesco, and to confine himself to condemning vices, "using gentle persuasion, and sticking to language befitting a good churchman."[40] In the same year, 1484, the Lords of Bologna invited Father Francesco da Bologna not to go too far in his sermons, so as not to provoke his listeners "to commit any evil against the Jews, to molest them, or to bring against them any impediment or violence."[41] In 1487, in the name of the Duke of Urbino, the same over-zealous monk was forbidden to incite the crowds of Gubbio, probably for fear that the threat to expel the Jews he had provoked the previous year might be repeated. The Lords of Venice were similarly irate in 1492, in their ducal epistle to the governors of Brescia and Crema:

It has been brought to our attention that Fra Bernardino . . . has been there or is on his way there to preach the divine word to the population. And since, very recently, while performing this duty in Padua, as well as in this and in other places, he incited the populace against the Jews, and there followed as a result great riots, perturbations, and scandals, which we would not like to see and hear repeated there or anywhere else in our territories, we have therefore deliberated to send you the present letter, to command you to call in the aforesaid Fra Bernardino and tell him in our name that, although we are well pleased that he should instruct and guide the people in the divine precepts and preach the word of the Lord, it would, on the other hand, be no less offensive and unwelcome to us if he were to stir up the people against the Jews, indeed nothing could be more pernicious to our ears, since incitements of this kind could lead to far-reaching scandals and unwanted novelties. Wherefore, as we have instructed you on other occasions, warn him that, if he values our favor, he must absolutely refrain from inciting the populace against the Jews, or even from mentioning them, openly or tacitly, or in any other way. And if he does not obey, inform us as soon as possible of the entire incident, so that we can take measures to deal with his disobedience in whatever way we see fit.[42]

The stability of juridical institutions was perhaps even more important. Whatever degree of autonomy the Jewish community may have obtained, and it will be seen in due course that it was not especially pronounced, as long as the plaintiff in the case was a Christian, the Jews remained subject to the Christian juridical authorities and to the Christian penal and civil codes. It goes without saying that the standards of criminal justice were far from being standards with which modern sensibilities could begin to feel comfortable. Thomas More regretted in his *Utopia* that thieves were often condemned to be hanged alongside murderers. Counterfeiters risked being burnt at the stake, homosexuals were hung and then burnt, traitors hung, drawn, and quartered. Torture was the order of the day. Executions served to inculcate respect for the law and for public order, though this was an area in which the men of the Middle Ages and the Renaissance seem to have had trouble separating the useful from the entertaining. The execution in the public square, in the presence of a crowd of spectators who flocked to attend out of morbid curiosity, constitutes perhaps the most telling example of the gulf that separates the modern mentality from the mentality of the time. At this point, however, it is possible to look ahead and formulate a general rule: a reliable juridical structure, the less authoritarian the better, would no doubt make the danger of a possible encounter with the law less distressful. Such a structure was therefore deemed a necessary preliminary to any choice.

ADDITIONAL FACTORS: SIZE, ECONOMIC CONDITIONS, THE EXISTENCE OF ESTABLISHED JEWISH SETTLEMENTS

NO ONE SETTLED, naturally enough, where it was going to be difficult to earn one's daily bread. Perhaps this proposition should be formulated in positive terms: localities in which it was possible to predict good business earnings were preferred. A moneylender of the day might have put it this way: he gave his preference to cities surrounded by an extensive *contado*, a nearby countryside with a large number of peasants, all of them potential customers for consumer loans, especially at seedtime or just before the harvest. In point of fact, the majority of what are now called the "seasonal poor" were made up of peasants, people who lived on the edge of poverty, to which they could be reduced by the slightest setback, and who were therefore frequently in need of ready cash to tide them over the lean months. It would in fact be a long time before the Italian cities would protect their peasants the same way they protected their citizens, which meant in practice that the moneylender could insist on a higher rate of interest from the peasants than was consented in the case of the city-dweller. As already pointed out, the Jewish moneylenders showed themselves no more sensitive about exploiting the poverty of Christian subjects than did the Christian authorities. Finally, those localities were preferred where the exploitation of the poverty of others did not bar the newcomers from assuming a real role in the local economy — localities, that is, where Jews were not forbidden to engage in commerce or to invest in local industry, as the Christian trade and professional guilds would have preferred.

The variables that determined the attraction for Jews of a particular locality were, then, manifold. It is impossible to present a universally valid descriptive model, particularly if one bears in mind that the variety of human idiosyncrasies also played an important role in the process of decision making. It was not unheard-of that, between two places close to each other, with identical socioeconomic characteristics and subject to the same form of political regime, one would appear attractive to the Jews, and the other not. A Jewish writer, who probably lived in the fifteenth century, wrote a parody of the world of the moneylenders in which he summed up in a few lines the whole problem of the choice of a place to settle: "The bank must be located in a city surrounded by walls, with its gates barred throughout the night, so as to be protected from armed and unarmed bands eager to get their hands on objects of value. This city must hold an annual fair, and a weekly market. There must be shops that sell bread and meat and other essential products. There must be a resident tribunal with judges and gendarmes, but the people who live in the *contado* must not enjoy the same rights as citizens. This city must be a heavily trafficked crossroads; it must be wealthy; and above all it must have a navigable river, though if the worst comes to the worst, a spring will do, or a freshwater well."[43]

The choice of a place to settle was strongly influenced by two contradictory factors. On the one hand, other things being equal, the best possibilities existed where other Jews had not yet settled, in other words, where one had no fear of competition from other Jewish moneylenders. Places fitting that description tended, however, in the nature of things to be smaller and smaller, since the bigger cities were obviously the first to be chosen. On the other hand, unlike the big cities, a small town did not offer many business opportunities. Another pair of contradictory needs must also be taken into consideration: the big cities were more attractive, not only for the economic opportunities they offered, but also because they frequently harbored a sufficient number of fellow worshipers to satisfy the most elementary cultural and religious needs of the group. In fact the Jews were seeking a situation where they could perform their devotional duties in groups of ten males over the age of thirteen, as required by the Jewish religious rule. They also wanted to be able to take part in some kind of study of the traditional texts and to hear rabbinical sermons on the Sabbath and on feast days. They hoped to provide a good education for their children, if possible in the company of children the same age, without having to pay for a preceptor out of their own pockets, and without having to send their children away to school. And finally they wished to be able to enjoy a minimum of social life with their fellow Jews, to eat with them and to drink a glass of wine without running into problems involving the dietary laws. In a word, they sought to enjoy the advantages offered by the existence of more or less organized groups: ritual services, the production of cheese and the ritual slaughtering of cattle, baths for the ritual immersion of women, a Jewish cemetery. All this could be found only in places where other Jews had already settled, possibly in considerable numbers, in other words, in the larger cities. But how many large cities were there in Italy in which a Jewish moneylender could find his little place in the sun?

In the mid–sixteenth century, Italian cities with more than fifty or sixty thousand inhabitants could be counted on the fingers of two hands: Rome, Naples, Bologna, Florence, Genoa, Milan, and Venice. The others, however important, rarely reached such figures: Ancona, Pesaro, Urbino, Rimini, Perugia, Siena, Pisa, Ferrara, Mantua, Cremona, Piacenza, Pavia, Verona, and Padua. Many Italian cities did not exceed ten thousand souls. Thus the choice was rather limited, all the more so because Jews were not accepted everywhere. It has already been pointed out that, toward the end of the period under examination, two of these big cities—Genoa and Milan—would only accept Jews in the most exceptional circumstances. These cities only granted residence permits under very special conditions to the occasional merchant or doctor, or a safe-conduct for a very limited period. The same may be said for Venice, except for a brief period (1382–1397) when extraordinary events convinced the leaders of the Most Serene Republic to admit Jewish moneylenders. In fact, it was not until 1509 that the Jews were admitted to Venice as war refugees (of the war in which the confederate League of Cambrai opposed Venice). When the war was over, the Jews were not required to leave, and in this way the ground was laid for that famous Jewish community.

The case of Naples was in a certain sense the opposite of that of Venice. The Jews of Southern Italy, after the expulsion of 1291 and the subsequent resettlement, went through a single short period of flowering shortly before 1492, concurrently with the grandiose and magnificent programs of King Ferdinand (1458–1494), who very probably encouraged the insertion of a number of Jews into the economic and cultural context of his realm. The subordination of the kings of Naples to Spanish policies became such that, after 1492, the atmosphere of the kingdom became quite unbearable; hence, anyone who had a slightly better alternative within reach moved out. The Jews were finally expelled from Naples in 1541. As for Florence, the Jews were admitted only in 1427, considerably later than the other cities of Tuscany, and even then they did not settle in a permanent manner. The competition of the trade and professional guilds made their settlement in this famous center of arts and letters difficult: add to this the interests of the Florentine bankers, who, though willing to leave small consumer loans to the Jews, did not welcome their competition outside of this very limited sector. In any case, the Jews were driven from the city on several occasions. For the entire period that interests us, then, Florence was not a center of particular attraction. Among the really large cities, the only one left was Bologna, where in fact, attracted by the particularly fortunate geographical position and by the possibilities of entering into the city's economic life, the Jews settled in considerable numbers throughout the first phase of our history, only to leave after the city became incorporated into the State of the Church and Pope Pius V ordered the expulsion of the Jews from his dominions in 1569.

One should not of course forget Rome. Jews had resided in Rome uninterruptedly for more than a thousand years. Nevertheless, in the period concerned, Rome ceased to be a center of attraction for anyone, and even less for Jews than Christians. By this time the possibilities of making one's fortune somewhere else seemed considerably greater. Those who were even slightly well off quit Rome for other localities, realizing they could earn their daily bread more easily as moneylenders elsewhere. Rome was no longer a privileged destination.

Where else could they go then? There were few choices, among the large or relatively large cities. Almost all of them have already been mentioned. It was in those localities that the highest demographic concentration of Jews was recorded. But they could not accommodate everyone. In order to heighten competition, and thereby reduce interest rates, rulers showed themselves ready upon occasion not to place any limits on the influx of Jewish moneylenders. For the same reason, however, the moneylenders who had settled there first were not at all favorable to the idea of increasing the number of their competitors. To prevent their settlement, they had a number of means at their disposal. They could, for example, quite simply obtain a monopoly from the Christian authorities. In the early decades of Jewish settlement in the Italian cities, the granting of monopolies was by no means rare. Still, one is left with the impression that, the more the years progressed, the fewer monopolies were granted. The phenomenon, however, has still to be studied in depth, and it is not sure to what it should be attributed.

Nonetheless, the Jews could prevent the settlement of newcomers by recourse to the traditional institutions of Jewish law. They could appeal, for instance, to the ordinances forbidding anyone to settle where he could not claim legitimate right of residence (*Ḥezkat ha-Yishuv*) under pain of excommunication (*Ḥerem ha-Yishuv*). Examples of this kind of opposition are not lacking. Nevertheless, it seems that such recourse was not very common practice. Compared with the large number of banks in the hands of Jewish moneylenders in this period, the evidence of suits based on this argument is truly negligible. Not that Jews did not litigate among themselves for reasons of this kind; quite to the contrary. Economic realities seem, however, in the long run to have been the deciding factor. In fact, before granting permission to set up a loan bank, the authorities insisted that the Jews make a minimum capital investment. It goes without saying that, the larger the city, the higher the sum. Moneylenders with little capital were therefore naturally driven out of the big cities and were forced to make do with small localities, or change their profession.

A second law determining Jewish migratory movements can therefore be formulated. On the one hand these movements seem to be characterized by a constant tendency toward marked dispersion, brought about chiefly by the complexity of the economic situation, whereas on the other hand, a contrary tendency came into play, driven by a complex set of social and cultural considerations. In the first phase of our period, this twofold tendency imposed a particularly intense dynamic profile on demographic distribution. Through the first quarter of the sixteenth century, more or less, one or two, occasionally three, families of Jewish moneylenders settled in scores of walled localities with one thousand, two thousand, up to five thousand inhabitants. These localities occupied an urban space of no more than a few square kilometers. Even today in Italy one can visit localities in which a spatial distribution of this kind is still perfectly preserved: we have only to think of San Marino, Macerata, Lucca, Castelfranco Veneto, Montagnana, and so on.

More than five hundred places could be listed in which the presence of Jews in this period is recorded, although the documents almost never provide proof of continuous settlement. In most cases, it is impossible to determine even whether documents that mention the same name and come from two different places are evidence of two separate Jews with the same name or of the same person in two different places at two different times. This makes it impossible to produce any kind of an accurate demographic profile: one must make do with an approximation. However, the phenomenon in question brings out a characteristic trait of the Jewish minority in Italy during the first phase, until, that is, the Jews who were expelled from Spain made their appearance: the omnipresence of a few thousand persons who settled throughout an extremely vast territory. We will return later to the inevitable repercussions that this situation had on these people's perception of group identity. For the moment it can be taken as read, as a touchstone by which to assess the radical transformation that occurred in the second phase, which covers most of the sixteenth century.

Second Phase:
The Ghettos

THE INFLUX OF IBERIAN REFUGEES

IN A CERTAIN SENSE, it would not be entirely mistaken to attribute the reversal of the trend to the appearance in Italy of the Jews expelled from Spain and Sicily. Not that their numbers were sufficient to cause a demographic revolution. On the contrary, they were more or less negligible, except perhaps temporarily at the beginning, when relatively large groups in transit to the Orient stopped off in Italy. In any case, even in the years immediately after 1492, they never reached the astronomical figure of 100,000 souls sometimes cited in outdated studies. All things considered, the impression is that Italy did not turn out to be very attractive to the refugees. Indeed, contemporary sources even tend to suggest that the tragedy of the Spanish Jews went practically unnoticed in Italy.

Why? Were the Jews of Italy more reluctant than Jews elsewhere perhaps to welcome their unfortunate fellow worshipers? Not at all. The insistence of many historians upon the few pieces of evidence available to confirm this interpretation—evidence whose significance has in any case been inadequately analyzed—seems to reflect the persistence of ideological conditioning rather than neutral attention to the facts. For the majority of Italian Jews, who had themselves experienced the bitter taste of expatriation and expulsion, the Spanish exiles were precisely that, refugees, and nothing more: to be welcomed or rejected in precisely the same way as refugees from Nüremberg or Regensburg. In fact, except for the sporadic instances already mentioned, in the absence of further testimony to the contrary, it does not appear that the Jewish communities in Italy ever even considered "the problem of the Spanish refugees."

The fact remains, however, that, unlike the Franco-German refugees of previous centuries, these fugitives did not choose Italy as their new homeland. Some of them probably found in Italy an atmosphere similar to that of the country they came from, in other words, potentially dangerous from more than one point of view. For years, a man of letters like Joseph Yavetz (1438–1539) existed in unjustified fear of the threat of the sword of Damocles, which he saw suspended over the heads of those who displayed cultural tendencies analogous to those of the "Averroistic" Spanish Jews, who had provoked the divine wrath: when nothing came of his prognostications, he left, disappointed, for the Orient. Others were doubtless attracted by the mythical El Dorado represented by the lands of the Great Turk. Once uprooted and on the move, it must have seemed natural to many of them not to let themselves be persuaded to remain in the lands of the Christians, by now to their eyes the symbol of the demon. The difficulties presented by practical considerations, such as language and culture, clearly more readily resolved in Italy than in the Ottoman empire, were probably minimized by the fact that these people migrated en masse, bearing with them their own shards of an imaginary Spain.

However that may be, and the question deserves further study, fairly few Spanish exiles opted for Italy. The *conversos* from Portugal were probably even fewer. The latter settled in Italy in greater numbers after the introduction of the Inquisition into Portugal in 1536. Pope Paul III adhered to the opinion of his counselors, who considered forced baptism null and void, and he allowed the settlement of conversos in the territories of the State of the Church, particularly at Ancona, where the newcomers were expected to make a positive contribution to the development of the economy. The same went for Venice. True, Venice ordered the total expulsion of the Jewish conversos in 1550, but this was no more than an exceptional circumstance. Generally speaking, the Venetian Republic went to no trouble to investigate the backgrounds of people who, once they disembarked in Venice, openly professed the Jewish religion. The dukes of Ferrara were, it seems, the most liberal and tolerant. In this period in fact Ferrara became the most important center of the Spanish and Portuguese presence in Italy, as will be seen later. Others sought unsuccessfully to imitate the example of Ferrara: Emanuel Philibert, Duke of Savoy, for instance, attempted in 1572 to give a powerful stimulus to the Piedmontese economy by settling a certain number of Spanish refugees. The attempt failed for various reasons, such as the refugees' fear of the proximity of the duchy to the Spanish royal troops, and the geographical position of the region, unpropitious to large-scale trade because of its remoteness from the main routes of communication. The attempts of the grand dukes of Tuscany were more successful. Their most notable exploit was the successful settlement of the Jews in Pisa and Livorno. But this development lies outside the chronological limits, not only of the phase of Jewish settlement presently under discussion, but of this entire work. Thus, one may sum up by saying that, except for the cases of Ferrara, Ancona, and Venice, and one or two other cities, though to a lesser degree, Jews of Spanish and Portuguese origin were not responsible for the aforementioned reversal of the topodemographic trend. In what sense, then, would it not be entirely mistaken to discern a relationship between the two events?

Actually, the Spanish and Portuguese Jews, whether or not they were conversos, were different from the Italian or German moneylenders dealt with so far. They were merchants and entrepreneurs with established business relations, usually reinforced by family connections, with the principal non-Italian cities, such as Amsterdam, Salonica, Constantinople, and Bursa. This is evidently the reason they tended to choose the large commercial centers. But it also explains why the attitude of the people in power toward them was quite different from that previously displayed toward the Italian or Franco-German Jews who preceded them. In fact, the basic economic difference naturally led to a modification of the reasons adduced to justify the invitation to the Jews to take up residence. The Jews themselves had already proved to be an economic force to reckon with: they were in a position to foster the development of commerce. Rulers therefore decided to integrate them into the local economy rather than continue to make use of them at the margins of society, where they had been relegated because of the despised roles they performed. This represented a radical change, and with it begins the second phase of the demographic configuration. A period of extreme geographic dispersion was followed by one of gradual but radical contraction and concentration. One no longer encounters, as one did previously, a few Jews scattered over many different localities. Entire regions were destined to remain completely devoid of Jews for centuries. In other areas, a gradual process of concentration began in the major cities. The settlement of Spanish and Portuguese Jewish merchants in the major Italian cities disposed to accept them was without a doubt one of the factors that led to the change, and in this sense it was paradigmatic. But there were certainly other factors involved.

SETTING ASIDE all other factors, whose specific importance is still open to discussion, the major cause of the upheaval can be found in a series of expulsions that forced the communities of entire regions to take the path of exile. Driven out of Sicily in 1492 as a result of the decree expelling Jews from countries under Spanish dominion, the Jews were subsequently also exiled from the Kingdom of Naples in 1541. Then, in 1569, came their expulsion from the Papal States (with the exception of Rome and Ancona), and, in 1597, from the duchy of Milan. In the course of approximately sixty years, the Jews were driven to concentrate almost exclusively in the territories of Mantua (which also included Monferrato), Ferrara, and Venice, and, to a lesser degree, in Tuscany and Savoy. The attitude of relative tolerance which had characterized the initial phase of our period had given way to one of extreme intransigence. The expulsions were merely its most acute symptom. There followed another symptom, no less typical of the reversed trend: wherever the Jews were tolerated, even in the most liberal states, they were sealed off in ghettos. The latter phenomenon parallels the former, in that it too contributed to the contraction of the space available to the Jewish presence.

It is not easy to identify the causes of the change in climate. They must be related to the whole complex of events that shook this century, so crucial and critical for the history of the West. At first glance it would appear that part of the responsibility must fall, on the one hand, on the anti-Jewish policies of the kings of Spain, who also ruled the kingdom of Naples and later the duchy of Milan, and, on the other hand, on the radical change in the papal attitude toward the Jews. After the expulsion of the Jews from the Iberian peninsula, the attitude of the kings of Spain vis-à-vis the "Jewish question" does not require explanation. That of the popes, however, was not perfectly in line with the traditional policy of the Church toward the Jews, and it is not easy to analyze. No doubt one may point to the Holy See's growing difficulties in opposing the Protestant offensive and the consequent desirability of distracting attention

A narrow street in the Jewish quarter of Ferrara, where Jews were first confined to a ghetto in 1626. Courtesy of Dr. Giulio Busi.

toward the Jewish problem. The Jews could provide a useful scapegoat, as well as a particularly vulnerable target for a weakened Catholic Church urgently in need of demonstrating its own orthodoxy and its devotion to the cause of Christianity. The vicars of Christ, however, had frequently found themselves in similar situations in the past without feeling compelled to turn to such an extreme policy. On the contrary, it might even be affirmed, without going too far, that the attitude of the Holy See over several centuries with regard to the Jews represented a stabilizing factor in comparison with the extreme fluctuations that took place in the attitudes of the leaders of secular states.

ONE MUST of course take into account the psychology and the personal tendencies of the individual popes, especially Paul IV (1555–1559), who played such an exceptionally important role in the period. In the sixteenth century, the folly or wisdom of a head of state could still be a critical factor in determining the course of history. In any case, we cannot separate the idiosyncrasies of the dramatis personae from the general context in which those idiosyncrasies might wither or flourish. From this point of view, Paul IV's policy toward the Jews is no exception. The decisions affecting the Jews made by the peremptory and choleric eighty-year-old patriarch cannot be isolated from the more generalized antisimoniac and reforming austerity cultivated by Paul IV in the face of the crisis of Catholicism. However, it would be a mistake to see in his approach to the "Jewish question" simply one more detail in papal policy, since his attitude toward the Jews was fed by a missionary fire so vigorous that it cannot be explained without reference to the man's idiosyncrasies. It appears that the various elements were complementary, and that for all practical purposes the Jewish component of Paul IV's zeal for reform, as well as his fundamentally anti-Jewish sentiments, were perfectly in keeping with the overall change in climate. In other words, the Pope's idiosyncracies functioned as the overt expression of this change, which was given a semblance of traditional continuity by a convenient collection of documents culled from the archives of the papal chancellery. As for the criteria to be used in describing the elements of the change and measuring its effectiveness, these, it seems, must be sought above all in the acceptance and reflection of papal policy in the policies of a number of other heads of state, including those to whom liberal tendencies might otherwise be attributed. A few facts and events will help to make the picture clearer.

As for Paul IV, the Jews did not have to wait for his elevation to the papal throne to discover his true sentiments. As head of the Inquisition prior to his election, the future pope Cardinal Caraffa had made no effort to keep them a secret. He had played a leading role in Julius III's decision to order the bonfire of all extant copies of the Talmud in Campo de' Fiori in September 1553, on the eve, that is, of the year 5314 in the Jewish calendar, and to invite other Italian heads of state to follow his example. Throughout the fifties and sixties of the century, one bonfire followed another, providing a foretaste of the general acceptance outside of the Papal States of the future policies of Pope Paul IV. This was one of the cruelest blows to the culture of the tiny Jewish minority and its ability to resist the impact of disintegration, as will be seen later. While he was still a cardinal, Caraffa made no secret of his opinion of the Portuguese conversos, whom, notwithstanding their past, Pius III had authorized to settle freely in Ancona. If it had been up to the cardinal, he would have had them burnt alive, at least according to the report of an ambassador to the Holy See.[44] The Jews of Italy had more than an inkling of disaster when, on 26 May 1555, Cardinal Caraffa ascended to the throne of Saint Peter. He kept his word as far as the conversos of Ancona were concerned. After first confiscating their goods, he sent to the stake all those who had not managed to flee in time. The episode underlined the weak position of the Jewish people. For a brief moment it looked as if there might be a vigorous international show of strength. At the solicitation of Doña Gracia Mendes Nasi, the Grand Sultan of the Turks intervened with the threat of reprisals. The overseas Jews threatened to impose an embargo on the port of Ancona and to transfer trade with the Levant to Pesaro. But nothing came of it. When the smoke from the auto-da-fé cleared, the Jews did nothing but demonstrate their confusion and their inability to agree on a single course of action. Their polemics still provide fuel for academic discussions: who or what was responsible for the setback? The jealousy of the Italian Jews toward their wealthy Portuguese rivals? The intransigence of the rabbis of Constantinople, who saw in the decision of the Portuguese to settle in Catholic territory a challenge to the divine wrath that past experience ought to have convinced them to avoid? Or, more simply, the historical combination of events, which made the threat of an embargo absolutely ineffective? The issue remains open to this very day.

This does not alter the fact that the pope's choices show him to have had very clear ideas on the subject of the "Jewish question." The Ancona affair, however unfortunate, played only a minor role in the general context of the revolution unleashed by the policies of Paul IV, which were to turn the condition of the Italian Jews upside down. Less than two months after his ascent to the papacy, on 14 July 1555, the pope published the bull *Cum nimis absurdum*, which marked the complete reversal of traditional policy with regard to the Jews and the beginning of a revolution in their condition wherever they might be, not only in the territories under papal government. Many of the ordinances specified in the fifteen articles of the bull would be later adopted by other Italian authorities, according to a pattern determined in part by their personal idiosyncrasies, as well as by socioeconomic circumstances, but which nonetheless demonstrates considerable overall uniformity.

"It is profoundly absurd and intolerable," thundered the pope in the programmatic preamble to the bull, "that the Jews, who are bound by their guilt to perpetual servitude, should show themselves ungrateful toward Christians; and, with the pretext that Christian piety welcomes them by permitting them to dwell among Christians, they repay this favor with scorn, attempting to dominate the very people whose servants they should be." On the contrary, he insisted, "considering that the Church tolerates the Jews in order that they may bear witness to the truth of the Christian faith," until the day comes when they acknowledge the error of their ways and accept the light of the Catholic religion, "they must show themselves to be the servants of Christians who are the true free men in Jesus Christ and in God." The Jews were condemned to live in a quarter set apart from the Christians; not to possess real estate and to sell immediately any property they might own; to wear the yellow insignia, the badge of infamy. From now on they were compelled to respect implicitly the ancient prohibition that forbade them to employ nursemaids or other Christian servants, or to have themselves referred to deferentially by poor Christians, to work publicly on Sundays or other Christian holidays, to engage in commerce (other than in secondhand commodities, the notorious "strazzaria" or rag trade), to dispense medical care to Christians, to have any relations with Christians, to gamble, eat, converse, or bathe in their company. Even moneylending was more strictly regulated and moralized, so as not to encourage Jewish cheating: the moneylenders had to keep their books in Italian, calculate the date according to a thirty-day calendar, and so on and so forth.

All this was certainly neither unheard of nor unprecedented. The precedent for most of the provisions in Paul IV's bull is to be found in the Fourth Lateran Council (1215). Under the direction of Pope Innocent III, that council had decreed, among other things, the ineligibility of Jews for public office, the imposition of the badge, the ban on appearing in public during Holy Week, the responsibility of Christians to limit the potential economic activity of Jews, and that of rulers in particular to create favorable conditions for the practical observance of this proviso. And what cannot be found in the deliberations of that particular synod can be found without much difficulty in the texts of other scattered papal promulgations or conciliar decisions. This did not prevent the massive reappearance of all these measures, for the most part long forgotten, coming as a profound shock to the Jews. Evidence of the shock is provided by a number of contemporary literary sources. How is it to be accounted for? Probably because the new experience brought them to the painful realization that this was no passing madness but the expression of a general reversal of policy, for which the Holy See was able to supply the ideological cement of a long-standing tradition, as well as the paradigm for its implementation. This awareness was definitively confirmed when they realized that this time they were not going to be able to commute the new papal dispositions into additional fiscal burdens.

THE INSTITUTION OF THE GHETTOS

PERHAPS the most obvious of these restrictive provisos, inasmuch as its effect had an immediate impact at the level of the civic space, was the institution of the ghetto—the most typical of the structural changes occurring in the attitude toward the Jews. In a sense, the institution of the ghetto became the symbol of the new Jewish condition. In

Above and next page: Paintings by Franz Roesler of the Roman Ghetto, established in 1555. Its gates and walls were removed only in 1846. Courtesy of Umberto Nahon Museum of the Italian Synagogue, Jerusalem.

this case too the precedent was set by earlier regimes in earlier times, and, even in the sixteenth century, the Holy See was not the first to revive the idea. This time it was Venice, the holder, incidentally, of the copyright on the term "ghetto," which led the way. In Venice the Jews had been confined within Cannareggio, on the extreme edge of the urban space, since 1516, a good forty years before the bull *Cum nimis absurdum*, when the air in the rest of Italy for the Jews was considerably more breathable than at midcentury. This circumstance may help us to grasp, in part at

least, the essentially ambivalent character of a measure that our modern sensibility automatically tends to see as a symbol of oppression, not to say discrimination.

As was already pointed out, Venice had been until then one of the Italian cities that had constantly denied Jews permission to settle officially. So, before it became a symbol of the desire to segregate the Jews, the institution of the ghetto in Venice marked the abandonment of the tradtional policy of excluding Jews from the city. In a certain sense, the institution of the Venetian ghetto was a compromise solution, designed to normalize the situation created when, during the war of 1509, the Jews had been given extraordinary permission to take refuge in the city. This did not represent a deterioration in the status of the Jews, but rather the opposite. The Venetian ghetto represented a kind of middle ground between unconditional acceptance, which was unthinkable, and expulsion, which would have meant a return to the *status quo ante*, which was equally undesirable. In Rome, however, the institution of the ghetto represented a definite deterioration in the conditions of Jewish life. And yet, if we look at it in the light of the Venetian attitude, even the Roman development can be seen to lend itself to a not entirely negative interpretation. When he formally revived the stipulations of the Fourth Lateran Council, without abandoning the traditional Christian theological conception according to which the presence of the Jews was necessary as a *testimonium veritatis*, Paul IV was asserting that the Venetian solution was consistent with his own. Though in the opposite direction, the institution of the ghetto in Rome was just as much of a compromise solution as it was in Venice. In the palpably anti-Jewish climate that had developed in Rome, the institution of the ghetto, understood as an alternative to out-and-out expulsion, undeniably changed the *status quo ante*, but it indicated at the same time that the pope had opted, at least for the moment, to preserve the presence of the Jews in the State of the Church.

One may be tempted to dismiss all of this as self-evident and banal. True enough, if we think of this compromise between the total rejection of the Jews and their unconditional acceptance merely in terms of a semantic dialectic, and especially if we think only in terms of the policy of Paul IV and the fact that not that many years later the Jews were in fact expelled from the Papal States. Still, despite the bull's emphasis on the continuity with medieval attitudes, the institution of the ghetto did represent a revolution. As a historical phenomenon it was not typical of the medieval Jewish condition but rather of the period between the Middle Ages and the Modern Period. Readily perceptible at the level of events, a new historical phenomenon seems to have been set in motion. Most ghettos were instituted in Italy at a later period than that which concerns us here. The sequence seems to be fraught with significance: Venice 1516; Rome 1555; Florence 1571; Siena 1571; Mirandola 1602; Verona 1602; Padua 1603; Mantua 1612; Rovigo 1613; Ferrara 1624; Modena 1638; Urbino, Pesaro, Senigallia 1634; Este 1666; Reggio Emilia 1670; Conegliano Veneto 1675; Turin 1679; Casale Monferrato 1724; Vercelli 1725; Acqui 1731; Moncalvo 1732; Finale 1736; Correggio 1779. On the eve of the French Revolution, ghettos were still being created! Is one to discern in this sequence a progressive deterioration of the situation of the Jews? The opposite is the truth. The overall attitude toward the Jews was in fact far more liberal during the period of the ghettos than it had been before. Accusations of ritual murder disappeared almost completely and the frequency of attacks and pogroms declined markedly, as did the tendency to expel the Jews. The series of expulsions stopped at more or less the same time the series of confinements in ghettos began, a symptom that should not be allowed to pass unobserved.

In my opinion, it is not in the least farfetched to believe that in the long run the institution of ghettos did not imply a simple progressive deterioration in the Jewish condition. Rather, following a circuitous route, the mental disposition of the Christian population toward the Jews began to be oriented in the opposite direction. In other words, the Jewish Other was no longer seen as someone to be acculturated, someone whose diversity must be eradicated, someone to be rejected should the attempt at acculturation fail. The Jewish Other could now be accepted without a prior commitment to acculturate him whatever the cost. (This did not mean, of course, giving up the Christian mission altogether.) Of course this acceptance took place on the only terms on which the mentality of the time could accommodate the Jew — segregation. Segregation was a necessity, given the lack of mental health of the Jews, which showed itself in an inability to identify with the majority, healthy precisely because it was the majority and because it was Christian. From this point of view, as Michel Foucault might have put it, the institution of the ghetto may be considered homologous with many other expressions of the change that took place in the Western mentality during the phase of transition from the Middle Ages to the Modern Period. A halfway house between acceptance and expulsion, the ghetto made its first appearance as a historically relevant phenomenon, characterized by distinctive features proper to the period that was ending and other features proper to the one that was beginning, on the very threshold of the modern age. It was a solution that represented a compromise between the tendency to welcome Jews practically unconditionally everywhere, characteristic of the period prior to the second half of the sixteenth century, and the tendency to expel them, characteristic of the period following the Council of Trent. The ghetto represented the latest expression of the millenary tradition of ambivalence toward the Jews: keeping them separate without actually rejecting them, accepting them only provided they were kept segregated.

The historical significance of the new process is underscored by the fact that this solution did not succeed in imposing itself in the same way as it would have done in the preceding period. The Jewish moneylenders were no longer as necessary as they had once been, and therefore arguments for their presence could be countered with even more telling arguments. The socioeconomic need for the Jews vis-à-vis the poor diminished as the Monti di Pietà were being transformed into modern credit institutions. According to the logic of the medieval mentality, the idea that one must rid oneself of the agents of the devil the moment they were no longer needed ought to have made itself felt immediately. But this is not what happened. The Jews remained in the cities of Italy, which tolerated them, even when they were no longer "necessary," at least in the sense in which they had been necessary in the fifteenth century. Their situation, nevertheless, obviously became somewhat more precarious. Throughout the period of transition into the modern era, the threat of expulsion seemed to hang over their heads. Not having yet developed mental categories altogether different from those of the preceding period, the Jews tried to avert this threat with the same old arguments. Simone Luzzatto (1582–1663), for instance, in that jewel of impassioned oratory that is his famous *Discourse on the Jews of Venice*, fell back on the old formula of the necessity of the Jews for the local economy. Luzzato in fact proposed to "demonstrate that the said [Jewish] nation was anything but a useless member of the common people of the said City [Venice]."[45] He therefore devoted long chapters of his work to sketching a positive portrait of his coreligionists and to an account "of the profits and advantages contributed by the [Jewish] Nation" to the Most Serene Republic (chapter 8). Luzzatto did not neglect to mention of course "the establishment of three Banks for the poor, set up by the Hebrews" (chapter 9). But the main emphasis fell squarely on the activities of the merchants. An entire chapter was devoted to demonstrating the truth of the proposition that "the Hebrews are marvelously suited to business" (chapter 4). In short, showing keen sensitivity to the new categories of the merchant economy, and remarkable historical and political insight, this Jewish rabbi simply substituted the term "merchant" for the term "moneylender." Realizing that the golden age of Jewish *necessity* was over and done with forever, he tried to pass their *usefulness* off as necessity. For all that, this discourse was not an anachronism. Rather, it was the expression of a world view that saw the changed historical circumstances as likely to provide Jews with an opening for their integration into the economic fabric instead of the role of despised service on the margins of society which had been reserved for them until now.

With the passage of time, the Jews returned to many minor centers from which they had previously been expelled. This return, however, was frequently ephemeral. And above all it never assumed the extremely widespread character it had had in the preceding phase of our history. Given that the opportunities for engaging in profitable activities based on the traffic in money were now considerably reduced, the Jews no longer felt, as they once had, the incentive to turn their backs on the big cities and give their preference to the lesser centers. They preferred to concentrate their presence in those of the major cities in which it was still possible to take up residence, the number of which was even less than in the preceding phase.

The institution of the ghetto led to the crystallization of the Jewish presence within the city's topography. The residential quarters of the powerful gradually moved out of the city center, in several instances following the tendency of the rulers to remove the center of secular power from the spatial orbit of the cathedrals and the bishops (such, for example, was the case in Ferrara). The Jews, however, had originally preferred to take up residence close to the market places, in the center of the city. Their dwellings were located along the main thoroughfares leading to the gates, along which the peasants from the contado, potential clients for the moneylenders, were obliged to pass whenever they came to town to buy or sell. The tendency toward urban decentralization thus had the effect of reinforcing the attachment of the Jews to the heart of the various cities: these were zones, incidentally, whose market value was constantly declining. In most cases, the institution of the ghetto "tied" the Jews, so to speak, to these quarters. In most Italian cities, the ghetto is paradoxically located at the very center, right around the corner from the cathedral, as a rule close to the market. A rapid glace at the maps of the principal Italian cities permits us to affirm that this was practically a general rule. The noteworthy exception, which nonetheless confirms the rule, was of course Venice. In the city on the lagoon, where, for the reasons already seen, the position of the ghetto was not determined by a prior Jewish presence, it was easy to plan the segregation of the Jews "logically," away from the center. In any case, the topographical distribution of the Jewish presence in the cities of Italy remained until very recently precisely as it was between the end of the sixteenth century and the first few decades of the seventeenth. Thus, the ghetto of Mantua can still be located only a stone's throw from the central Via dell'Orso, that of Ferrara right behind the cathedral, that of Padua between what is today Via Roma and Piazza delle Erbe, and so on.

In this new demographic arrangement, everything had to go back to the beginning in the most difficult circumstances. The condition of inferiority was considerably worse than in the preceding period. Above all it frequently became necessary to change professions, abandoning moneylending for commerce. Moneylending became impractical without the capital investments that only the biggest moneylenders possessed. Many Jews of Italian or German origin who had chosen to leave behind the lesser centers and settle in the more populous cities no doubt continued to struggle to make a profit in the money trade, the field of their expertise. But conditions were no longer as favorable for this kind of activity as they had been in the past. Even if they had not chosen to give up moneylending and seek other ways of earning a living, they would have been forced to do so anyway, because they certainly could not hope to replace the wealthier lenders, who had cornered the market some time previously. For most of them, trade was the most immediate alternative. Unable to compete with the great merchants, they had to make do with small trade, especially in secondhand objects, though they were also prepared to try their hands at other professions. To the demographic transformation was added a no less far-reaching change in the socioeconomic profile of the Jewish minority in Italy. We will return to this in more detail in the next chapter.

The radical transformation of economic opportunities served as a major incentive to abandon the small centers for the large cities. The variety of choices offered by big cities obviously made them more attractive than a small locality. The natural attraction of centers with an established Jewish community must have provided an additional incentive that was by no means negligible. On top of all these factors, which are part of the logic informing the choice of emigrants in all times and places, one should probably add the change in safety conditions within the cities. The increasing use of artillery fire had made it unsafe to live in the smaller centers, which could not afford fortifications strong enough to withstand attacks by the powerful new weaponry. One may therefore suppose that there ensued a tendency to "go into shelter" in the big cities, which meant living differently and perhaps more poorly, but certainly in conditions of greater security. Given, on the one hand, the fact that it was no longer as easy as it had once been, because of the general change in attitude toward the Jews and the success of the Monti di Pietà, to earn a living as a moneylender in a small center; and given, on the other hand, the ever more precarious security conditions in the small centers, one might just as well change professions and seek one's fortune in a large city, where, if nothing else, it was also easier to pursue a "Jewish lifestyle."

It is quite likely that there is a connection, albeit on an unconscious level, between the new tendency on the part of the Jews to congregate in the larger cities and seek a place in the economic fabric of commercial enterprise, and the change, apparently unforeseen, in the policy of the Holy See regarding authorizations to open consumer loan banks. Between the end of the sixteenth century and the first decades of the seventeenth, in fact, thousands of such authorizations were issued. Nothing like this had ever happened before. Did it represent an attempt to curb the tendency toward concentration and integration by now under way? Or was it a paradoxically conservative gesture on the part of the Holy See? The question deserves to be studied in the light of the historical context, which was certainly different from that of the preceding century.

To conclude, the topographical distribution of the Jews in Italy presents itself, at the end of our period, as radically different from what it was at the beginning. Sicily and Southern Italy were without Jews, as was Central Italy, with the exception of Rome and Ancona, which had populations of a few thousand Jews. The remainder by now resided chiefly in the regions of Northern Italy: in Venice, where there dwelt a Jewish population of approximately 2,500, concentrated in a restricted area that was permitted to develop only in a vertical direction; in Mantua, where, when the ghetto was instituted in 1612, there were 2,325 Jews out of a total population of approximately 50,000; in Ferrara, a city for which no full-length study exists, and for which the data is therefore imprecise; in Verona, Padua, Casale Monferrato, Florence, Modena, and Parma, all centers with Jewish populations numbering in the hundreds; and finally, in a number of other localities, whose Jewish communities were even smaller.

II

TRADES AND
PROFESSIONS

SICILY

THE EXPULSION of the Jews from Sicily in 1492 considerably dis-
torted the historiography of the Jews of Italy. The paucity of the
documentation so far published regarding the Jews of Sicily, combined
with their total disappearance from the Italian scene at the very moment
when they were beginning to be of particular interest to historians, has
led to their passing practically unobserved in the pages of history. The
extent of the distortion can be better appreciated when we recall that
there were as many Jews in Sicily as there were on the entire peninsula.
We have already observed that between thirty and forty thousand Jews,
the equivalent of 1 percent of the local population, were living in sixty or
so towns and villages on the island. A good half of them were concentrated in Palermo, Syracuse, Messina, and Catania, whereas the rest were
scattered in localities where the number of Jews did not exceed forty or
fifty families.

During the period that concerns us, the Jews of Sicily continued to
live according to socioeconomic and institutional structures formed over
the course of the centuries by the particular historical and political conditions of the island. The many features of a Spanish or Moslem nature
that characterized the condition of these Jews are the result of the island's
proximity to the Islamic area of North Africa, as well as to the persistence
of Moslem traditions in Sicily itself. These traditions had never entirely

disappeared, just as they had never completely vanished in Spain, to which Sicily had close political and administrative ties. This takes us back to the distinguishing features of the "Mediterranean Society" so masterfully described by S. D. Goitein.[1] When the Moslems abandoned the Christianized island of Sicily, the Jews remained as the only representatives of an Otherness that preserved distinctive traits of the Islamic past. The synagogue, for instance, was called the *meschitta* (i.e., mosque), the poll-tax the Jews were expected to pay was called the *gyzia* (after the head tax Moslem legislation had imposed on Christians and Jews alike), and so on. All of this, including local semantics, was founded on a substratum going back to the Byzantine period: the leaders of the Jewish community, for example, were known as *proti*.

The continuity with the tradition of the past is also apparent in the fact that the Jews of Sicily continued to be called *servi camerae regiae* ("serfs of the royal chamber"), according to the terminology used in 1236 by the emperor Frederick II. This was not always a complete drawback; indeed it might at times prove an advantage. The Jews were usually included among those with the right to claim the privileges granted by the Crown to the Communes in the text of the charters. This, however, was not enough to guarantee them equality with other citizens. There are many documents that bear witness to various attempts to harass the Jews on the part of feudal overlords, ecclesiastical dignitaries, and communal administrations. In all these cases, the Crown was the sole arbiter in whom the Jews could place their trust, and they did not hesitate to invoke its protection, rightly appealing to their special status as serfs of the Royal Chamber. As for the royal authority, it appears to have been constantly guided by appetites of a fiscal nature rather than by coherent ideological or religious principles. However, numerous documents testify to the fact that this same traditional attitude with regard to the Jews, which could be defined as juridical in nature, can be traced back to older patterns of behavior inherited from the Moslem domination. The privilege of riding saddled mules, for instance, granted in 1491 to two Jews from Messina,[2] must be related to an explicit interdiction of the same prerogative, evidently inherited from the statute of Omar regarding the *dhimmi* minorities (Jews, Christians, and other minorities whose presence was tolerated under Islamic rule).

Past tradition also explains the fact that, in the urban context of the city, the Jews of Sicily presented a model of topographical settlement very similar to the one later destined to prevail in the cities of the Peninsula and already discussed in the previous chapter. The Jews, apparently of their own volition, generally resided in their own neighborhoods (called *giudecche*), in which the synagogue constituted the center of community, administrative, scholastic, and social life. The term *giudecca* ended up designating the Jewish community as a whole, even when many Jews lived in other neighborhoods, as was the case in Palermo. To the eyes of the Others, the giudecca presented itself as an organically structured whole, clearly defined within the civic space.

It comes as no surprise therefore to note the existence in Sicily of socio-economic and institutional structures profoundly different from those of the rest of the Peninsula, where Jewish settlement was based on the "colonizing" trend already alluded to. Rabbi Obadiah of Bertinoro (c.1450–1515), known above all for his commentary on the Mishnah, universally adopted as a classic text in traditional Jewish society, took note of these differences during his stay in Palermo. Obadiah was on his way to Jerusalem, where he arrived in 1488, to settle permanently. In his own account of his journey, set down for the benefit of his aged father who had stayed behind in Italy,[3] he jotted down some of the interesting features he had observed. Obadiah stressed the size, quite extraordinary to his mind, of the Sicilian communities, the demographic density of the Jewish quarters, the shops of the Jews open onto the main thoroughfare, and the crafts and agricultural occupations of his coreligionists, a good number of which he found particularly odious. The impression he had of the lot of Jewish workers was a miserable one for the most part. They were filthy, dressed in rags, and subject to harassments from which the Jews of the Peninsula were still practically exempt: prohibited from employing Christian servants and using Christian slaughtering facilities; compelled to wear an identifying badge and to perform a number of services for king, nobility, ecclesiastics, and communes; obliged to attend the sermons of Christian missionaries and the Christmas functions of the Church; pelted with stones by the population along the route they had to use to go to church. Perhaps the last straw was being forced to act as public executioners, a role imposed on the Jews of Sicily in accordance with an ancient tradition mentioned in the documents of the Moslem and Byzantine worlds.

Rabbi Obadiah was not surprised to find that most Sicilian Jews were merchants. There were plenty of merchants, to be sure, in his own place of origin, though their presence was marginal in comparison with that of the moneylenders. However, he made no comment on the incidence of moneylending among his Sicilian coreligionists. Moneylending was in fact formally forbidden on the island. According to the official documents, it was the Jewish communities themselves who, in one of the provisions of the ordinances solicited earlier, in 1363, requested its prohibition, without explaining the reasons for the request.[4] In a subsequent document presented to the Crown in the name of all the communities of the kingdom, the Jews were more explicit and requested that "lending at usury be prohibited among Jews as well as between Jews and Christians, as it was prohibited in the past and as it has always been prohibited among Jews, and this on account of the great detriment that may result from this activity."[5] Are we to interpret this as a sign of extraordinary ability to foresee the evils connected with the practice of moneylending, an ability demonstrated by the Jews of Sicily considerably in advance of their peninsular brethren? Or could it reflect a decision of the Crown, which the rules of the diplomatic game suggested should be registered in the form of a request coming from the Jews? For the moment, the question must remain moot. The repetition of the interdiction, combined with the evidence of trials for its violation, would seem to suggest that the Jews were not overscrupulous in their observation of its provisions and were not totally devoid of interest in moneylending. Perhaps this was why Rabbi Obadiah did not notice anything unusual in this regard.

He also made no comment on the presence of Jewish doctors, most of whom enjoyed important privileges and were close to the Court and the nobility. He evidently saw in this a circumstance similar to that of his place of origin, a point to which we will return shortly. Furthermore, the socioeconomic stratification of the Jewish population must not have seemed too different from what he was already familiar with, since he makes no comment on it. Official documents help us grasp some of its features and present us with a community governing body organized according to the medieval model, which was omnipresent in Aragonese and Italian municipal structures of the period, made up of representatives of the three "estates": a third of its members came from among the rich (*de statu majori, di li ricchi*), a third from the middle classes (*de statu minori*), and the last third from the poor (*di li poviri*). The same documents permit us to assess the social prestige and influence exerted by the more powerful Jews (the *maiorentes*) on their less influential brethren, over whom they asserted their authority, resorting at times to violence. The powerful, favored by the Crown, had few scruples about getting themselves assigned key positions in the exercise of power within the community or about getting themselves exempted from the payment of community taxes.

Many documents bear witness to this.[6] A permanent conflict was inevitable between the aspirations toward autonomy of the various groups and the ambition of the maiorentes to exercise power independently, as formal delegates of royal authority. For the time being, suffice it to conclude that the social structures and economic activities of the Jews of Sicily possessed distinctive features such as to further justify the basic dichotomy already suggested.

PENINSULAR ITALY

IN THE PENINSULA, as opposed to Sicily, the Jews were newcomers almost everywhere. We have already seen how the "novelty" that they represented came to be justified by citing the needs of the poor or some other necessity, such as ensuring the services of a doctor for the community. It was of course preferable to kill two birds with one stone, by securing the services of a moneylender who was also a doctor. The settlement of Jews in a place where they had not previously resided required formal residence permission, a *privilege* in the most elementary meaning of the word, a document justifying the exception to the rule. At first this document could only be issued *ad personam*: the rulers gave permission to this or that individual Jew to take up residence in their city for the purpose of carrying on a specific activity, according to a set of reciprocal conditions, listed in detail in the documents known as *condotte* or charters. These Jews naturally brought with them additional coreligionists, connected in some way to the titulary holders of the privilege: employees of the bank, servants, tutors, and so on. A "family" nucleus could in this way consist of as many as ten or fifteen individuals, whereas two families could include twenty to thirty people, a far from negligible number in most instances. The three Jewish families residing in Trent at the time of the deplorable accusation of ritual murder mentioned in the previous chapter made up in fact a total of thirty individuals. The connection or affiliation with the holder of the privilege might even be nothing more than a camouflage; from the majority of the cases examined, however, one does not get the impression that this was a frequent occurrence. It does appear, though, that the persons actually connected with the moneylender or doctor had in addition other professions or occupations of their own. In this way, people nominally without a residence permit, whose right to live in a given place was nonetheless not called into question, prepared the ground for the existence of groups or individuals who were not dependent on the titulary holders of the privileges at all. Their right to reside in a given place was de facto reinforced when the privileges, rather than being granted to a single individual, were vouchsafed to groups, to the *universitates* or "nations" of the Jews, without further distinction between moneylenders and the rest. This was the basis on which later Jewish *Communities* were formed.

T HE CONDOTTE were bilateral contracts of limited duration, usually lasting for from three to five years, in rare instances for fifteen or more, stipulated by the rulers of the city and the Jews. When they expired, these contracts could be renewed, which is what usually happened, thereby establishing a certain continuity of the Jewish presence in many centers from which the Jews had been completely absent in the period immediately preceding. The Jews were not automatically expelled from the city even when they were unsuccessful in obtaining the renewal of their condotta: their residence was simply no longer founded on the legal basis of the privilege. In theory, they became *liable* to expulsion. De facto, however, it meant that they fell under the provisions of the *jus comune* rather than under the *jus speciale* as defined in the terms of the privilege. This was a very different situation from a regularly authorized residence, but it was still preferable to expulsion. In any case, throughout the period in which the residence of Jews was regulated by the system of the condotta, that residence was everywhere formally and essentially only *temporary*. This detail should be added to what was said in the preceding chapter regarding the difference between the first and second phases of the period. Though there are examples of condotte being issued at a fairly late date, for instance in Padua and Verona, the system based upon them is in fact characteristic of the phase prior to the establishment of the ghettos.

The documentation regarding the condotte is extremely plentiful: there are hundreds of these documents extant today, all of which present a more or less homogeneous set of general characteristics, whereas in points of detail they reflect a variety of local circumstances, in addition to the specific characteristics of the individuals involved. The condotte define in precise detail the terms and limits of the protection afforded the Jews, their rights, and, above all, their duties. The Jew or Jews mentioned in the document agree to exercise the function for which they were invited to take up residence in the locality, usually consumer lending, sometimes trade, more rarely the medical profession. The last two

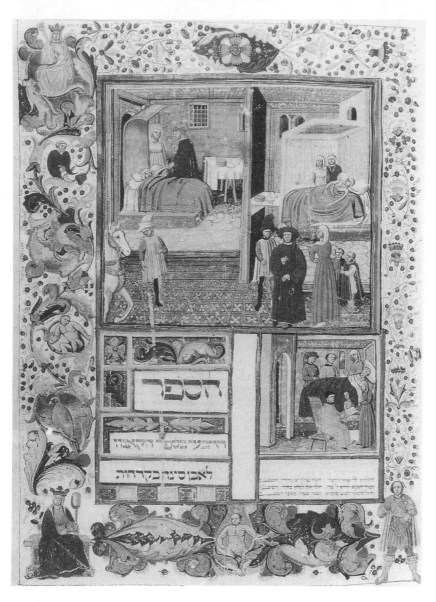

Jewish doctors and medical cures as depicted in the late fifteenth-century illustrations found in a Hebrew translation of Avicenna's Canon *(a medical treatise) currently in the University Library of Bologna (Ms. n° 2187, folios 492ʳ and 402ʳ).*

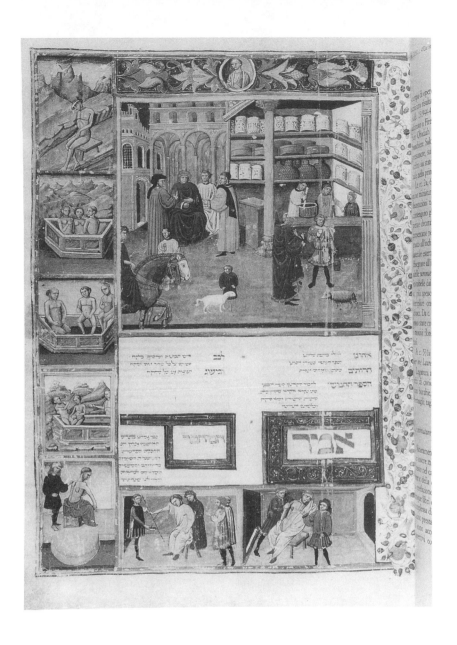

types of profession were supplementary to that of moneylending, which was absolutely predominant in the first phase of the settlement, according to the features already described in the preceding chapter. These Jews agreed to conduct a business that can only very improperly be called a bank and which must not be confused with our modern commercial deposit institutions. In fact what was involved might more properly be designated a "pawn shop." As we saw above in passing, quite often the "bank" was located in a building adapted for the purpose, but not infrequently it amounted to little more than an ad hoc stall set up in the market place or in its near vicinity. The beneficiaries of the condotta agreed to invest a certain capital sum, whose minimum level was sometimes specified, usually between 3,000 and 6,000 ducats, to be placed at the disposal of the poor. Despite the fact that from the middle of the fifteenth century until approximately the third decade of the sixteenth century, or the end of the first phase of our period, Italy was blessed with remarkable monetary stability, it is nonetheless difficult to give a precise idea of the actual meaning of these figures. With 3,000 ducats, at the University of Padua in the second half of the fifteenth century, it was possible to pay annual stipends to three outstanding scientific luminaries. At the same time, however, less renowned and less sought after professors had to be content with less than 100 ducats a year. Three thousand ducats was, then, a considerable sum, though not excessively so. As to the possible impact of sums of this kind on the overall money supply circulating in the cities of Italy, we refer the reader to our summary observations on this topic in the preceding chapter. A detailed study of this aspect of our period is much needed. Everyone was of course aware that this capital investment represented a kind of fiscal contribution by the Jews in a context in which they were there to provide a social service rather than being fully integrated into the various local economies. Nevertheless, there was nothing in principle to prevent the Jews seeking and finding more remunerative ways of earning a living, over and above the loans they made to the city's poor.

The terms of the condotte also stipulated the conditions under which money could be lent: the highest approved rates of interest, the procedures for the auctioning off of unredeemed pledges, the terms under which a monopoly might be granted, the nature of the taxes to be exacted, as well as the fiscal exemptions granted, and so on. Some condotte also specified the local government's commitment to guaranteeing the recipients freedom to profess the Jewish religion, as well as the equal status of local citizens and Jews before the civil and penal magistratures, while occasionally they went so far as to concede noninterference in the exercise of Jewish self-government, or even, with certain limits, to be specified in greater detail in chapter 5, in the actual autonomy of the Jewish communities involved.

Despite the extraordinary abundance of the documentation, or perhaps precisely because of it, a systematic and detailed analysis of the way the terms of the condotte are formulated has yet to be undertaken. An examination of the kind would certainly serve to clarify a number of points regarding the actual conditions of Jewish life in the period which remain unclear. An analysis of the stipulations referring to fiscal exemptions granted to Jews and denied to Christian citizens could help define the nature of the Jewish component in the complex local sociopolitical and economic balance. At first glance, for instance, there would seem to be a correlation between the degree of liberality in the concession of customs exemptions and the role of the merchant middle classes in the exercise of power.

As has already been remarked, the concession of a condotta implied a payment on the part of the Jews. This was clearly specified in the record of the rulers' decision, but it was not usually mentioned in the condotta itself. Indeed, it would be impossible to reconstruct its existence or quantify the amount simply by examining the stipulations contained in the various condotte. Our initial tendency in fact would be to conclude that the condotta represented some kind of act of grace on the part of the government, and the payments a form of prepayment of taxes, calculated globally on the basis of the highest rate of interest consented to the lender. In other words, the introduction of the Jews to a city was presented as something occurring outside the framework of a normal exchange relationship, a form of give and take whose terms were laid down in the condotta. Not that it was difficult to say who was the giver and who was the taker in the transaction: rather it was the transaction itself that was inadmissible according to the normal mental categories of the period. What we are dealing with in fact is a concession to human weakness, as was also the case, for instance, for relations with prostitutes — a failing that had to be regimented in the interests of public order, that certainly had to be taxed, though one had to be careful not to elevate it to the level of an interpersonal relationship openly and normally integrated into the fabric of social activity.

THE LOAN BANKS

THE VERY CONDUCT of the loan bank was based on an ambiguity similar to the one just witnessed. The bank was supposed to be plainly visible, but at the same time sufficiently out of the public eye, present and absent, precisely as was the case with Jews and prostitutes in the framework of Christian society. The anonymous author of the *Book of the Moneylender and the Borrower* has given us an invaluable sketch of the "bank" as it was perceived through Jewish eyes:

The building must be strong and constructed in stone, so that outlaws cannot get inside under cover of darkness. It must not have many doors and windows, so as not to be exposed to the danger of burglary. The windows must be protected by gratings, anchored to the walls at the top and bottom. The bank must be located in the best section of the city, close to the central crossroads, so that it is easy to reach, but off the main street, away from the market square, so that rich people aren't ashamed to be seen going in. The entrance must be low and narrow, protected by a curtain to stop passers-by seeing in, so they don't recognize the faces of those taking out a loan. The curtain must be blue, so that the bank is easily recognizable.[7]

The "bank," then, was discreet in the way it presented itself, like a house of prostitution, to all intents and purposes disguised, so that the outside gave no precise clue as to what went on inside, except to those who had already had occasion to enter. To those who had not yet succumbed to the temptation, the insignificant modesty of the outside allowed the imagination full scope, stimulating it to go beyond any conceivable reality. This discrepancy between reality and appearance introduced a peculiar imaginary dimension to the perception of the Jew on the part of the medieval Christian mentality, as well as a sense of alienation in the Jew's perception of his own vital space that should not be underestimated.

Unlike its outside apprearance, the interior of the "bank" was expected to be well-lit and functional and to inspire a sense of security, in keeping with the activities that took place there. Once again, the author of the *Book of the Moneylender and the Borrower* supplies us with valuable details:

> Inside the bank there must be several doors and windows, so that it is well illuminated, and it is possible to tell the good man from the bad. The windows however should be sealed with paper, or with oiled parchment, if the banker is poor, or with glass, if he is rich, to keep out drafts, because they could affect the functioning of the weighing scales. The counter must be in the middle and must stretch across the room from one side to the other, completely separating the moneylender from his customers. It should be wide and deep, so that the inner edge is out of the customers' reach. The bank, then, should be so constructed as to ensure that moneylender and customers are separated and maintain a respectable distance from each other.[8]

Paolo Uccello translated some of these details visually in a six-panel po-·lyptych in 1468, painted no doubt in the general climate of hatred liberally sown by the itinerant friars. The polyptych represents the "Miracle of the Profaned Host": a poor Christian, to humor a Jewish moneylender, brings him a sacred host, which the Jew proceeds to throw into the fire. The host thereupon begins to bleed, and the blood, flowing out into the streets of the city, brings the profanation to public light. The poor Christian is hanged, and the Jew and his family burned. One of the six panels in particular represents the interior of a loan bank.[9] The fact that the details of the panel correspond fairly precisely to what is described in the *Book of the Moneylender and the Borrower* leads to the conclusion that Paolo had firsthand knowledge of what he was painting.

Just as the outside appearance of the bank did not in the least correspond to its interior, so the economic activity of the Jews was not limited to the loan of petty sums. On the contrary, these loans were only the

A Jewish pawn shop as depicted by Paolo Uccello of Florence (d. 1475). Courtesy of Galleria Nazionale, Urbino.

excuse for the Jews' presence, and they turn out to be in reality a mere camouflage for other more profitable activities, adding to the Jewish condition a further dimension of alienation all the more significant in that it is difficult to characterize unequivocally. In point of fact, small loans against pledges were not sufficient by themselves to ensure a living; the banker was therefore compelled to engage in other activities. Moreover, from the anti-Jewish point of view, common to the Christians of the time and to antisemites throughout history, the situation was seen as nothing more than a ruse on the part of the Jews. From the modern historian's point of view, however, this gap between the real and the imaginary, associated with the profound sense of alienation which was part and parcel of the Jewish condition at the time, constitutes the highest price imposed by Christian society on the Jews. It is precisely this gap that, in the final analysis, reflects the insuperable barrier to true integration.

OTHER OCCUPATIONS

JEWISH CAPITAL could be, or, to put it more precisely, had to be, invested in commerce and industry in order to produce reasonable profits. The investors operated as a rule in association with other Jews, less often with Christians. Such activities indeed provoked the most energetic opposition from the Christian guilds, which had everything to lose from an increase in competition. Of course, Christian opposition was not determined by purely economic considerations, and protectionist tendencies were linked to an undercurrent of anti-Jewish sentiment, stirred up and fed by the propaganda of the religious orders. Furthermore, it is worth stressing that membership in the craft and trade guilds was forbidden to Jews, who were thereby barred from competing with Christians "from the inside," so to speak. In spite of the antisemitic tendencies so widespread at the time, the documents available testify to a number of economic activities carried on by Jews in fields other than moneylending. Besides the medical profession, Jews were active in trade and in more or less all other fields of endeavor. Thus, among the Jews of the time we find blacksmiths, goldsmiths, tailors, fullers and dyers, skilled craftsmen, even experts in arms manufacture and the production of gunpowder. There were Jews in the agricultural sector also; however, "naturally," Christians served as intermediaries for Jews' investment in agriculture: business associations between Jews and Christians in this area were of many kinds, but a detailed examination of them is beyond the scope of the present brief outline.

The evolution of Jewish professional activities followed the same broad lines as the successive phases of the topodemographical distribution dealt with in the preceding chapter. The phase of concentration, which followed the period of extreme dispersion, corresponds to the gradual transition from a situation of extreme specialization in the area of moneylending to one of vast diversification of employment. This diversification increased in direct proportion to the decreasing possibilities of earning a living through moneylending. The attention paid by current historiographers to the traffic in money seems to have obscured, possibly involuntarily, the rich spectrum of trades followed by the Jews, thereby distorting their history in another way that it would be well to eliminate.

It should also be pointed out that many Jews were actively involved in the publishing business. The invention of printing gave many of them the chance to combine intellectual activity with capital investment or manual labor. Throughout the first phase of the period, that is, from the second half of the fifteenth century to the first decades of the sixteenth, the Jews flung themselves enthusiastically into the new occupation: a by no means negligible number of the incunabula published in Italy were in fact printed in Hebrew. As in other economic sectors, the Jews worked in association with or in service to Christian printers; rarely were they completely independent. The quality of Italian paper and printing shops ensured the rapid spread of works printed in the Peninsula to foreign markets, so that for Jews active in the printing industry the potential number of customers was vastly superior to the number of their coreligionists in Italy. Many Jewish scholars of the period devoted themselves to the editing of the texts to be printed or to the correction of proofs. Jewish culture owes a great deal to these editorial labors, which can rightly be considered the forerunners of our modern critical editions, and which determined the form of the texts, still in use today, of classic works like the Talmud, the Midrashim, and the Bible itself.

ROME

ONLY ONE CITY formed an exception to the picture outlined above: Rome, where the situation was the exact opposite of the cities where the Jewish population was made up of newly arrived Jews. The Eternal City could already count a fairly large number of Jews at the outset of the period we are dealing with. In the course of the centuries, Rome constituted a strong center of attraction for the Jews of the dias-

pora, who settled there in the century before the Christian era and remained there until our own day without interruption. The Roman community had known moments of glory. Proof of this, for the early
centuries of the Christian era, is to be found in the visual evidence of the
catacombs and the numerous funerary inscriptions, invaluable for the re-
construction of a more complete picture of the society of the Jewish diaspora of the time. There exists, of course, in addition abundant literary
evidence. The golden age of the Roman community can be placed perhaps immediately following what Georges Duby called "L'An Mille," the
period of the "Birth of Europe." It was then that the Jewish scholars from
Rome, like Nathan ben Yeḥiel (c. 1035–1106), the author of the famous
Talmudic encyclopedia 'Arukh, reached the height of their fame. Everywhere, even in the France of Rashi, even in the Franco-Rhenish regions
in the full flood of their cultural development, people sought out the
light represented by the wisdom of the Roman scholars. The communities of the diaspora also saw in them their own natural representatives to
the Holy See. It was doubtless as a result of the intervention of the Jews
of Rome that the popes published in the twelfth century the bulls of protection known as the *Constitutiones Judaeorum*, or, better yet, as the *Sicut
Judaeis*, from the first two words of these bulls. Nevertheless, in the period
we are concerned with, the golden age was already a thing of the past.
The prime responsibility for the decadence lies in the particular set of
circumstances that came into existence from the thirteenth century on.
As was pointed out in the first chapter, owners of capital were attracted
to the cities of North-Central Italy, where conditions were more favorable to the practice of moneylending. In the course of the fourteenth century, the vicissitudes of the Eternal City, including the so-called Baby-
lonian Captivity of the papacy in Avignon, were such as to reinforce the
tendency toward an exodus. In fact, the greater part of the Jews who "col-
onized" the cities of the central and northern Peninsula in the first phase
of our period were more or less closely related to the famous four historical families of mythical origin reputed to have been deported by Titus to Rome after the destruction of the Sanctuary in Jerusalem: the Min
ha-Anawim, or Anau, a family name variously translated into Italian as

delli Mansi, delli Piattelli, and delli Umani; the Min ha-Ne'arim, corresponding to delli Fanciulli; Min ha-Adummim, or de Rossi; Min ha-Tappuḥim, or de Pomis. But others too laid claim to these prestigious origins: the Min ha-Zeqenim, corresponding to del Vecchio, and the Min ha-Dayyanim, or del Giudice. In addition to these, the most renowned of the colonizing families from Rome seems to have been that of the Mi-Beth-El, or de Synagoga. At the time, Jews with this family name were to be found practically everywhere.

In the area of occupations, professions, and trades, then, from the very beginning of our period, Rome presented a picture similar to that found much later in the other cities of the Peninsula. In a certain sense, the social structure of the Roman community can be considered an intermediary between that of the most distant past, encountered in the discussion of Sicily, and that of the future, destined to be dominant from the end of the sixteenth century. In the governing body of the community, for instance, we find documented, as early as 1525, the tripartite division into bankers, the rich, and persons of middling condition,[10] which recalls the division encountered in Sicily between *de statu majori*, *de statu mediocri*, and *de statu minori*. We must, however, stress the fact that in the case of Rome we are dealing with two categories of the wealthy: the superrich, namely the bankers, and the plain rich, evidently the merchants. As for those of middling condition, this group included all those who were not poor, in other words, those engaged in the practice of the liberal professions or those who had some kind of trade skills. The supersession of the Sicilian "model" is evident. In fact the structure documented in 1525 in Rome is fairly similar to the one found at the end of the century in Mantua: first, the bankers, heirs to a privileged social position because of their past as first "colonizers," next, the merchants, the *nouveaux riches*, and then, in last place, all the others.

In light of what has been said, it is my conviction that, *mutatis mutandis*, Rome may be included in the above picture. The chief difference between Rome and the other cities was that, whereas the latter were going through a phase of economic blossoming and development, the Eternal City found itelf in a completely different situation. This difference obviously had unavoidable repercussions on the history of the institutions and culture of the Roman Jews, but it did not have any particular consequences as far as the socioeconomic characteristics of the Jewish community were concerned.

THE DECLINE OF MONEYLENDING

IN THE SECOND PHASE of the period the proportion of moneylenders to other callings, especially merchants, is reversed. We already listed in the preceding chapter a number of factors that led to this reversal: the gradual transformation of the public pawn shops into actual banking institutions, the settlement of Jews of Spanish origin, with a different economic orientation and significantly greater capital resources than the Italian and German Jews, the growing necessity to concentrate in a few large cities, with the result that fewer and fewer persons were able to continue to prosper in the moneylending business. To these factors, we must also add a number of factors of a more general nature, to some extent contradictory, which affected the entire peninsula. Among them, one should stress the dawn of mercantilism on the one hand, and on the other the attraction of the idea of a "return to the land." For the Jews, for whom a "return to the land" was largely confined to the sphere of the imaginary, these additional factors boiled down to an encouragement to become involved in commerce. The diminished importance of the moneylenders was so marked that in more than one instance the demands of those engaged in commerce that the change be reflected in a parallel change in structure of the ruling cadres became the occasion for long and bitter controversy. In practice, however, only a privileged few, especially those of foreign origin, could hope for success. Many had to be content with the secondhand trade, to which, the reader will recall, they had been condemned by Paul IV in his bull *Cum nimis absurdum*. Others went to swell the ranks of the small-time dealers and artisans. Not a few were sadly compelled to cross the poverty line and to sign up as charity cases.

In the second phase of our history we witness, then, a radical revolution in the socioeconomic structure of the Jewish population. The overall picture is much more miserable than in the preceding period, as well as being violently polarized: alongside a fairly sizable group of "rich" Jews, in reality no more than middlingly well-off, we find an equally large group of the really poor, living hand to mouth and on charity. Whatever advantage the Jews might have derived from the prosperity of the Italian Renaissance, once the promise of that period was over, they were certainly in for a great deal of suffering. To attempt to follow the thread of this transformation, however, would take us considerably beyond the period it was our intention to describe here.

PART TWO
STRUCTURES
OF CULTURE
AND SOCIETY

III
THE PROBLEM OF
SOCIOCULTURAL
IDENTITY:
SOME PRELIMINARY
OBSERVATIONS

THE IMPACT OF RELIGIOUS OTHERNESS

AFTER READING the account presented in the preceding chapters, one may well ask why the Jews of the time, living as they did so demographically dispersed, were not caught up in an irreversibly centrifugal dynamic leading to assimilation. True, even today, there is no dearth of examples of families belonging to religious minorities, especially Jewish minorities, who choose to live in isolation rather than join the communities organized elsewhere by members of their religious group. Nevertheless, even though, from the point of view of the psychology of minorities, the similarities between these modern day cases and those of our period are noteworthy, there is still one conspicuous difference: the importance of religion and its impact on the social life of the people, and on their perception of the reciprocal relations between religion and society, are radically different.

Any interpretation that does not take this elementary fact into proper account risks being seriously skewed. In my view, however, this fact seems to have been neglected, and continues to be neglected, in many of the current presentations of the issues, especially those that attribute the greatest weight to economic factors. These presentations are often modeled on the "three-level" interpretive framework: economy, society, and culture. Such a framework, if applied rigidly and in that order to the present case, makes it impossible a priori to give proper attention to the factor of religious otherness. In a certain sense, traditional historiography has followed this same path: a little like Molière's *Bourgeois gentilhomme*, Monsieur Jourdain, who finally becomes aware that he has always spoken in prose without realizing it, traditional historiography has likewise tended to apply the above interpretive framework without realizing it, and without really knowing what it was doing.

As it has been applied to our topic, the framework may be summed up as follows: since they were *necessary* to the economies of the Italian cities, the Jews were *integrated* fairly easily into the socioeconomic fabric of these economies. An accelerated process of acculturation inevitably followed, a process that the modern eye can only interpret in terms of cultural assimilation. From this point of view, the fact that the Jews lived in conditions of extreme dispersion, especially in the initial phase of our period, could only contribute to the reinforcement of such a tendency. All this seems so patently clear that to doubt it would be tantamount to denying the evidence. And yet most of the elements that make up this very simple interpretive formula are more the fruit of the historian's fertile imagination than a phenomenon of the reality of the time.

First of all, as we have pointed out in previous chapters, the economic role played by the Jews in Christian society did not lead to a dynamic of social integration backed by the Italian people. The Jews of Italy in the Renaissance lived in the same conditions of social inferiority as their brethren elsewhere. Moneylending at interest, which was how most of them earned a living, served to make them hated rather than loved. Seen from this perspective, the substantially positive change in the attitude of the Italian cities with regard to the "Jewish question" which occurred toward the end of the period under consideration can no doubt be linked to the decline of Jewish involvement in moneylending. Moreover, even if it were possible to measure the intensity of anti-Jewish feeling and to prove that it was weaker in Italy than elsewhere (which in my opinion was not the case), this finding would have no real consequence as far as the existence or nonexistence of barriers to social integration was concerned. We should therefore be extremely careful not to interpret the various expressions of cultural interaction between Jews and Christians as a *result* of the alleged high level of social integration, or to present them as manifestations of Jewish assimilation. These examples of interaction should not, however, be ignored. On the contrary, they should be given every consideration, since they are indispensable to understanding the model by which the self-awareness characteristic of the Jewish society of the time was attained in relation to the Other.

Certainly, many Jews at the time were quick to accuse their Jewish adversaries of behaving like Christians, of having become assimilated, of not being sufficiently orthodox in their behavior, in their cultural interests, and so on and so forth. Thus it was that Leone di Vitale (1420–c.1495), the medical doctor and learned rabbi usually known as Messer Leon, was accused of assimilation because he adopted the custom of wearing the red "hood," the distinctive dress of medical practitioners. The accusation was, however, rebuffed by the unquestionably orthodox rabbi Joseph Colon (1420–c.1480), who devoted a long and detailed *responsum* to the subject.[1] A similar accusation was even leveled at the extremely orthodox following of the Paduan rabbi Judah Mintz (c.1410–1508) for having adopted certain fashionable burial customs on the occasion of their rabbi's death. The accusation was far from persuading the parties concerned to reconsider their actions. As is readily apparent from an analysis of the chronicle of the events to which we will return in detail in chapter 11, rather than expressing genuine concern, the accusations amounted to nothing more than factious criticism, which exploited the rhetoric of assimilation in order to denigrate their enemies. Messer Leon himself did the same thing when he accused those who professed kabbalistic ideas, which he could not abide, of "going over to the Christians."[2] Many more such examples could be adduced. But this is no reason to mistake accusations for reality. On the contrary, what we really have here are affirmations of the accuser's own orthodoxy by appealing to a stereotype recognized by the common consensus of opinion. In other words, the rule was that whatever was considered an exclusive characteristic of the Other became *ipso facto* negative with respect to the definition of the Self.

For the mentality of the time, Jewish *difference* and especially Jewish *inferiority* were *taken as a given*. For the Christians, these facts were the logical consequence of the perfidiousness of a people blinded by the Devil; for the Jews they were part and parcel of their existential destiny, marked by the irreversible facts of a history for which they themselves were responsible, because they had not proved worthy of Salvation and Redemption. For Christian and Jew alike, these facts signified a social barrier that it was impossible to eliminate.

THE SUMPTUARY LAWS: EVIDENCE OF ASSIMILATION?

A FAIRLY EMBLEMATIC example of what we have been talking about is provided by the sumptuary laws adopted by the Jews of the time, which some historians have chosen to regard as an irrefutable demonstration of the assimilative influence exerted upon them by the Renaissance. The evidence in fact seems to suggest that the Jews, in imitation of the Christians belonging to the upper social classes, liked to make a show of luxury and ostentatiously display their clothing and jewels. Anyone wishing for further confirmation of the fact that the Jews really did dress like their neighbors is encouraged to leaf through one or two of the many illustrated Jewish manuscripts of the time. Even if the artists sometimes represented the figure of the Jew in accordance with more or less familiar stereotypes designed to make them recognizable to the common observer, the miniatures present countless proofs that the general tendency was certainly to dress like everyone else. How is one to interpret this evidence?

Let us admit without further ado, since it has been sufficiently proven by the most detailed studies of the sumptuary laws in medieval society, that the idea people wish to convey of themselves is best rendered by how they present themselves to others, that is to say, by the style of their dress, as well as by other forms of social display: the way they receive their guests, their festivities, and so forth. Through the way its members dress (which has been defined as a delicate balance between the desire to imitate the majority and the desire to stress one's own difference), a society may evince a general tendency: toward closure upon itself (through the systematic adoption, for example, of a uniform), or toward openness to external influences (through its willingness to adopt the fashions of others). This latter case, therefore, could be used as the index of an authentic tendency toward acculturation. Let us also agree that the way the ruling classes react to the tendencies of the society of which they are a part, as well as the expressions of their desire to influence its tastes and behaviors, are extremely important indices for the study of the mentality of the period. What the historian finds in the sumptuary laws is mostly evidence of opposition to particular tendencies and customs. This opposition usually manifested itself in the form of ordinances designed to impose strictures, and inhibit the display of luxury, and therefore to educate according to a model of virtue considered ideal. Sumptuary laws of this nature are already long familiar to us. Their elements are religious, social, political, and economic in nature. Designed to protect the fortunes of the great families, they were aimed at promoting the sense of conservatism that would help reinforce the stability of the social order. Sometimes the laws were intended to safeguard local industries by prohibiting certain imports, but they were also meant to impose an ideal of austerity, of virtuous morality, designed to combat the ostentation of wealth and luxury, all the more since such ostentation, according to the medieval mentality, was analogous to a claim to power. Today, we could perhaps draw up a quantitative chart of the prohibitions according to their sources, according to the authority, that is, which issued them, royal, communal, and so forth, with a view to reaching conclusions pertinent to "histoire sérielle." We could also define the sociopolitical factors that contributed, in the course of the thirteenth century, to the shift in emphasis from the public to the private sphere. With the passage of time, the prohibitions focused in fact more and more on fashions of dress, rather than on funeral and wedding rituals. This could represent a particular case of the more general shift of interest toward the individual, the single human personality, in preference to the social group. We may also be dealing with an evolution in the means of exercising power and making social control more effective by limiting the prestige of the aristocracy and encouraging, instead, republican virtues; or perhaps we are faced primarily with mani-festations of the intensification of the religious spirit, associated with Franciscan propaganda. One cannot exclude the possibility, however, that the message of the Franciscans may have been turned to their own account by the governing bodies of the commune. Furthermore, in a so-ciety in which the transfer of capital from one family to another took place chiefly through marriage, did the prohibition regarding the osten-tation of feminine luxury express an aspiration to socioeconomic stabil-ity? Or was it not purely and simply a question of male chauvinism over-laid with moral and religious prejudice? The language of the sumptuary laws lends itself to more than one reading, and it is in any case fraught with metaphoric meaning, which, in its turn, reflects the current *Weltan-schauung* as regards the social order. Finally, it is not difficult to read be-tween the lines of the sumptuary laws the reactions of the governed to the political structures proposed by those in power: the dynamic rela-tionship between the two groups was frequently resolved, quite simply, on the fiscal plane, itself an expression of the notion that one has of self and others.

There is something at this point that strikes me as particularly signif-icant. In the Christian sumptuary laws, there is no mention of Jews until at least the sixteenth century. Why not? Wouldn't it be reasonable to ex-pect the sumptuary laws, promulgated by the local governments, to treat everyone, Christians or Jews, alike? But if that is the case, why did the Jewish leaders themselves at times consider it necessary to publish sump-tuary laws addressed to their coreligionists? And furthermore, why do the Jews begin to be explicitly mentioned in subsequently published general legislation? All this might lead one to conclude that the general rules did not apply to the Jews, in the same way as they did not apply to anyone else who was excluded from the social order, such as prostitutes, to cite one example.

An excellent recent study seems made to order to fit our case: it is a study of the evolution of the Christian attitude toward the use of ear-rings.[3] The religious sensibility of the fourteenth and fifteenth centuries associated such ornaments with concupiscence and vainglory: earrings were viewed as the distinguishing marks of social exclusion and were designed to identify Jews and prostitutes, both obliged to wear them so they could be told apart from virtuous Christians, who were forbidden their use by the provisions of the sumptuary laws. But the ladies of the aristocracy seem to have found it difficult to forego the pleasure of wearing earrings; they therefore ended up being reintroduced into fashion, first in aristocratic circles, then among the middle classes. The aristocracy in this case performed a mediating function: the aristocrats, excluded from observance of the regulations because of their social superiority, could permit themselves the use of what was forbidden to the others as a sign of the latter's exclusion or inferiority. Earrings thus became the prerogative of the members of the upper classes. It therefore became necessary to forbid their use by everyone else. The result was a radical reversal of the tendency of the sumptuary laws, which, in the sixteenth century, aimed more at protecting the social hierarchy than public morals. The Jews were not forgotten: they were prohibited the use of what, until shortly before, had been considered distinctive signs of their inferiority: earrings. A rapid glance at the sumptuary laws promulgated by the Jews themselves may allow us to establish a link with these developments.

The first sumptuary law of the Jews of Italy known to us goes back to 1418: this and all subsequent provisions seem to be characterized by a constant preoccupation on the part of the Jews with not attracting attention, not standing out. The fiscal motivation is obvious in every instance: the idea was not to spark the envy of the Christians, who might have been tempted to impose high taxes. Naturally, moral and religious motivations are also present, similar to those revealed by analogous Christian documents: "The Community of the Jews of Rome desiring . . . to repress the exorbitance of Pomp, Entertainments, Luxury, & other Incentives to Vice, that serve as pernicious Bait to Youth, diverting them from that Justice, and moderate living instituted by the Prophet Micah in the name of God . . . & further considering the economically depressed state of this Community, and desirous of procuring through greater savings the means of alleviating the burden of the heavy requirements of Collections and Taxes, that daily are imposed . . ."[4] So goes the preamble to the regulations promulgated by the Council of the Community of Rome in 1661. In the regulations of one or two hundred years earlier, the accent is placed on women, rather than on youth, but for the rest there is little change. "With a view to bending hearts to behave humbly and not to attract the attention of the Gentiles" the delegates of the Italian communities gathered at Forlì in 1418 forbade, for example, open or silk-lined sleeves, linings of ermine, sable, marten, or other kinds of costly fur, jackets and dresses of silk or velvet, gold necklaces and the gilt hairnets worn by women, and belts with silver buckles weighing more than six ounces for men and more than ten for women, as well as a number of other accoutrements.[5] The constant preoccupation with not attracting the gaze of others, with promoting morality and austerity, assumes, however, different shadings when considered in the light of changes that took place in Christian regulations. From the most general point of view, we are concerned with an evolution parallel to other changes recorded in the passage from the first to the second phase of our history. In fact, whereas the earlier non-Jewish regulations were intended to curb extravagance, permitting it nonetheless to Jews so as to highlight their social exclusion, the regulations of the Jews seem concerned with concealing, rather than prohibiting, aiming at the establishment of a semblance of integration as far as austerity went. This becomes evident in the passage from the regulations of 1418 cited above: there, "not attracting the attention of the Gentiles" is placed on a par with "behaving in a humble fashion." This is why the contents of the regulations do not seem to differ in any way from the non-Jewish regulations of the same period. Though the differences are almost imperceptible, in my opinion the documents of the succeeding period appear to indicate an increased tendency toward rigor. These regulations, however, seem no longer to be at pains to stress the element of Jewish morality, which had been geared, or so it was claimed, since the most remote antiquity, to placing a curb on luxury. Instead, there is an attempt to present the prohibitions as a necessary result of the "noblesse" of the Jewish nation and its attendant responsibilities, such as the need for emulating illustrious examples from Jewish history, of *be-*

having better than the Christians, even more than avoiding their envy, and so forth. What we have here is a method, in a sense paradoxical, of rejecting the condition of exclusion by asserting one's distinctness, of aspiring to be like everyone else while cultivating one's difference from them, of claiming one's position within the larger society while at the same time preaching a retreat within the group! This tangle of paradoxes expressed itself in the simplest of ways, by stressing the fact that the display of luxury could lead to the danger of expulsion, a divine punishment that would be brought about through the earthly agency of unbearable taxation.

Over and above the human aspiration to be considered no different from everyone else, what we seem to be observing here is a condition of existential inferiority which the Jews attempted to ease by means of community legislation aimed at reducing its effects as far as possible. In other words, rather than expressing a conservative reaction to centrifugal and assimilative tendencies, the Jewish sumptuary laws reflect a desire to mitigate the condition of inferiority to which the Jews were condemned by their diversity. Otherwise, one would surely find references in the sumptuary regulations to a negative assessment of the assimilative tendencies that those same regulations were intended to combat, and yet no such references are to be found. As has already been remarked, this in no way excludes concerns of a moral, religious, or social nature, similar to those expressed by Christian legislators: indeed it would be strange not to find them.

Let there be no mistake. The general mentality was that of the men of the Middle Ages for whom bright colors, obtained by means of costly dyes, were the symbol of riches and power, whereas dark colors in general, or, more simply, undyed clothing, were the signs of poverty and a humble station. By adopting a model of austerity more rigorous than that of the Christians, the Jews aspired to an image of poverty even more extreme. No furs, then, and absolutely no fabrics woven with gold or silver threads. In clothing, dark colors seemed to be the ideal: black or grey, green or dark blue at the outside. The impression is of a group of people determined to fit into society, but on an inferior level, the level decided by the Other, because it was the only one appropriate to the social order. Unable to think for the moment in terms of aspiring to equality, the Jews thought in terms of fitting in as inferiors, while continuing at the same time to cultivate a sense of their repressed superiority.

But other phenomena, admittedly few in number, imply that, viewed from inside the small Jewish society, the social order could only be conceived in the image and likeness of the larger Christian society. It is not surprising, then, to find similar exemptions from the observance of certain obligations and customs being extended to members of the upper classes, for no other reason than because of their social prominence. Here again, the idea of mediation between two opposites is associated with the idea of social prominence, though on a different plane from that described above. Thus, for example, in the Venetian sumptuary provisions of 1548, it was explicitly stated that "the daughter of Messer Israel Klemperer must also consider herself subject to the ordinances, with respect to all the provisions as regards luxury issued by the Gentile authorities, but when she goes outside the ghetto, it is not our intent either to prohibit or permit them."[6] In other words, the aristocrats of Jewish society were entitled to forego the distinction of poverty typical of the Jewish condition! Dignitaries and persons in power were permitted to have the same exterior aspect as the Christians. This was justified by the conventional wisdom that cast them in the standard role of mediators between Christians and Jews for the benefit of the latter: it was therefore logical that those in positions of power among the Jews should appear externally equal to their Christian interlocutors: had Joseph not shaved off his beard and altered the style of his dress to stand before the Pharaoh?

In the course of time and in other locations, the natural tendency to make a virtue out of necessity was to modify this tendency that the Jewish sumptuary laws encouraged to distinguish oneself by the austerity of one's dress. This has encouraged some historians to imagine some sort of Jewish orthodoxy characterized by a specifically Jewish attire. This image in turn gave rise to the current tendentious interpretation of the behavior of the Jews of Italy in the period that concerns us. It is claimed that there would have been no need to publish such regulations at all unless the Jews had shown a tendency to assimilate in their style of dress. Nothing could be further from the truth. Assimilation, in circumstances in which it was invoked to encourage desired behaviors, was associated with *luxury* pure and simple and had nothing to do with *fashion*. In other words, assimilation was invoked as a dissuasive argument and not as the object of an actual concern. Dressing like Christians was not prohibited so as to prevent Jews mixing with them: the Christians could take care of that all by themselves. Dressing lavishly was prohibited because it was considered evil and a Christian characteristic, and as such it was to be avoided. Imitating negative Christian behavior was what had to be avoided, not merely the exterior aspect of their style of dress.

"SWEET SINS OF LOVE" AND SOCIAL INTEGRATION

THERE IS A CLAUSE in the sumptuary laws of 1418 which is worth considering in close connection with the phenomenon we are about to examine. The Jewish representatives, "concerned with the numerous transgressions involving vain oaths and with sexual licentiousness, involving even married women . . . to the point where *even Christian women seem to be allowed them* . . . ," decided to nominate commissioners in each city and province whose task it would be to find a remedy for the situation. Are these to be seen as exceptional cases that caused scandal precisely because they were so extraordinary, alarming the more pious spirits, or does this document bear witness instead to the widespread nature of the phenomenon and to the opposition on the part of the Jewish establishment to the centrifugal tendencies of their coreligionists? If we follow current historiography, which presents the evidence of sexual relations between Jews and Christians as proof of social integration encouraged by the general climate of permissiveness that is supposed to be typical of Renaissance Italy, it would seem a foregone conclusion. In Jacob Burckhardt's interpretation of the Renaissance, in which deviation and crime are seen simply as the darker colors in an aesthetically harmonious picture, Jewish adulteries (especially with Christians), Jewish prostitutes, and of course sexual relationships between Jews and Christians would be no more than expressions of the Jewish participation in the general ballet — sweet sins of love, then, in a climate of idyllic symbiosis.

It is difficult, however, to accept this view. I am not of course about to deny the existence of evidence of sexual promiscuity; indeed, a good number of cases are known. There are even some that involve authentic love affairs, more eloquent, to my mind, than the mere sexual relations with prostitutes which usually receive so much attention. All this testimony, however, is drawn without exception from the dossiers of the police and tribunals summoned to judge the guilty parties, who were accused of strictly forbidden sexual relations punishable by death. The executions of the condemned speak clearly: the penalties were not metaphorical. All of this explains why the evidence of sexual relations between Jews and Christians is in fact not very plentiful: of the 2,286 documents relative to the Jews residing in the duchy of Milan over the course of the fifteenth century, which constitute almost all of the sources identified up to this point regarding the history of that group,[7] there are not more than forty cases of this type; and among them there are several accusations made by zealous functionaries in the hopes of blackmailing the accused. The documents are certainly interesting from a human point of view, in addition to the light they shed on the attitudes toward sexual relations held by the Jews of the period, in this respect not very different from their Christian neighbors. But they are far from providing the evidence of tolerance and social integration that some people claim; and still less is it possible to recognize traces of a centrifugal tendency on the part of Jews encouraged precisely by that tolerance and integration.

The death penalty could generally be commuted to a fine. This, too, was part of the rules of the game consistent with the mentality of the period. It also helps explain many accusations, which would otherwise be incomprehensible. The documents speak for themselves. Take the case of the administrators of Tortona who in 1459 informed the Duke of the possibility of enriching his coffers by two or three thousand ducats by lodging an accusation against a Jew for sexual relations with a Christian. A quarter of the sum would have to be handed over to the informant as compensation for services rendered, but it would be well worth it! In the same category is the case of the *capitano* of Milan who in 1470 informed the Duke that a certain Crassino was cohabitating, at the ripe old age of seventy-five, with a Christian woman. Even though there was no way of proving beyond doubt that the two were living together *more uxorio*, and despite the fact that Crassino was poor, money could still be extorted from the Jew's wealthy relations.

Over and above the existence of a certain number of cases of sexual relations between Jews and Christians, documented and explicable in terms of the personal histories of the various dramatis personae, their idiosyncrasies, and their particular circumstances, the one undeniable fact is that they led to judicial proceedings, a clear indication of how these relations were viewed by the mentality of the time: as deviations from the norm, which society was not in the least disposed to tolerate. The rare cases of sexual promiscuity, far from being evidence of a dynamic of integration, demonstrate instead the existence of rigid social barriers. The above-cited clause from the sumptuary laws of 1418 may also be read in this light, seeing in it, in addition to a perfectly natural tendency to moralize, a concern for the socioeconomic implications of the instances of deviance. In other words, one may read the clause as evidence of the concern not to disturb the social order, an order within which the Jews had their position, inferior certainly to that of the Christian burghers, yet superior after all to that of the peasants or the urban poor.

A balanced view of the historical reality must of course take all of these phenomena into account, as well as others to be mentioned further on. What is in question is certainly not the existence of an interaction between the Christian and Jewish worlds. It is clear that such an interaction did exist and that things could hardly have been otherwise. The point is rather to know how to evaluate this interaction. In my view, for the Jews of the time, their manner of expressing their Jewishness did not have the innovative aspects that their modern-day admirers are so quick to perceive, and a balanced consideration of the various aspects of the culture and behavior of the Italian Jews of the period cannot help leading to a changed interpretation. It is time to reexamine the cultural significance

of the various evidence of contacts between Jews and Christians, precisely because those contacts have been interpreted upon occasion as particularly convincing by reason of their exceptionality.

ASSIMILATION, ACCULTURATION, INTERACTION?

OBVIOUSLY, THE JEWS, as part of the geographic and chronological world of the Italian Renaissance, developed attitudes similar to those of everyone else who participated in it. To presume axiomatically the contrary, as some historians appear to have done,
unconsciously following tendencies whose source might be worth analyz-
ing, involves as a corollary the assumption of an essential difference between the Jews and other people. I refuse to subscribe to such a point of
view. Consequently, the very idea of imitation and assimilation must be
reconsidered in this context. It goes without saying that just as it would
be inappropriate to state that the merchant of Prato Francesco Datini
imitated the Renaissance or assimilated himself to the men of the time
in the way he dressed, it would be just as inappropriate to maintain that
Francesco Datini's Jewish contemporaries imitated the men of the Renaissance or assimilated themselves to them because they dressed, ate, or
spent their free time in a way similar to Francesco Datini.

Therefore, just as we would not classify under the heading of "imitation and cultural assimilation" the facts that the Jews dressed according
to the current fashion, used perfume, or displayed their own "importance" by the number of guests taking part in their wedding receptions
and other social functions, so we will choose not to follow Cecil Roth
when he places in this category the case of the Jewess Anna of Rome, an
expert in cosmetics who, in 1508, ordered a shipment of creams for Ca-
terina Sforza to hide the wrinkles of her aging face. Evidence of individual acts of courage or violence is also not lacking: Jews, for example, took
part in the defense of their cities under siege, a case in point being Siena
in 1552; young Jews, moreover, took part in the sack that followed the
1509 entry of the imperial forces into Padua.[8] Yet these phenomena too
could hardly be placed under the heading of "imitation and cultural as-

similation." Still less could we classify in this way the evidence as to moral or social "deviation," such as gambling, adultery, sexual relations contrary to current norms, or prostitution. In short, it is neither logical nor permissible to postulate an ideal model of the Jew, one who does not gamble or give way to the temptations of the flesh, a Jew, in other words, *absent* from his own surroundings, in order to explain the contrary indications of Jewish *presence* as deviations from that model! The result would be absurd characterizations, such as the one perpetrated (once again) by Cecil Roth, when he presented the rabbi Moses Provenzali of Mantua as an example of an enlightened individual simply because among his *responsa* there is one concerning the permissibility of playing tennis on the Sabbath and might, therefore, be classified as "liberal" by our own modern mentality.[9] Actually, it is difficult to imagine a man more rigidly fundamentalist than Moses Provenzali!

Generally speaking, I find it quite inappropriate to classify as examples of assimilation, or of the centrifugal dynamic of Judaism, the numerous cases involving the Jews' adoption of attitudes, aesthetic tendencies, tastes, and cultural behaviors, to say nothing of cultural themes, ideas, and concepts, similar to those in fashion among their neighbors. One could argue that what we are dealing with is a tiny minority immersed in the sea of the Christian majority who were setting the tone, whereas the former were culturally conforming. Yet this, too, would be an erroneous, mechanical vision of the true state of affairs, even if we must not deny that it contains a kernel of truth, since it is quite clear that the Jews were far from being the principal artificers of the Italian Renaissance, and for this reason it is not completely inappropriate to say that they "imported" certain cultural contents elaborated by the majority outside their circles.

From the phenomenological point of view, there is nothing exceptional in all this. Every cultural expression includes a dialectical component resulting from the encounter between the Self and the Other. The definition of cultural identity through comparison, indeed confrontation, with the identity of the Other always implies a dynamic moment of creation. The creativity of the Jewish people like any other emerges from the encounter between their traditional cultural legacy and the culture of the Other. Consider, for example, the history of the encounter of Jewish culture with Greek culture, and subsequently with the Roman, Persian, and Arabic cultures. The encounter with the culture of the Christian West follows these illustrious antecedents.

THE PHENOMENON OF JEWISH CONVERSION

WE ARE TEMPTED to ask whether the encounter with the behaviors and ideas of the majority, to say nothing of their adoption, was responsible for setting in motion a dynamic process of acculturation that subsequently led, as a matter of course, to the annihilation of the Jews' own identity, in other words, to conversion — that is, whether remaining Jewish and becoming acculturated were two mutually exclusive choices that created tension and therefore alienation. From the point of view illustrated here, the response to this question is clearly negative. Conversion and the acculturation of which we are speaking belong to two substantially different types of assimilation. The first has to do with one's religious faith, whereas the second has to do with more general attitudes and cultural tendencies. The first is the result of a conscious choice, whereas the second is unconscious. There are no doubt broad channels of communication between the two, and it would be worthwhile to study them in detail, though this does not alter the essentially diverse nature of the two phenomena. Conversion is a consequence of the choice of abandoning the field of Difference, of adopting the identity of the Other, and this necessarily involves the annihilation of one's own current identity. Acculturation, however, is a redefinition of this identity: in the face of the challenge presented by Christian identity, Jews who wished to remain Jews ended up constructing a Jewish identity of Otherness. The common denominator of both phenomena is represented by the desire to arrive at a satisfactory definition of the identity of the Other, and consequently of all that pertains to the legitimacy of coexistence among different groups.

Conversions are also of course an index of the pressure exerted by the Christian world and of Jewish lack of faith or religious apathy, elements that are always excellent catalysts of opportunistic choices in matters of faith, as is well known even in our own times. All these elements were naturally present in Italy during the Renaissance, as they were elsewhere, as they always are for that matter. I would not be at all surprised if the number of those who opted to abandon Judaism in Italy during the Renaissance was greater than is currently known. On this topic, we have no comparative studies weighing Italy with other Western countries. Nonetheless, one fact emerges with relative clarity: in the period we are considering, conversion was a large-scale phenomenon. Frequently those involved were poor devils who fell victim to the illusion that the water of baptism would rescue them from their condition as outcasts. Paupers converted and in some instances were driven to repeat their abjuration and baptism several times in different cities in the hope of scraping together a few pennies from the missionary alms fund—a poor enough gain for Christianity. Cardinal Carlo Borromeo came to realize with horror the existence of this phenomenon toward the end of the sixteenth century, as his recently published correspondence attests. "In such people . . . I have little faith, and have been disappointed more than once by this sort of person, and by the way former converts turned out, . . . because under the pretext of rallying to our faith, I have found that many of them were seeking and pursuing other temporal purposes and interests, with fraudulent and deceptive means," wrote the Cardinal, for example, in 1584, as he neared the end of his life.[10] These examples involving the destitute can clearly not be classified under the heading of cultural assimilation.

Yet, many others certainly converted as a result of an authentic spiritual crisis that we have no right to label as an example of opportunism. In such cases, the comparative dialectic between the Self and the Other led to the effacing of the Self and to regeneration. (Many Jewish converts were indeed renamed *Renato*, that is, born again.) Many became wealthy and famous and gained access to social distinction. No doubt some saw this as the just reward for their efforts to reunite with the Truth. Their personal conviction that they had finally acquired the Truth caused some converts to turn into outstanding persecutors of their ex-brethren. Such convictions, in fact, frequently involved a willingness to resort to violence in order to make the whole world participate in the happiness discovered and obtained after so many trials. The fact is that behind many of the episodes of violence against Jews, we find (then as always) the actions of a Jew-turned-Christian neophyte. The history of the polemical diatribe against the Jews and the censure of Jewish books in Italy is studded with the names of neophytes, who, once baptized, dedicated their own Jewish learning to the cause of Christianity: Vittorio Eliano, Alessandro Franceschini, Domenico Gerosolimitano, and Domenico Carretto are just a few of the more regrettably famous. Alessandro Franceschini, for instance, seems to have been at the center of the inquisitory proceedings in Bologna, shortly before the expulsion of the Jews from that city (1569), against Rabbi Ishma'el da Valmontone, in the course of which the elderly rabbi was not spared the torture of the *strappado*, though he did manage to survive, however, and to set down in writing the contents of his own arguments in response to the neophyte.[11] Wherever he appeared, Alessandro sowed panic among the Jews, who were almost always invited to take part in public debates with him.

But, even after taking into account the whole range of possibilities, one incontrovertible fact remains: conversion was, then as always, the result of a personal choice to adopt the identity of the Other. In all such cases, it was a matter of people deciding to cross the proverbial Rubicon and to exit from Jewish history. Their cultural and spiritual background has not been studied in sufficient detail, and we do not know how far the chance to participate in the general culture may have influenced the decision to choose the Christian faith. The majority of the testimonials left by this type of neophyte, however, leave no room for doubt: their decisions were the outcome of a crisis fundamentally religious, rather than generically cultural, in nature. Those who betook themselves to the baptismal font for reasons other than opportunism were guided by a concern for the salvation of their souls, by meditation on the nature of the Messiah, by the witness borne by the story of Christ and Christianity to all humanity, and by the discovery that the Christians were right and the Jews wrong to refuse the Light of Truth. The arguments of Christian theology were certainly no stronger and more convincing in the Renaissance than in other periods, nor does it appear that anything new had emerged in the field of theological disputation. The reasons that convinced the neophytes to abandon the Jewish for the Christian identity were of the same type that reinforced their brethren in their conviction to remain Jews. All things considered, it seems impossible to classify these cases as examples of acculturation. Even if we wished to consider these conversions as setbacks suffered by certain people in the attempt to define their own identity within the Jewish sphere, the fact remains that such abjurations do not pertain to the cultural history of the Jews. Those who changed their religion followed in this case the paths of faith. Culture no more led the Jews out of Judaism than it led the Christians out of Christianity. There is nothing to prove that the choice of those who converted was imposed by their choice of the pleasures of the middle class lifestyle — poetry, music, theatre, sports, society games, and all the other phenomena customarily cited when describing the alleged tendency of the Italian Jews to limit the significance and definition of their own identity in terms of its Otherness with respect to Christian identity.

THE EXCEPTIONAL NATURE OF THE HISTORY OF THE JEWS IN ITALY

IT MAY FINALLY BE ASKED what the reasons are for the apparent exceptionality of the available evidence. In this connection, it should be simply stated that one cannot afford to lose sight of the general historical situation: in other words, we must not forget that the Italian Renaissance occurred in Italy and not somewhere else, and at that particular time! The French Renaissance occurred later than the Italian one and in any case is without importance from a Jewish standpoint, since in France at that time there were no Jews. The same can be said of England, from which the Jews were expelled in 1290, and for Spain, from which they were banished in 1492. We are left perhaps with Poland, where we find late expressions of a Renaissance imported from Italy, and where, in fact, there is considerable evidence similar to what we have been discussing. An initial explanation is therefore to be found in the peculiarity of Italy in that period. It is pointless, then, to insist on the fact that the Jews loved music and nature, the good life and the hunt, walks in the country and country vacations, or that as a rule they dressed no differently from the Christians, except in the details imposed by the sumptuary laws. If the prominent members of Jewish society discovered these pleasures in Italy as opposed to somewhere else, it is first and foremost because the leaders of Christian society also discovered them in the Italian peninsula long before they did on the other side of the Alps. A second explanation, which also has to do with the particular nature of the historical situation, is related to the exceptionality of the demographic profile characteristic of the Jews of Italy. How could we imagine, in such a situation of dispersion and extreme isolation, a complete lack of social contact with the Christian world? In the majority of cases, Jews wishing to engage in social and business relations could do so only with Christians. This does not imply, however, that all barriers were abolished. We are dealing with a complex interaction, and only by perceiving its nuances can we understand its nature and limits.

A third explanation that carries some weight is the fact that the parameters used to assess orthodoxy with respect to religious deviance were quite different in that period from ours. The same may be said, in fact, for the parameters of decency or of morality in general. This is an aspect of the mentality of the period whose importance should not be underestimated.

THE BASIC AMBIVALENCE OF THE JEWISH CONDITION

B EFORE CONCLUDING these preliminary considerations, it would be well to insist once more on the fact that the figure of the Jew unquestionably involved more than one element of ambivalence. We have already seen some of these in chapter 1, when we spoke of the social role played by the Jews with regard to the poor, a role rulers were disinclined to take upon themselves. In this capacity, the Jews found themselves cast in the role of mediators between those in power and the particular strata of the population that needed their services. In such a context, the Jews were the object of the ambivalence characteristic of participants on both levels—which could be interpreted in two antithetical ways. Situated on the fringes of the upper orders of society, they could be considered as belonging to them, thereby attracting the hostility that the wretched and the disinherited might nourish toward those in power in moments of particular economic difficulty. But from another point of view, the Jews' place was at the top level among the outcasts, and they could also be assimilated to the latter, which could result in their being treated with a mixture of contempt and fear, and consequently hostility, attitudes usually generated by the destitute. In the eyes of the Christians, the mediating function performed by the Jews, whichever way it was seen, was in any case perceived negatively. Besides, in such a situation there were incidental advantages for the Jews which they did not hesitate to exploit: how could they have been expected to do otherwise.

The fact that Jewish settlement was founded on the granting of a condotta involved questions of privilege, in the most straightforward sense of the word. The gesture of defining the juridical status of the Jews on the basis of the extraordinary nature of the condotta—which at the same time eliminated any possibility of their organic introduction into the municipal fabric—also defined a number of fields in which their uniqueness was transformed into undeniable privilege in comparison with certain strata of the Christian population. By virtue of these privileges, the Jews could on occasion be exempted from the risk of incurring supplemental taxes, usually levied on well-to-do citizens. In this way too they enjoyed a considerably more favorable juridical situation than did the peasants, and it has already been noted how they took advantage of it. Nonetheless, the fact remains that, on the whole, theirs was an unusual situation; ordinariness, under the circumstances, was quite out of the question.

These are certainly not the only examples of ambivalence, nor perhaps are they the most important. Other examples will be mentioned below. For the moment, it should be stressed that the ambivalence conferred upon the presence of the Jews in the Christian social panorama by virtue of their apparent "absence" was inevitably projected onto the Jews' way of perceiving their own sociocultural identity.

The fascination and attraction that the atmosphere of the cities in which they worked held for the Jews could not help shaping their attitudes and leading them to take very definite stands on ideological and practical issues. That atmosphere was made up of the countless things, great and small, in the routine of daily life which act to shape the mentality of the people. To imagine that the Jews were not a part of that atmosphere, or that their participation consisted in a set of *compromises*, never satisfactory by their very nature and therefore a source of tension and alienation, would be tantamount to seeing them as inhuman or constantly alienated. This, however, is certainly not what we find in our sources.

Thus, the Venetian Jews, when they drew up their sumptuary laws, expressly defined social preeminence *within* the group as a function of the position achieved *outside* it. The model may be found throughout the whole of the Jewish history of the diaspora, and unequivocal examples can also be found in the modern sociology of minorities. In a certain sense, the ambivalence described above was projected onto the *elite* members of the minority, where it was immediately exacerbated to the fullest extent, precisely because it was those elites who played the mediating role between minority and majority. They thereby participated in the world outside their own group and were at the same time an integral part of their own world. Seen from below, that position aroused a combination of admiration, even veneration at times, and criticism. Seen from above, however, the position was accompanied by frustration at the impossibility of becoming integrated into the social context that their inclinations and mentality led them to consider appropriate to their personalities. This frustration was also accompanied by pride stemming from the fact that the reason for that impossibility was their conscious choice to remain Jewish, a choice imposed by their ideology, in other words by their religious faith. Seen from the outside, their position brought with it a combination of advantages and disadvantages, and it would be absurd to assess these in isolation from the whole. Seen in terms of the potential for social integration, the ambivalent situation of the Jewish elites had in the final analysis negative consequences that only the decision to embrace the Christian faith could neutralize. In fact, only in this way could the Jews of the period *become like everyone else.*

We will take a look later at other examples of the mental and practical affinity between Jews and Christians. Let it suffice for now to conclude these preliminary observations by restating that the natural tendency of the Jews to model their own sociocultural identity on the basis of specular reflection on the Other (Christian) is not in conflict with the affirmation that the contacts (especially economic) between the Jewish and Christian societies did not modify the basic situation in which the structural opposition between the two societies was absolute and fundamental, whereas the contacts were wholly accidental. In other words, if one may put it this way, the Jews *thought* like the others, shared the same kind of *mentality*, and *aspired to be like everyone else*, but since "being *really* the same as everyone else" would have meant becoming Christians, that aspiration had to remain repressed because of their own refusal to integrate in that way, and because of the corresponding refusal of Christian society to integrate them in any other way.

In my view, to insist on presenting this conclusion, in many respects obvious, as invalidated "by prejudicial questions of an apologetic and integralist nature," and hence as an obstacle to an "objective analysis" of the historical phenomena studied, is itself proof of an incapacity, or unwillingness, to recognize the complexity associated with the ambivalence of the Jewish condition in a medieval Christian context.[12] When it comes to the history of the Renaissance Jews, the tendency to succumb to the temptations of analogy are thwarted by the ambivalence of the figure of the Jew itself. This has led to the revival in recent historiography of the kinds of distortion I mentioned earlier when speaking of the late nineteenth- and early twentieth-century historiography. To be unwilling or unable to grasp that ambivalence in all its complexity leads the historian to exaggerate one or the other of the opposing aspects underlying the ambivalence itself. This is why in some descriptions we find an emphasis on the themes, apologetic or denigratory, of traditional non-Jewish historiography: "the Christians, on the whole, would have liked to integrate them, but the Jews, basically, refused"; or "the Christians would, generally speaking, have preferred to integrate the Jews, and in fact did so, except for a few extraordinary events whose significance should be minimized." Then we have the apologetic or denigratory themes of traditional Jewish historiography, chiefly concerned with the question of how advantageous it was for Jews to persist in their difference: "the Jews would have liked to be integrated into Christian society, but the Christians basically refused to allow it"; or alternatively: "it was 'fortunate'/ 'unfortunate' that the Christians put a curb on the integration of the Jews, since, had this not been the case, the tendency of the minority toward acculturation would have inexorably led to total assimilation, in other words, to the 'end' of Jewish history"; or again: "Jewish society attempted to limit external influence through compromises and expedients aimed at maintaining their difference in a flexible manner." This is the same thing as saying that thinking and acting like everyone else, since this is the real issue, involved some degree of negation of one's own ideological diversity and its substitution with another ideology — a "pragmatic ideology of survival," based on the "search for a compromise, that would allow the compromiser to have his cake and eat it, at least *as far as appearances were concerned.*"[13]

In conclusion, I consider it essential to approach the problem of the definition of Jewish cultural identity from within, from the point of view of those who had no hesitation about choosing to remain in the Jewish camp and on the basis of that choice were not afraid to ask the burning questions of their time. To be in a position to do so, we must retrace the paths that led to the formation of this cultural identity, starting from childhood.

IV
EDUCATION
AND THE
RABBINICAL IDEAL

THE STRUCTURES OF ELEMENTARY EDUCATION

THE EDUCATION of the young has always and everywhere been the ground where old and new, *juventus* and *senectus*, meet. The period we are studying was no exception to the rule, valid alike for the Jews and for their Christian neighbors. In the case of the Jews, however, the encounter of opposites seems to have been somewhat more complex than in that of the Christians. The achievement of Self-awareness by a process of specular reflection in the Other called for the introduction of a second element, namely the Other, to all intents and purposes absent in the case of their Christian neighbors. Consequently, this awareness of Self was achieved in the context of a more than usually complex version of the delicate balance that any type of education is wont to produce between the adherence to the old world of tradition and the innovative rejection of that world. In this case, the interplay between adherence and rejection also included the interplay between adherence to the mental and cultural categories of one's environment, necessarily shaped by the Christian majority, and the rejection of such of those categories as might have threatened one's own individual identity. It will soon be seen that, for the Jews of the Renaissance, the conservative elements turned out to be more powerful than the innovative elements and that this state of affairs was paradoxically due to the new course that was being taken by the premodern mentality at the time.

Even a cursory glance at the traditional structures of education immediately reveals a decidedly conservative factor. As was also the case with their Christian neighbors, the education of Jewish children took place in different circumstances depending upon their socioeconomic background. In cities with any kind of community organization, there was usually a tutor hired by the community, but only the poor availed themselves of this service. The rich generally engaged a private tutor. The less-well-to-do sent their children to study away from home, to a tutor who transformed his home into a school, or to the home of someone else who could afford to hire a private tutor, usually a rich relative whose house thus came to serve as a boarding school for young men from outside.

Private tutors and their families received room and board from their masters. In this one may discern a form of patronage similar to that practiced by the Christians of the time and with which we are already familiar. The higher the rank of the patron, the better the qualifications of the tutor had to be. In any case, the tutor's responsibilities were not confined to teaching the children. He also wore the hats of counselor, lawyer, and private rabbi and took care of anything else in his area of competence demanded of him by his patron, for whom he also played the more general role of cultural "expert." As such, his was an extremely ambivalent position, characterized at the same time by its servile and its exalted nature. Outstanding scholars and men of letters earned their livings as tutors without their social status being thereby diminished: Johanan Treves (c.1480–c.1557), for instance, or Moses Provenzali (1503–1576), or Isaac Emanuel Lattes (died c.1570). The last was a doctor who worked as a private tutor, winning such renown that in 1557 the community of Pesaro offered him the directorship of the local Academy (Yeshivah) with an annual salary that for a Jew of the time was astronomical: 100 gold *scudi*, in addition to a dwelling "suited to his rank" — all for the task of leading the daily morning study group, a charge that usually did not take up more than an hour, as will be seen in due course. In the letter in which they made the offer, the community leaders of Pesaro also told Lattes that he would be free to spend the rest of the day as he saw fit.[1] At the same time, the rabbi of the community of Verona was earning an annual salary of a mere 6 ducats, more or less the equivalent of 6 scudi! We will return later to the rabbis' stipends and to their relationship with the community.

The transformation of private homes into public or semipublic institutions was one of the many ways in which Jews tried to overcome the difficulties consequent upon their dispersion over a vast territory and the lack of adequate public structures to satisfy the basic necessities of group life. Private synagogues played a similar role and cannot therefore be considered merely as a consequence of the social differences between rich and poor: such differences did exist of course, but they do not explain the phenomenon in and of themselves. Actually, the young men who studied in families other than their own were not always poorer than their hosts. On the contrary, according to the mentality of the time, in order to be effective education had to be severe, and one aspect of its severity often consisted of separating children from their parents. The extremely scattered nature of the Jewish population, especially in what we have defined as the first phase of our period, made it more necessary for Jewish boys than for Christians to travel far afield to pursue their education. It was not rare, then, to find rich young men studying in other people's homes, often members of the same family who lived in other localities. Even more frequently the person who directed the "family boarding school" was an elderly grandmother residing in another city. It was the general consensus that she, if anyone, would succeed in combining satisfactorily the necessary kindness and severity. "Directing" such a "boarding school" provided these elderly ladies with a more than worthwhile occupation. To sum up, the majority of young men received their education away from home, often at a considerable distance, and this fact must be borne in mind when we attempt to evaluate their psychological formation.

Having to put up with the habitual violence of a tutor, without being able to count on the understanding of a sensitive mother, having to adapt

Jewish teacher and advanced students as shown in a Maimonides code (Mishneh Torah) *currently in the Vatican Biblioteca Apostolica, Ms. Rossiana 498, f. 2ᵛ.*

to being on one's own and to solving one's problems by oneself, tended to accelerate these young men's sense of being already grown up. This last feature should be added to the elements common to the mental categories of both Jews and Christians, categories that underlay the behavior of both. As I have already stressed, we should not, however, imagine that there was complete affinity between them. When we come to study the contents of education, the image becomes more complex.

METHODS AND CONTENTS OF ELEMENTARY EDUCATION

THERE IS ONE characteristic of the cultural profile of Jewish society of the time that deserves to be particularly stressed. Whereas the Christian culture of the Renaissance increasingly cultivated the consciousness of a break with the Middle Ages, in method as well as content, Jewish culture tended to stress its continuity with the past. We find nothing among the Jews comparable to the revolutionary fervor of the humanists in revolt against the *Auctores octo*, the *Cartula*, and the *Graecismus*. The texts consecrated by tradition as the basis for the education of the young and their preparation for entry into society, for their participation, in other words, in the religious and cultural life of the group (though in the period that concerns us, the two levels are almost impossible to distinguish) remained the same. The educational structures inherited from preceding ages also remained unaltered.

As previously suggested, the general tendency, in keeping with time-honored tradition, confirmed by medieval notions, was to urge young people to break with childhood and enter the adult world as early as possible. Children were scrutinized so as to discover in their faces the tenderest indications of maturity and to encourage their precocious apparition. Did the Bible not teach us that man is prone to evil from birth (see Genesis 8:21)? The sense of the brevity and precariousness of human existence, much more marked then than now, led to an equally powerful sense of the importance of not letting time go by in vain. The consequence was to exaggerate the aspiration to save children from their childhoods and to have them assume the role of adults, dressing them as grown-ups, teaching them to speak, behave, and correspond like grown men with their peers as well as with people of the older generation. From this point of view, the particular existential situation of the Jews brought with it a further contributing element.

According to the Mishnah, children should be taught to read the Bible from the age of five (Avoth V, 21). But everyone tried to go one better: they therefore began at the age of three, even earlier if the child was especially gifted. We should not be surprised, then, to read what Leone Modena writes in his autobiography when he states that at the age of two and a half he read aloud in public the passage taken from the Prophets (Haftarah) during the Sabbath morning service.[2] The whole educational process was geared to achieve from the very beginning small concrete results at ascending levels of socialization: first of all, performing such liturgical functions in the synagogue as were compatible with their status as minors; then writing and performing other religious functions whose social component seemed inferior to the liturgical service in the synagogue; and so on. In this way, they perfected themselves by climbing one by one the various rungs of the traditional ladder of knowledge, indispensable to a complete education. This is how a father recorded the different phases of his son's progress: "At three Joseph encountered his Creator [in other words, came into contact with the world of religion]. He began studying the first day of the month of Iyar 5320 [= 1560]. At four and a half he read the Haftarah in the synagogue, on the occasion of the wedding of Messer Baruch of Arles. . . . At five and a half he learned to write. At six he started wearing the phylacteries [tefillin]. At eight and a half . . . he was studying the *Alfassi* [a famous medieval talmudic compendium]. At twelve and a half he began reading the Torah in the synagogue . . . and the same year he learned ritual slaughtering. . . . During the feast of Simchat Torah in the year 5322 [= 1571] he recited the morning liturgical service in the synagogue."[3] After this, he records nothing further: a sure sign that he considered the chief stages of his son's social apprenticeship to be over.

There are many revealing details in this brief text that we cannot allow to pass unobserved. First of all, the complete absence of any rite of passage from childhood to adolescence. The bar mitzvah ceremony, a universal custom today for young Jewish boys who have reached the age of thirteen, and which for Jewish law marks the entry into majority and full assumption of adult responsibility, goes unmentioned in our text. The scattered evidence on this point, still not satisfactorily studied, seems to indicate a gradual increase in sensitivity to the bar mitzvah ceremony, which the Italian Jews began calling at about this time "entering *minian*," by which they meant "becoming a member of the adult world." Little Joseph had joined the adult world long before he had the formal right to do so, showing his sense of responsibility and wearing the phylacteries at the age of six, following the ancient custom mentioned in the Talmud ("the father will purchase the phylacteries for his son whenever the latter is ready to take care of them" — Sukkah 42b). It should come as no surprise, then, if at eight and a half Joseph began studying the text of the Talmud — from the compendium of Isaac Alfassi, since, as was noted in chapter 1, the Talmud had been condemned to public burning a few years earlier. Joseph's father did not record the stages that succeeded this one. He was clearly only interested in the various degrees of his son's social integration, and the study of the Talmud, or its equivalent the *Alfassi*, represented the final stage in this process.

We know, however, from other sources the paths that led up to this final stage. In the first place, the systematic study of the Pentateuch (the Torah), which was learned by heart in Hebrew, along with the literal word-for-word Italian translation and the Aramaic translation (the *Targum*). The Aramaic version, written in the language once spoken by the Jews in the Holy Land and in the entire Mediterranean area, was in fact also canonized alongside the original text by a centuries-old tradition. There followed the study of the other books of the Bible, as far as possible committed to memory and always accompanied by the literal Italian translation. Then came a few elementary texts from the *Mishneh Torah* of Maimonides and the Mishnah, each complementing the other. These constituted the basis of the child's knowledge in the area of religious practice — the various blessings and prayers, the precepts relative to what was considered ritually permitted or forbidden, the rules for ideal moral behavior. There was no formal curriculum. The study of the Talmud began when this preliminary practice had led to a sufficient degree of maturity. From that moment on, the study of the Mishnah and the Codes was incorporated into the study of the Talmud.

Before he could consider his paternal duty accomplished, little Joseph's father taught his son how to slaughter poultry and other edible animals according to the ritual norms. The fact that the Jews were extremely dispersed made this knowledge practically indispensable. In a period in which refrigerators were unknown, a family living isolated in a small town had no way of obtaining meat unless one of its members knew how to butcher it. The rabbi Judah Mintz expressed his most profound concern in this regard when, in a series of ordinances, he forbade young people under the age of eighteen to take it upon themselves to butcher animals.[4] He was concerned lest children be forced to assume responsibilities beyond their years. And perhaps he hoped to impose a check on the extreme demographic dispersion of his brethren, whose risks and pitfalls he was not unaware of. However that may be, he was unsuccessful. Unlike his other ordinances, these went unobserved. Many documents bear witness to authorizations to butcher poultry and other animals issued by rabbis to young Jews no more than twelve years old. They were compelled to make a virtue out of necessity.

FEMALE EDUCATION

IN ITALY it was not only Jewish young men who were forced to learn the butchering trade in order to find a satisfactory solution to the prosaic problem of obtaining meat to eat. Women too learned butchering. The particular demographic distribution of the Jewish presence in Italy made it necessary upon occasion for widowed women with dependent children cut off in small towns, where they had been left to run the bank, to take over the "male" role. Talmudic law in any case did not exclude women from the task of ritual butchering, so the solution adopted by the Jews of Italy was really not abnormal. Still, the circumstances were exceptional, and in some ways paradigmatic of the special nature of the history of the Italian Jews. Aside from this, however, the course of study pursued by young Jewish girls was no different from that pursued by Christian girls of the same age. The daughters of the rich were better educated than the daughters of the poor, and on rare occasions they were better educated than the male children. Still, the examples of exceptionally educated women, however frequently they may be cited, serve only to confirm the rule. The time was not yet ripe for female emancipation, not even in Renaissance Italy.

Nevertheless, in this, as in a number of other fields, we occasionally come across expressions of doubt regarding the perfection of the status quo. The collection of epistolary models composed in his youth by Samuel Archivolti (1515–1611) contains two letters whose interest resides precisely in the fact that they are offered as models and therefore point to problems that the youthful author saw as typical of the problems of his time.[5] The first is a letter addressed by a young woman to a rabbi in which she asks if she may be permitted to study the materials of Talmudic law explicitly forbidden by the Talmud to women; the second is the rabbi's reply. The rabbi grants her permission to study the materials requested, but not without pointing out the absolutely exceptional nature of the case. According to the rabbi, the young woman, a real virago, has the right to behave like a man precisely because she is so *different from her peer group*. During the period we are studying, most women confined themselves to leading the type of life they had always led: they were kept busy in the kitchen alongside their mothers or in other work traditionally labeled as "feminine" while they waited for the time to come when they would leave their father's house in order to marry.

A YOUNG BOY'S STUDY DAY

FROM THIS POINT of view, the life of a male child was more demanding, as was only to be expected considering the greater responsibility he would be expected to assume. The text of a letter addressed by a tutor in the service of the wealthy Rieti family of Siena to the mother of a boy who was attending his classes gives us a number of interesting details. This was the program for the day:

In the evening we study until the fourth hour [i.e., until the end of the first third of the twelve hours of the night, according to the system current at the time, in which the twenty-four hour day started and ended at sunset]. Then we go in to supper. . . . While we are at table, three times a week one of the pupils speaks on a topic of Talmudic law, while his fellow students fire questions at him. . . . This goes on for an hour and a half, sometimes two hours. After that, we go to bed and sleep until the tenth hour [about four in the morning]. We get up and, since it is not yet daylight, we devote ourselves for three hours to the study of the text of the Talmud. When it gets light, we go to the synagogue for morning prayers, after which we study another Talmudic text. Then we go and have breakfast. Then we proceed to the study of the glosses on the Talmud (*Tosafot*), until we have perfectly absorbed the text. At the nineteenth hour [an hour after noon], we eat lunch, and after that we do not study again until evening. This is because I have left the afternoon open for the teaching of grammar [i.e., Latin], which is taught by a Christian instructor.[6]

We should not of course take this schedule too literally. Although the tutor clearly cites the precise times of day, study time was still fairly elastic: more than by the striking of the clock, it was determined by daily rhythms, the sequence of liturgical services in the synagogue, the abilities of the pupils, the instructor's personal judgment. The above description, however, constitutes a declaration of the tutor's intentions, an ideal manifesto of what he would have liked to accomplish, though he may never actually have succeeded. It should be observed that no thought was given to leaving free time for recreation or sport: the children would have felt guilty wasting their time playing. There is a great deal of other evidence to confirm explicitly what we can read here between the lines.

The subjects studied were generally speaking what the Jewish tradition considered orthodox. One should, however, take note of the fact that a certain level of utilitarian instruction in subjects essential for contact with the outside world was required. Our text mentions Latin: the boy in question was probably an adolescent. Other texts speak of the instruction of younger children in other subjects that the mentality of the time considered as lying halfway between the useful and the pleasant: arithmetic, of course, but also music, drawing, and occasionally dancing. Dancing masters were fairly common among Jews during the period we are studying. Their services were available to both the Jewish and the Christian populations, a circumstance that did not fail to create apprehension among religious spirits in both camps, who considered such association undesirable. It is clear that the same "Renaissance" atmosphere that characterized the lives of their neighbors also prevailed among the Jews. According to the mentality current among Eastern European Jews on the eve of the modern period, such a climate of tolerance was to be avoided like the plague, so as to reinforce the distinction between the Jews and the rest at all levels. This was not, however, the mentality of the Renaissance. In Renaissance Italy, as had been the case in Spain, behavior of the kind described was in no way considered a deviation from Jewish orthodoxy, the fruit of an irresponsibly liberal spirit already headed for assimilation. Instead, it was the course chosen by the Jews of Eastern Europe that signaled an unmistakable involution in this sense. The famous Judah Loew (or Maharal) of Prague (c.1525–1609) was fully aware of this when he criticized the study plan championed by his brethren and proposed a reform similar to the one already practiced for some time by the Jews of Italy.

ADVANCED EDUCATION: THE YESHIVAH

THE ABOVE DOCUMENT penned by the Sienese tutor has led us almost imperceptibly into the climate of those studies that little Joseph's father, the author of the text previously cited, no longer considered relevant to his parental duties. In fact, Talmudic studies were an affair for adults. But adolescents mingled with adults of all ages during the study sessions presided over by the head of the Talmudic Academy (Yeshivah). Elijah Capsali (c.1483–1555) has left us, in his *Venetian Chronicle*, quite a lively description of the study activity of the Paduan Yeshivah directed by Judah Mintz during the final year of his life (1508). The passage reads as follows: "The rabbi received from the community one hundred florins a year, in addition to a large house as his personal residence. In exchange, it was his duty to act as tutor to the children of the poor, whom he was also expected to provide for, furnishing each of them with a room in his house. He ministered to them according to their condition and their merits. These students were expected to procure their own food, but they took their meals in common, discussing the texts they were studying."[7] The Master, then, acted as tutor to the students who lodged in his residence. This was the organization of the day's studies:

In the morning, after leaving the Academy, where he had engaged in discussion with the other rabbis, the Master [the head of the Academy, Judah Mintz] went back to his own home, where he taught the text of the Talmud to the less gifted students, though he was not obliged to devote a specifically defined portion of his time to that activity. After lunch, in the afternoon, the other students went to him, and all together under his guidance they studied the glosses (*Tosafot*). The rich members of the community took into their service private tutors who did the same thing. The following morning, after morning prayers, the Master went to a small room in the courtyard of the Great Syngogue with the students lodging with him. This is what is known as the *Yeshivah*. There were desks and benches, and everyone sat down, the rabbis and the other [private] tutors with their pupils. At this point, the Master would ask a series of questions, and everyone answered according to his ability. Then they began a discussion, asking each other questions. This is what they call an academic disputation (*pilpul ha-Yeshivah*). Everybody discussed with his neighbor, grown-ups with grown-ups and youngsters with youngsters. The discussion was done without consulting the text, since everyone knew it perfectly. The only book in the room was the book of the Master, in which he would indicate the passage for the day's study. Everyone stayed here for about an hour, depending on how the discussion went. Afterwards, the Master opened his book and indicated exactly what was to be studied for the following day. Then they rose, left the room, and went home, where each of them studied with his own pupils the same way the head of the Academy did with his. This was the practice each day of the week except Friday, when everyone studied on his own account.[8]

One cannot help noticing the similarity of this description to that in the letter of the Sienese tutor quoted earlier. It is precisely on account of this similarity that the Sienese institution has been classified by some historians as a Yeshivah, but this is inaccurate. A Yeshivah like the one described by Capsali was not in operation in Siena. To be sure, the private tutor guided his pupils' lives as if they were part of a Yeshivah, distinguishing, that is, between the study of the text of the Talmud and the *Tosafot* and the discussion that followed the morning liturgical service in the synagogue. Beyond that, however, his activity was confined to what Capsali's text clearly defines as *preparatory* study. The Yeshivah was an institution of higher learning. The question is therefore legitimate whether the *Yeshivot* (plural of *Yeshivah*) were the Jewish equivalents of the Italian universities of the time, which allowed the participation of auditors, according to ability and not according to age: the young mingled with the more advanced in age and often showed themselves better prepared and more astute. In fact, the Yeshivah was usually perceived as a kind of Jewish university. Period documents in Latin refer to it as a *Studium* and define the rabbis as *Doctores*, or, more rarely, *Doctores legis hebraicae*. It is therefore logical to conclude that in such a context the title of rabbi was considered the height of academic and consequently social success to which a Jew could ordinarily aspire.

THE RABBINICAL IDEAL AND RABBINICAL TITLES

THE RABBINICAL HIERARCHY was divided into two principle levels, to which there corresponded two separate titles: *Morenu ha-Rav* (the Rabbi our Master, or alternatively, our Lord and Master) and *Ḥaver* (Colleague [of the Rabbis], or Associate Rabbi). Toward the end of the sixteenth century another intermediate title was added: *Ḥakham* (Learned Man). There can be no doubt that the people of the time considered the title of *Ḥaver* subordinate to that of Morenu ha-Rav. Elia Levita in his Hebrew dictionary defined the former as indicating "a man with rabbinical credentials who has not yet acquired the right to emanate decisions on the law and has not yet been named *Morenu ha-Rav*."⁹ The "associate rabbis" were entitled to the honors set aside for those whom society recognized as dedicated to study and who were on the way to achieving the status of wise men. These honors were quite conspicuous on the social level: they were called to read the Torah with their relevant title, they had the right to a place of honor within the synagogue, on

A Jew engaged in study, as shown in the Rothschild Miscellany, Northern Italy, c. 1470, currently in Jerusalem, Israel Museum, f. 44ᵛ.

public occasions they were sometimes exempted from observing the restrictions contained in the sumptuary laws, and the like. As a consequence, the distinction between the title of Morenu ha-Rav and that of Ḥaver was reflected at the social level, thereby projecting into that dimension an opportune reflection of the hierarchical order of knowledge established in an academic context. The addition toward the end of our period of the intermediate title of Ḥakham, with all that it implied for the restructuring of the hierarchy, might be interpreted as an expression of the tendency to emphasize still more, in what we will see was a period of intellectual crisis, the importance of whoever was at the top of the ladder, in other words, the rabbis properly so called.

From the formal point of view, the title of Morenu ha-Rav was the only qualification that entitled its holder to exercise the highest functions of the rabbinical office, specifically, the right to pronounce opinions in the area of Jewish law and to be considered a spiritual leader. As long as people continued to see in the knowledge of the rabbi the true bulwark of Jewish society, the rabbinical credential and title continued to represent an ideal worthy of pursuit. The tutor from Siena, whose observations from a letter written to the mother of one of his pupils were quoted earlier, expressed this general opinion when he described the progress made by the boy entrusted to his care: "Your son never pauses from study for an instant. . . . There is no doubt that he will be the honor of his family. . . . For my own part, I am certain he will become a rabbi, and that people everywhere will have recourse to his wisdom."[10] A young father expressed a similar wish on the occasion of the birth of one of his daughters: he hoped he would see her grow up in good health, a happy wife, and the mother "of sons who were students of the Torah, observant of its precepts, and rabbis of Israel."

Seen from a broader perspective, this is a feature common to the general mentality of the period, for which knowledge was the only way for a person of humble origins to improve his social lot. In the light of what was said above, however, it should be stressed at this point that for the Jews the only "true" knowledge was the knowledge linked to their traditional culture. Other cultural fields were considered at best a sort of supplementary superstructure. This is a fact of major importance which must be borne in mind when approaching the question of Jewish participation in Renaissance culture. Combined with elevated socioeconomic status, knowledge served to further highlight the social excellence of the rabbi and his family. As was the case with their Christian neighbors, who were frequently ambitious for at least one of their sons to embrace an ecclesiastical career, the Jews too hoped that one of the more talented members of the family would obtain the title of rabbi. We have many well-known examples that provide ample confirmation of this general tendency: Solomon Modena, Ishmaʿel Rieti, Yeḥiel Nissim da Pisa, Menaḥem Azariah da Fano.

A common problem was how to avoid abuses of rabbinical rights and prerogatives. How could one guarantee, for example, that the principle of the sovereignty of the public in the choice of its spiritual leaders did not come into conflict with the claims of qualified rabbis to exercise power? Or, alternatively, how was it possible to ensure that rabbinical titles would not be conferred on unworthy candidates, or that the conferring rabbis would not manipulate the granting of titles to promote their own students and thereby extend and perpetuate their own influence? The measures evolved to cope with these various possibilities serve merely to confirm the enormous importance attributed to the possession of a rabbinical diploma and the social prominence it conferred upon its holder. Efforts were made to raise the age requirement for candidates for the title of rabbi to forty, to limit the number of titles bestowed by making it a rule that they could only be awarded by a committee of three rabbis of recognized renown, or by introducing the notion that only a diploma granted by the head of a famous Yeshivah could truly be considered valid. But, all things considered, these and other measures proved ineffective. As is invariably the case in such circumstances, the temptation to take advantage of the situation for personal gain was often more powerful than the sense of what was necessary to safeguard the interests of society. Only the exercise of full sovereignty on the part of solidly organized communities, which, as will be seen in chapter 6, only became typical during the second phase of our period, proved capable of introducing effective countermeasures: thus it came to be stipulated that no diploma was a sufficient qualification to exercise rabbinical functions without the express consent of the Community Council. In Rome, for instance, a community ordinance in effect at least until the end of the seventeenth century made it a rule that "no one could be called Rabbi without the consent of the *Congrega* [Congregation]," in other words, of the Community Council.[11] In Mantua in 1597 it was decreed that only a candidate who had obtained the approval of the majority of the qualified rabbis belonging to the Community could be recognized as a Rabbi.[12]

RABBINICAL PREROGATIVES

THE CHIEF PREROGATIVES of the rabbis, specified in detail in their diplomas, consisted of the right to issue decisions in ritual matters, to act as judges in accordance with the precepts of Jewish law, in particular regarding matrimonial disputes, and the right of excommunication. From the normative point of view, all of these prerogatives obviously produced in the public *a state of dependency on the rabbi.* Nevertheless, the only power that played a particularly significant role, as far as the exercise of public authority was concerned, was the power of excommunication. It seems that, apart from one or two exceptional cases that confirm the rule, for the entire period under investigation excommunication remained in the hands of the rabbis. It was the rabbis' responsibility to pronounce the formulas of excommunication, and it was to them that the Christian authorities granted the necessary authorization to do so. Given the fact that the system of taxation would not work unless the delinquent were threatened with excommunication, it proved a practical impossibility to dispense with the role of the rabbis in community administration. Efforts designed to reduce the arbitrariness of rabbinical decisions regarding excommunication could as a consequence only be intensified.

Nonetheless, we must also take into consideration the element of clerical sanctity that the very nature of the act of excommunication added to the distinguishing features of the rabbi's role, as well as to his public authority. This consideration served to further stress the affinity between the mental attitude of the Jews toward their rabbis and that of the Christians toward their priests, an affinity confirmed by a number of examples. For instance, rabbis were called in to hear the confessions of the dying, thereby playing a role similar to that of the Christian priest; people also turned to them to interpret their disquieting dreams. The rabbis themselves attempted, unsuccessfully, to lay claim to the priestly prerogative of the *kohanim* to be the first called upon to read from the Torah. In other words, they tried to push the analogy that the mentality of the time tended to make between the social dignity of their learning and the dignity of the priesthood, to the point of interfering with ritual itself. Similarly doomed to failure was the rabbis' attempt to use the provisions of Talmudic law to escape paying taxes: the economic circumstances of the communities made the application of this principle out of the question.

RABBINICAL DIPLOMAS AND UNIVERSITY DOCTORATES

IN FACT, THE FIGURE of the rabbi was essentially ambiguous. Insofar as he was a "man of religion," he was above all a "man of learning." So, however similar his figure might be to that of the Christian priests, it was also comparable, indeed still more so, to that of the medieval *doctores*. Far from undermining the analogy with the Christian mentality of the time, this characteristic serves to reinforce it. The rabbinical diplomas of the time are remarkably similar in their wording to the stereotyped formulas of the doctorate, as the latter had been handed down by a centuries-old tradition. We find the same fulsome praises of learning, the same mention of the rights of the learned to a series of privileges and prerogatives, and the same meticulous listing of the latter. It goes without saying that there are inevitable differences in content. Unlike those of the rabbis, the prerogatives of the doctors only marginally involved the exercise of power in the true sense of the word. In other words, although it was easier for someone with a doctoral title to gain access to power than for someone without, and although the doctors enjoyed far from negligible privileges in the realm of social life, that did not alter the fact that in the judicial structure of the Italian cities only the magistrates had a role comparable to that of the rabbis. A doctorate was sometimes a necessary condition for becoming a magistrate — but it was never a sufficient condition.

In teaching, however, the parallel between the rabbi and the doctor was almost perfect. We already alluded, referring to the Paduan Yeshivah, to a certain affinity between the Yeshivah and the University. The types of activity performed by Judah Mintz in that Yeshivah were in fact extremely similar to those exercised by the *doctores* in the University; the activities of the *doctores* were meticulously described in the diplomas that qualified their bearers for *legendi, disputandi, docendi, interpretandi, glosandi, cathedram magistralem ascendendi illamque regendi, insignia doctoratus recipiendi* (reading, disputing, teaching, interpreting, commenting, ascending to the teacher's chair and occupying it, receiving the doctoral insignia) as well as *privilegium doctorandi* (the right to confer the doctorate on other scholars). From the strictly professional point of view, therefore, the sequence of the various teaching activities was the same as that followed by Judah Mintz. The privilege of elevating others to the rank of doctor was analogous to that of conferring the title of rabbi. The rabbis, then, presented themselves in Jewish society not only as "priests" but also as "*doctores*" and university professors. This concept had made headway among the Jews as a consequence of the Latinization or Italianization of the word rabbi, which was and is impossible to translate: in the documents of the time the rabbi is almost always referred to as *doctor legis hebraicae* or simply *magister*.

The figure of the rabbi is in a way emblematic of the complexity characterizing the contemporary Jewish conception of culture. In the light of what has been said so far, it is time to reconsider the theory current among historians of a dichotomy between a rationalistic tendency dominated by a centrifugal attraction toward the world of culture in general, which is supposed to represent the general tendency of Jewish society, and an "antirationalistic" tendency dominated by a centripetal attraction toward the traditional Jewish world. An integral part of this dichotomy is the stereotyped picture of the rabbi, intent on pursuing an ideal of total "isolation" of Jewish culture from the rich culture of the Italian Renaissance. Another theory that must be called into question is that which posits a difference in attitudes between Italian and Transalpine Jews, the first being more "liberal," the second "conservative," not to say "obscurantist." As will become apparent in the next chapter, the concrete examples offered by the representatives of the Jewish culture of the time are too far removed from these clichés for us to continue to condone them. Throughout the period in question, among the Jews of Italy, most of the authors of works of a cultural nature were qualified rabbis. Whatever their ethnic affiliation, the rabbis were an integral part of the public group to which they belonged, and their culture represented the highest level attained by the Jewish culture of which they were a part. Consequently, whatever the general characteristics of the culture in question, its fundamental tendencies were orthodox and conservative, at least as far as the declared intentions and social rank of its official representatives went. This, therefore, is the proper context in which we must investigate the nature of the encounter with the culture of the outside world.

V

JEWISH CULTURE, HEBRAISTS, AND THE ROLE OF THE KABBALAH

JEWISH CULTURE AND THE CULTURE OF THE RENAISSANCE

I T WOULD BE a well-nigh impossible task to attempt a concise summary of the characteristics of the culture of the Jews of Italy during our period. This is not simply because it would call for far more than the available space, but also and above all because modern historical research is still in its infancy when it comes to the problems that the topic entails. On the one hand, one has to contend with the slowness of Jewish historiography to assimilate new trends in the fields of intellectual and, more generally speaking, cultural history, to say nothing of their implications for social history. On the other hand, one cannot ignore the dead weight exerted by the point of view imposed by the historiography of the socio-political majority, whatever its special bias. In the present instance, the latter point of view produces a distortion that might be defined as "colonial," inasmuch as it perpetuates the relationship historically prevailing between the Christian majority, in a position of strength because it controlled the reins of power, and the Jewish minority, tiny by comparison and in a position of weakness because excluded from power, in a conceptual relationship that opposes the stronger to the weaker culture, and implies, in the final analysis, a value judgment in favor of the former.

The distorting effect characteristic of this point of view is apparent from the start in the very choice of research topics and historiographic methodologies, choices one would expect a serious scholar to make *sine ira et studio*. Rather than addressing the major issues that should be raised relative to any sociocultural group, the tendency in the present case is to give preference to questions normally considered subordinate, questions whose real importance is often unmistakably secondary. The question is posed, for instance, whether Italian Renaissance culture influenced Jewish culture, and, if the answer is in the affirmative, how and to what extent, long before the culture on which this "external" influence is to be sought has been adequately defined. This procedure constitutes on the one hand an implicit assumption that the *Italian culture of the Renaissance* ("Italian," note, not "Christian") and *Jewish culture* are two quite different things, without pausing to define the parameters that define this supposed diversity. On the other hand, the preliminary work of historiographical selection ends up unjustly favoring the kind of documentation that seems, at least at first sight, to lend itself better to the definition of areas of contact between the internal and external cultural spaces. From this perspective, for instance, the analysis of a philosophical work looks more promising than that of a commentary on the Talmud. And yet, in the cultural economy of Renaissance Jewish society, this does not reflect the actual situation.

BOOKS AND LEARNING

ONE WOULD DO WELL, therefore, to inquire in the first place what the basic elements of Jewish culture were. We have already obtained a general idea by examining the system of education in force at the time, as well as the human ideal that the system set itself. We may now take a further step forward and ask ourselves what were the sources that served as models for Jewish cultural activity and how was that activity reflected in the literary production of the time. A systematic diachronic analysis of the degree of Jewish literacy still remains to be undertaken. Nevertheless, ever since the late Moses Avigdor Shulvass and Isaiah Sonne called our attention to the importance of a quantitative analysis of the libraries of the Italian Jews, considerable progress has been made in this field, so that one is now in a position to hazard, with a fair degree of assurance, a few preliminary obvservations. The literary achievements of Jewish men of letters do not suffer by comparison with those of their most illustrious Christian contemporaries. Of course we will not find among the Jews libraries comparable to those of Vespasiano da Bisticci, Niccolò Niccoli, or Lorenzo de' Medici. Even after the revolutionary invention of printing, books still continued to be luxury items. In the manuscript period, only the very rich could afford to acquire them. Bearing in mind that the Jews were on the average considerably less wealthy than the Christian bourgeoisie, a comparison of the known library inventories nevertheless appears to indicate a literacy gap in their favor. We need only recall, for example, that the books owned in the first quarter of the fourteenth century by a rich merchant from Prato like Francesco Datini did not amount to many more than a dozen, and that the library of the famous Duke of Ferrara, Borso d'Este, numbered no more than 148 volumes in 1467. The inventories of Jewish libraries show far higher numbers: Abraham, son of Elia of Imola, a contemporary more or less of Francesco Datini and considerably less wealthy, was the owner of 32 volumes.[1] Lists of the books owned by the entire community of Mantua survive, thanks to the censorship purges ordered by the Inquisition in 1595 and again in 1605. An excellent detailed study recently confirmed two general impressions, partly advanced as a result of the preliminary investigation carried out fifteen or so years ago by the present author on the basis of a conspicuous number of inventories of books owned by Jews.[2] The first of these impressions was that the degree of literacy of the Jewish public was in fact quite high, and the second that practically all of Jewish cultural activity, at least down to that time, was based on texts written in Hebrew and was unquestionably modeled on "sacred literature." An analysis of the lists of books inspected by the Mantuan Inquisition shows in fact that, even toward the end of the sixteenth century, 98 percent of the books owned by the members of that community belonged in the category of "sacred literature." Only 11.2 percent of the libraries contained books written in Italian, and in any case the number of the latter did not exceed 0.6 percent of the total number of books owned. These facts supplement and confirm my own preliminary research, which showed that, down to the mid–sixteenth century, the vast majority of the books that formed part of these collections were liturgical works, works of biblical exegesis, works dealing with questions of ritual, and especially copies of the Talmud. As things currently stand, therefore, one can be quite categorical in affirming that, throughout the entire period under examination, the books that Jews kept in their libraries, and the works that they read and studied, were almost all in Hebrew. The language of cultural communication of Italian Jewish society was Hebrew and Hebrew alone. Setting aside for the moment the problem of the Christian scholars of Hebrew, to be discussed later, one cannot escape the conclusion that this cultural phenomenon appears to be confined within the Jewish social space.

This state of affairs is confirmed by the lists of Hebrew works the first printers chose to publish in the last quarter of the fifteenth and the first half of the sixteenth centuries. With very few exceptions—and these exceptions can be considered as indicative of future developments—these works are the same as those found most frequently in the private libraries: classics of Hebrew literature and thought of the Middle Ages, and first and foremost those particularly linked to the cultural traditions of the Jews of Italy. It should be noted that although the first dated Italian edition of a Hebrew work is Rashi's commentary on the Pentateuch (Reggio Calabria, 1475), it seems certain that other more ambitious works were printed earlier, works such as Jacob ben Asher's treatise on Jewish ritual, *Arba'a Turim*. Among the first Italian editions in Hebrew, however, the Talmud deserves special mention. The fact that the priceless first editions of the Talmud, accompanied by Rashi's commentary and the medieval glosses (*Tosafot*), were produced at the end of the fifteenth century (Soncino, Pesaro, 1484–1520) and the beginning of the sixteenth (Venice, Bomberg, 1520 and on) by Christian Italian printers, whose collaborators, as textual editors and proofreaders, were the most notable Jewish scholars and converts of the day, is sufficient proof both of the importance attributed to the study of the Talmud and the abilities of the Jewish scholars of Italy. Also, let us not forget that the text of the Talmud edited and printed by one of these men, Bomberg, was destined to become the standard text and is still used today by the entire Jewish world.

LITERARY PRODUCTION

TURNING NOW to consider the literary production of the Jews of the period, we will arrive at similar conclusions. The works into which the Jews of Italy poured their creative energies were also composed in Hebrew. Many of these works are still awaiting publication, though in the last decade notable progress has been made in this field. The bulk is made up of works relating to Jewish law, especially rabbinical responsa, for the most part having to do with questions of ritual, though not exclusively so. The first two responsa contained in the collection of Moses Provenzali, rabbi of Mantua (1503–1576), for instance, deal with questions of an eminently philosophical nature (the first explains a passage in Gersonides on the nature of celestial matter, the second is a detailed explanatory commentary on the twenty-five propositions that open the second part of Maimonides' *Guide for the Perplexed*). These many thousands of rabbinical responsa do not strike modern scholars — disinclined as they are to venture into the thicket of technical disquisitions that were the bread and butter of the scholars of the fifteenth and sixteenth centuries, and which call for a technical training no longer easy to come by — as particularly inviting. And yet it is precisely these texts that give us an idea, not only of the kinds of problems that occupied the minds of the day, but also of their approach to the problems, their points of views, and the solutions they put forward. The fact that only under exceptional circumstances were one or two of these works ever printed, a fact that has given rise to various explanatory hypotheses, can probably be attributed to the limited numbers of Italian Jewry, the only group interested in many of the questions debated, and consequently of the potential market. Whatever the printers saw as a good investment, however, was printed, and usually well received, even outside Italy. Such was the case, for instance, of the responsa of Joseph Colon, which in fact went through two editions in the sixteenth century (Venice, 1519, and Cremona, 1560).

Particular mention should be made of Obadiah da Bertinoro's commentary on the Mishnah, which, though composed in Jerusalem, where this scholar settled permanently in 1488, should nevertheless be considered typical of fifteenth-century Italian rabbinical culture. This commentary is still printed in the traditional standard editions of the Mishnah, just as Rashi's commentary accompanies the Talmud.

In a related category are works of biblical exegesis, among which may also be included collections of sermons, exclusively based on biblical themes and associated with the passages from scripture read during services in the synagogue on the Sabbath and holidays. Some of these works enjoyed extraordinary popularity among the Eastern European Jewish public of the last century—a fact that proves that these works were perfectly in keeping with the spirit of that public, which, rightly or wrongly, one is accustomed to regarding as emblematically typical of Jewish orthodoxy. Such was, in particular, the case of the commentary on the Pentateuch by Obadiah Sforno (c.1475–1550), which was habitually included in the standard editions of the Bible accompanied by the classical commentaries, and which remains to this very day one of the most popular texts of its nature.

All of this should of course be compared with what was said in the previous chapter about the education of the Jewish public of the day. That it was typical of the whole of Jewish society and not just of a few learned rabbis is more than confirmed by the enormous epistolary production of the period. These letters, hundreds of examples of which have recently been published, are perhaps the most obvious demonstration of the phenomenon at hand. However well one may know Hebrew, and however many dictionaries and concordances one may have, it is difficult for a modern reader unfamiliar with the modes of the literature in question to grasp the full significance of these letters. This is another type of production that amply confirms the fact that the phenomena of culture were strictly confined within the Jewish space.

The fact that the principal representatives of Jewish culture were qualified rabbis is extraordinarily important for a proper characterization of the Jewish culture of the period. There can be no doubt whatsoever that, taken as a whole, these authors shared many ideas, mental attitudes, and to some extent even topics of interest with the members of the society of the Other, in other words, with Christian society. This fact has already been clearly demonstrated in a large number of detailed studies. An example or two will be given later in the course of this chapter. What I would particularly like to stress at this point, however, is that this incontrovertible fact must be seen as a part of what I have been trying to demonstrate: that this entire literary production was essentially conceived and experienced as the creation of Jewish culture for Jews. In other words, the affinity between Jewish and non-Jewish literary production manifested itself at the center, not at the edges, of the Jewish cultural space. It must therefore be considered an integral part of their awareness of belonging to Jewish culture, as well as a way of conceiving their Jewishness, especially on the part of the most legitimate representatives of its conservatively "orthodox" tendency. If it had not been thus, this awareness would have manifested itself instead in feelings of tension and alienation, which, as far as we know, occurred only in the imaginations of modern historians.

THE SIGNIFICANCE OF THE IMPORTATION OF "OUTSIDE" CULTURE

IT FOLLOWS from this that the *importation* of elements of the outside culture must be understood as the adoption and manipulation of contents considered "neutral" as far as their potential impact on their consciousness of a Jewish identity—perceived as different from, or better yet, *opposed* to Christian identity—was concerned. This importation took place along lines similar to those of any group that today borrows technology from another. It might be objected that such importation could not fail to influence the group's awareness of its cultural identity. This is no doubt true. What we are getting at will perhaps become clearer if we go back for a moment and consider what was said about diplomas of rabbinical ordination and the figure of the rabbi. The rabbinical diploma exhibited unmistakable similarities with the doctoral diploma; and at the same time the Italian rabbi tended to have more in common, in his sacral function, with a Christian priest than with a doctor of the law. From the point of view proposed here, this means that the ideals of the Jews of Italy regarding learning and how it should be presented were no different from those of their neighbors. In this case, the "neutral" contents are not represented by the role of the Christian priest, upon whose distance from their ideal figure the Jews would have been more likely to insist, nor by the university doctor, but by the abstract *model of learning* and by the *model of the mediating role of the man of religion in the ideal functioning of society.* The ideal learning of the Jew was one thing; however, the learning of the university doctor was another. When the latter did not seem to the Jews to be completely at odds with their Jewishness, it might seem complementary at best to the learning necessary for the more perfect practice of Judaism. Thus, for example, the ideal of the learned rabbi, for David, son of Messer Leon, was the man who united Talmudic learning not only with Kabbalistic learning but also with the learning of the university.[3] And he translated this concept into practice in the formulas of the diplomas granted to the rabbis he ordained.[4] It was a still more obvious truth that the religion of the Jew was one thing, the religion of the Christian something altogether different. In other words, we are not faced with a reduction of the gap between two different religious conceptions, or between two different social groups, but with a natural communality of mental structures shared by people living in the same historical context, structures that, when they operated within the specifically Jewish sociocultural space, led to results whose Jewish contours were very clearly defined.

We can therefore safely affirm that these Jews indeed displayed a cultural profile different from that of their coreligionists in other countries, but without being for all that any "less Jewish" than they were. Just as the Italians in the Renaissance exhibited a markedly different cultural profile from that of the other countries of Europe, especially the Germans beyond the Alps whom the Italian mentality of the day tended to view as barbarians, so the same thing was true of the Jews. Their coreligionists from beyond the Alps seemed to them crude and lacking in cultural sensitivity, in a word "primitive." They criticized certain of their customs, which in an Italian perspective appeared decidedly superstitious, such as the custom of *Tashlikh*, or going to the banks of a river or spring to cast their sins into it on New Year's Day. This was the opinion, at least, of Elijah del Medigo, who came himself from a ritual and cultural tradition of the German type (Ashkenazi).[5] Others criticized their primitive understanding of the Talmudic legends, which in Italy people preferred to read from the metaphorical and symbolic perspective of Maimonides. This at least was how Don Isaac Abravanel (1427–1508), an illustrious exile from the Iberian peninsula, whose works enjoyed a great success in Italy, saw it.[6] And to cite only one of his many criticisms, Messer Leon found barbarisms in the Germanic pronunciation of Hebrew.[7]

Considering that the Jews of the time shared tastes and behaviors with their Christian contemporaries, it would have been strange indeed if they had not allowed themselves to be inspired by the more narrowly literary aspects of the culture of their neighbors when it came to expressing their specific identity. Indeed, given the mentality of the time, such affirmations of one's identity could only express themselves in terms of comparison and emulation, in other words, in the context of an effort geared to demonstrate one's superiority over the Other. It was not just a question of inflating oneself with national pride in difficult times, but rather of aligning oneself with the tendencies of nascent nationalism, of staking one's claim to emulate the other nations and competing on an equal footing in the cultural encounter, which could only find expression in affirmations of superiority. What it was all about was *playing the game*, in the real competitive meaning of the phrase.

Generally speaking, it can be said that in every field the literary production of the Italian Jews selectively imported cultural trends and values, fashionable literary and prosodic genres and motifs, norms and conventions, philosophical problems and solutions. The Jews of Italy were simply following along a road already opened in Spain in previous centuries. In fact the literary production of the Italian Jews exhibits the same characteristics as that of the Jews of Spain, who imported literary trends, genres, and themes from the Arabic world of which they were a part, remaining faithful to them even after the Christian *reconquista*. These same literary influences, mediated by the Jews of Spain, were later adopted by the Jews of Italy in the course of the thirteenth and fourteenth centuries. Now, the fact that the majority of the Jewish poets of the Renaissance were of Italian or Spanish origin has given rise to suppositions concerning a fundamental difference in attitudes and aptitudes between these groups and those of French or German origin. In my opinion, these suppositions are unfounded: Jews of French or German origins had no trouble whatsoever in fitting into the Italian cultural context if they immigrated into it. What must be stressed, however, is that, generally speaking, if cultural expressions are to flourish, what is needed is a soil capable of communicating the necessary vital juices. This was not the case with the transalpine countries. In the Italy of the Renaissance, in the Spain of the Golden Age and earlier, in the Islamic period of the tenth century, stimuli, sources of inspiration, and subjects worthy of competition were not lacking. In Renaissance Italy, as in the period immediately preceding, the Jews were prepared to draw inspiration from others, to import "neutral" forms and contents that they would proceed to amalgamate with the forms and contents of the biblical and postbiblical tradition, thereby opening the way to a specifically Jewish cultural production.

A FEW EXAMPLES

I MMANUEL OF ROME (c.1265–1335), for instance, who was born in the same year as Dante and who enjoyed friendly relations with Bosone da Gubbio and with the poet and jurist Cino da Pistoia, seems to have been the first to introduce into Hebrew poetry forms inspired by the Italian poetry of his time, such as strophaic compositions and sonnets. Thanks to Immanuel, Hebrew literature appears to have been the first non-Italian literature to adopt the sonnet form. Immanuel was without a doubt a follower of Dante's *dolce stil novo* school of poetry. The work of Dante was the model he chose to follow in the composition of his famous *Maḥbarot* (plural of *Maḥberet*, Hebrew *Maqama*). Nevertheless, Immanuel's *Maḥbarot* are full of references and allusions to Talmudic and

Mishrashic literature, as well as to medieval Jewish philosophy, especially that of Maimonides. The modern reader, who has less difficulty recognizing the features in common with the Italian production of the time from those that derive from the Hebrew tradition, is not aware of any tension between the two elements. On the contrary, it is precisely these additional Hebrew levels of meaning that give Immanuel's work greater complexity and richness than that of the majority of his Christian contemporaries. Immanuel's philosophical works, as well as those of his nephew Judah, which have not so far been the object of systematic study, fully confirm this impression.

The way opened up by Immanuel was followed by others. Moses ben Joab da Rieti (1388–c.1460), the doctor of Pope Pius II Piccolomini, tried his hand at the composition of a Hebrew "Divine Comedy," the *Little Sanctuary* (*Miqdash Me'at*), in which the protagonists are Jewish rabbis, men of letters and poets (after what was said in the previous chapter, we are tempted to add: *naturally!*). Semantics is not without its importance here: the title "Little Sanctuary" is a Hebrew expression indicating the synagogue, the sacred space, the symbol of Jewish identity, perceived, in relation to that of their Christian neighbors, in terms of total Otherness, with the vast series of cultural polarities that are a necessary consequence. The work of Moses da Rieti brings out the clash between two opposing conceptions of history. The history of the Jews is presented as a history of men of culture, very different from the view of history envisioned by Dante.

The extraordinary flowering of Jewish historiography in the course of the sixteenth century, the work for the most part of authors belonging to the Italian geopolitical sphere, though parallel to the similar flowering that took place among Christian authors in the same period, was profoundly influenced by this conception of the uniqueness of Jewish history. Jewish history in fact, according to the parameters in vigor at the time, came across as a *nonhistory*: politics had no place in it, and still less feats of arms; there were no kings or princes intent on dividing up the world by means of war or dynastic marriages. The problem of inserting Jewish history into the context of world history was undoubtedly therefore the major problem of the Jewish historians of the Renaissance. Elijah Capsali (1490–1555) transcribed into biblical rhetoric the Greek and Italian chronicles of the wars against the Turks, as well as the history of Venice, in his Hebrew *Chronicle of Elijah* (*Seder Elijahu*), of which the previously cited *Chronicle of Venice* is merely a part; Joseph ha-Kohen (1496–c.1576) in his *Chronicle of the Kings of France and the Ottomans* gives us a Hebrew version of works with the same title popular in the mid–sixteenth century; Ghedaliah Ibn Yaḥya (1526–1587) borrowed freely from Joseph ha-Kohen in his *Chain of Tradition*. Since their conception of history was identical to that of their Christian neighbors, the Jews had somehow to cope with the problem of defining and restructuring their own cultural identity in such a fashion as to bring out its simultaneous opposition to the Christian identity and its congruence with it. Their efforts were geared to constructing a *Weltanschauung* such as to permit the uniqueness of Jewish particularism, the result of a basic difference in religious belief, to find a way to insert itself organically into the general context. This uniqueness could not therefore be conceived in terms either of closure or still less of alienation. The fact that the vein of historiographic production dried up almost immediately after producing its first fruits is to my mind ample demonstration of both the *direction* of the Jewish effort and the practical *impossibility* of obtaining results in that particular instance: since there was no Jewish history in the usual sense of the word, it was only natural that every attempt in the direction of integration should fail, precisely because it revealed itself in the final analysis as bearing the seeds of closure and alienation. This does not alter the fact that the historiographic production of the Jews provides one more confirmation of the general picture sketched in these pages.

TWO OPPOSED OTHERNESSES

THIS OBSERVATION has more general implications. What strikes us as particularly significant in the case of the Jews is the way in which the profane element was fused with the religious one. Schematically speaking, one could say that this way was the *opposite* of what occurred among the Christians. For Christians, in fact, it was easier to keep cultural expression separate from religious expression. The cultural identity of the Christian humanists of the Renaissance, and here we should keep in mind above all the general trend toward secularization, was formed as a result of their specular reflection on a single Other culture — that of the preceding period of classical antiquity. The cultural identity of the Christians could be constructed along the lines of gradual detachment from the field of religion in the proper sense of the word, without necessarily endangering their Christian identity. Things were quite different in the case of the Jews. Jewish Otherness was essentially a matter of religious belief, so that any cultural deviation from a religiously based culture would have immediately put their Jewish identity in crisis. To have allowed secular cultural tendencies to develop toward an ever increasing detachment from religion would have meant anticipating problems that have become typical of the modern period: how a nonbeliever is supposed to set about defining his/her Jewish identity, or the problem of the believer's greater or lesser cultural alienation. The result would have been a crisis of Jewish identity similar to that prevailing in the modern era. This did not occur.

One cannot altogether exclude the possibility that the discriminatory attitude of Christian society toward the Jews may have contributed to some extent to delaying the development of the crisis. In my opinion, however, a more telling factor was the universal human tendency to react instinctively against the introduction of anything new, usually perceived as a source of danger and uncertainty, and the resulting reinforcement (at times radical) of preexisting structures. In all such cases, the intensity of the instinctive reaction is directly proportional to the degree of perceived danger. Since, as we have already remarked, this danger was in the present case felt more strongly by the Jews than by the Christians, the tendency of the former toward "closure" was much more pronounced. In the initial phase, then, the encroachment of secularization on the overall mentality was apprehended by the Jews from the inside, in the context of a complex process of osmosis essentially medieval in nature. The problems of medieval theology, then, remained very much alive for the Jews, with all the anachronisms such a state of affairs implied. Once Jewishness had been identified with the sacred space, the coherence of that space with every aspect of cultural expression was a logical consequence. It was somewhat as if the Jew had declared, *Nihil humanum alienum a me puto* ("I think nothing human alien to me")—but from inside the synagogue! Whereas the Christians marched on toward modernity *separating* secular thought from the strictly religious sphere, the Jews continued to follow the opposite course: that of an ever closer link between secularization and religious expression. The context of the cultural affinity between Jews and Christians was thus fundamentally conditioned by their religious Otherness. This is precisely the reason why the manifold cultural expressions of the Jews of the time seem so ambivalent, indeed deceptive, to our eyes. Only in the seventeenth century was the Jewish camp to begin the laborious search for new solutions.

PHILOSOPHY

A BETTER IDEA of the overall situation can be obtained by turning from the field of literature to that of philosophy. One of the most easily manipulated parameters historians appeal to in order to demonstrate the allegedly centrifugal tendency of Italian Jewish culture is the frequency and intensity with which they applied themselves to the most important philosophical texts. There can be no question that the Jews of Italy devoted themselves at the time to the reading and study of philosophical texts. The relationships between Jewish and Christian scholars of the period are also well documented. We have only to think of the examples of Elijah del Medigo (1460–c.1493), Johannan Alemanno (1433–c.1504), Judah ben Jehiel, also known as Messer Leon (1435–c.1495), Joseph Ibn Yahya (1496–1539), Azariah de' Rossi (1511–c.1575), Judah Moscato (1532–1590), and Leone Modena (1571–1648). It should, however, be stressed (though it usually is not) that philosophical texts were transmitted within a specifically Jewish tradition of rewriting and translation, which gives a somewhat different meaning to the importance of the parameter in question. Here too we should speak of a tendency on the part of Jewish scholars to approach the texts of the Other culture on the basis of their "neutrality," in the sense spoken of above. In the field of philosophy, this tendency was even more pronounced than in that of literature, though perhaps one would be better advised in this instance to speak not of a "neutral" but of a "scientific" approach.

The men of the Middle Ages classified as "scientific" many texts that we can no longer consider as such. As Michel Foucault justly remarked, whereas our modern notion leads us to accept the scientific validity of a text only after we have verified its contents in the light of a coherent conceptual system of well-founded assertions and methods of authentication, the medieval mentality took the scientific truth of a work for granted the minute it was attributed to an author whom the common consensus judged an authority.[8] The Bible was certainly one such work, but there were others: the entire corpus of rabbinical literature (Mishnah, Talmud, Midrashim) enjoyed among Jews an authority practically equal to that enjoyed by the Bible, or by patristic literature among Christians. In the cultural space of the Mediterranean, the Maimonidean tradition was quite firmly ensconced among Jews, at least as firmly as the Thomistic tradition was among Christians: both were based for the most part on Aristotelian texts, and Aristotle was considerable as an incontestable authority. His works were accordingly viewed as "neutral" by the Jews. Only if a patent incompatibility had been found between his teachings and the teachings of faith would it have occurred to them that the two needed to be reconciled, and it is far from certain that such a confrontation would have automatically meant the rejection of Aristotle's theses. It was easier to follow the classical route of exegesis of the letter of the text. This was after all what Averroës and Maimonides had done. The same thing could be said, *mutatis mutandis*, of a number of other medieval authors, such as the exegetes of the works of Aristotle: they too were considered authorities. Let us look at the case of Averroës. When medieval authors quoted "the Philosopher," referring to Aristotle, they were referring in reality to the texts they had before their eyes, in other words, to Averroës's paraphrases of Aristotle's texts. In circumstances such as

ARISTOTELIS

STAGIRITAE
OMNIA QVAE EXTANT OPERA

Nunc primum selectis translationibus, collatisque cum græcis emendatissimis
exemplaribus, Margineis scholijs illustrata, & in nouum ordinem digesta:
Additis etiam nonnullis libris nunquam antea latinitate donatis:

AVERROIS CORDVBENSIS
IN EA OPERA OMNES QVI AD NOS PERVENERE
COMMENTARII,
Aliique ipsius in logica, philosophia, & medicina libri:

Quarum aliqui non amplius à Latinis visi, nuper à IACOB MANTINO sunt conuersi:
Alij ab eodem clarius ac fidelius, quàm vnquam antea ab alijs, translati:
Cæteri ex manuscriptis, optimisq́ codicibus Philosophorum hac nostra ætate
celeberrimarum, innumeris penè locis diligentissime castigati:
Singuli compluribus marginei. scholijs exornati.

LEVI GERSONIDIS Annotationes in Auer. expositionem super logices libros,
Latinis hucusq̨ incognitę, eodem Iacob Mantino interprete.

Græcorum, Arabum, & Latinorum monumenta quædam, ad hoc opus spectantia.

M. Antonij Zimaræ in Aristotelis & Auerrois dicta Contradictionum Solutiones.

IO. BAPTISTAE BAGOLINI VERONENSIS LABORE, AC DILIGENTIA.

Hæc autem omnia tum ex Præfatione, tum ex Indice Librorum
clarius innotescunt.

BERNARDO SALVIATO EPISC. S. PAPVLI
ROMAE PRIORI DICATA

10277

Cum summi Pontificis, Gallorum Regis, Senatusq́; Veneti decretis.

VENETIIS APVD IVNTAS M D LII.

*Frontispiece of the complete works of Aristotle, Venice, 1552. Jacob Mantino, who
translated the commentary of Averroës from Hebrew to Latin, had served as physician
to Popes Clement VII and Paul III.*

this, the mode of access to the texts did not play a critical role when it came to taking a stand on their interpretation. The Jews preferred to read philosophical works in Hebrew not only because this was the language they knew best, but also because a text already translated into Hebrew posed fewer problems of legitimacy — the textual tradition was evidence of the fact that others before them had come to grips with it, and that as a rule was regarded as sufficient.

It was pretty much the same for the Italian Christians of the period of Humanism. This is the only possible explanation for the fact that serious-minded and highly cultivated men like Pico della Mirandola and Marsilio Ficino accepted the authenticity of texts which a minimum of critical reflection would have led them to reject outright. This is also why their efforts at syncretism were so short-lived: they were still using essentially medieval mental categories and study methods in a time of rapid intellectual change.

One should not attribute any particular importance, then, to the fact that in this period the Jews of Italy showed an interest for works of a general cultural nature. All they were doing was following a route marked out by a millenary tradition. The number of quotations from Aristotle, Plato, Averroës, Avicenna, Al-Farabi, and others is not evidence of centrifugal tendencies among Jewish scholars, since they themselves considered these authors an integral part of their particular Jewish culture. What one should insist upon instead is the way these texts were read, through a prism, that is, which allowed to filter through only such contents as could be appropriated in order to reinforce the perception of Jewish cultural identity in relation to that of their Christian neighbors. This is the context in which they proceeded to restructure Jewish religious Otherness as a consequence of reflection on Christian Otherness, many aspects of which seemed quite attractive. In a period of cultural absolutism still essentially medieval in character, all truths but one's own were rejected: obviously therefore the self-perception we are discussing found expression in terms of superiority. As a consequence, for Jews convinced of the scientific validity of certain aspects of the general culture, there was nothing more natural than to place these aspects at the service of an affirmation of their own cultural superiority. The efforts of the Jewish intellectuals of the Italian Renaissance were therefore directed toward "Judaizing" anything and everything that seemed worthy of being presented within a Jewish context.

This tendency led them to affirm over and over again the uninterrupted presence in the arsenal of traditional Hebrew culture, since the earliest antiquity, of everything that the mentality of the period considered noble and elevated. In so doing they tended to apply to the Hebrew tradition the current criteria for cultural nobility, in the first place the criterion of classical antiquity. Their line of reasoning can be reduced to a simple syllogism: the mentality of the time considered as ideal those aspects of culture that could be proved to have been part of classical culture; the presence of a given cultural phenomenon could be ascertained in classical, and especially biblical, Hebrew culture; therefore classical Hebrew culture, of which the Jews claimed to be the uninterrupted depositors and proprietors, was the bearer of that ideal content. There followed an extremely important corollary: since Hebrew culture preceded Greco-Roman culture, it was obviously superior to it, and all the more so since it was free of pagan traits. Hebrew culture was therefore superior to all other cultures!

Arguments like this may make us smile today. Nevertheless, from the point of view of emulation, so typical of the period, they constituted the principal aspect of the perception of Jewish cultural identity. As for the scholastic philosophy of Obadiah Sforno (c.1475–1550), who claimed to have discovered all philosophical truths in the Bible (which was of course to be read, in accordance with the humanist persuasion, in Hebrew), it was simply a latter-day reprise of a theme that had already been fashionable for some time. Maybe this is the reason why Obadiah Sforno is better remembered for his works of biblical exegesis than for his philosophy, a close reading of which permits us to discern the typical themes of Averroistic mysticism in vogue in contemporary university circles, starting with Padua. Obadiah Sforno was so convinced of the universal validity of his work that he had it published in Latin for the benefit of the entire scholarly world. The Latin title of his book published in Bologna in 1548 is significantly *Lumen gentium* (The Light of the Gentiles), which was translated from the Hebrew, *Or 'Ammim*, published in Bologna in 1539. It constitutes a rare example of a product of rabbinical culture addressed to a Christian audience. Before Sforno, Jewish thinkers preferred to address their Christian audience through translations from Hebrew into Latin of classical philosophical texts, mostly of Arabic authors, chief among whom was Averroës. One would do well to recall in this connection that during the Renaissance the Jews of Italy played a by no means negligible role in propping up that same Aristotelian-Averroistic tradition that humanism had done so much to undermine. We owe, for instance, to the Averroist Elijah del Medigo, the master in this field of Pico della Mirandola, the publication, sponsored by Domenico Grimani, of a considerable portion of the works of Averroës. The classical edition of Averroës (Venice, 1552) contains more than one translation by Jewish scholars. There was of course no question of Jewish influence on Christian culture and still less of the influence of the Renaissance on the Jews. It was simply that the medieval *Hebrew* literary tradition appeared, to Christians and Jews alike, perfectly compatible with the common ideals of knowledge of the time.

THE SIGNIFICANCE OF LITERARY BORROWING

THE SAME CAN BE SAID for those literary "borrowings" that have been philologically ascertained. The phenomenon should not give rise to misunderstandings. One might be led to insist, for example, on how much certain Jewish scholars, such as Judah Romano or David, the son of Messer Leon, borrowed from Thomas Aquinas's *Summa Theologica* — as if these borrowings "demonstrate" the capitulation of the Jews in the face of the seductions of "non-Jewish" science. But these scholars were not behaving any differently from Thomas himself, when he borrowed methods and contents from the *Guide for the Perplexed* of Maimonides, the same Rabbi Moises Egyptius whom Thomas abhorred no less than he abhorred other Jews. In other words, David B. Ruderman's recent balanced conclusion seems perfectly adapted to these men and to their works: "It was necessary to formulate their Jewish faith by reference to Aristotelian texts or through scholastic modes of study and investigation."[9]

All that was done in literature and philosophy was done in fields that Jewish culture considered relevant to the definition of its own identity. Judah Moscato, who lived in the second half of the sixteenth century and was one of the period's most talented Jewish thinkers and preachers, claimed that it was the Jews who had first discovered music. In Mantua, where Moscato was living at the time, Judah Sommo (1527–1592), actor, director, playwright, and theorist of the theater, likewise claimed that the Jews had been the first to invent the theater and that the first tragedy in world culture was the Book of Job. Inspired by the Bible, the Jews had also developed the most perfect political system: this is proved, according to Azariah de' Rossi, by the Letter of Aristeas, considered part of the canon by the Christian tradition. Isaac Abravanel also traced back to the Bible the principles of the Venetian republican model, whereas Johannan Alemanno preferred to discover there the model offered by the Florentine principate. The examples could be multiplied without difficulty. The origins of every cultural phenomenon whose absolute validity was axiomatically accepted were to be found in the Jewish tradition. Rather than continuing to list them, it seems preferable to examine in some detail the mechanisms of these operations by considering a famous example that combines humanistic literature and philosophy.

What was more noble at the time than humanist rhetoric? The works of Cicero and Quintilian, recently rediscovered, were authentic best-sellers during the period of the first printed books. To unearth the quintessence of classical rhetoric in biblical literature, the chief basis of Jewish education, was therefore a natural development of Jewish cultural self-perception. It was the task of Messer Leon, a rabbi and medical doctor who received his diploma from the Emperor, in his classical work of Hebrew rhetoric *Nofet Tzufim*, published in Mantua in 1475. Messer Leon incorporated in his work the entire *Rhetorica ad Herennium*, then attributed to Cicero, and a good portion of Aristotle's *Poetics* in Todros Todrosi's medieval Hebrew translation of the paraphrase of Averroës, as well as other illustrative passages taken from other classical and medieval works: Cicero's *De Inventione*, the *Rhetorica ad Alexandrum* attributed to Aristotle, Quintilian's *De Institutione Oratoria*, Vittorino's commentary to the *De Inventione*, and other works. The book is a marvelous synthesis of the humanist sensibility, however anchored in the medieval world as far as contents and method are concerned. And all to what end? All to demonstrate that the best of classical rhetoric was already present, at a higher level, in biblical rhetoric: in other words, a humanistic variation, adapted to rhetoric, of the old theme, formulated by Hebrew culture in the Hellenistic period, later taken up by the Fathers of the Church and finally by the Jews of the Middle Ages, according to which the Ancient Hebrews were already masters of all the sciences, which were subsequently claimed as their own by other peoples. It was God Himself who revealed to His chosen people the whole of knowledge. In the words of Abraham Farissol, a contemporary of Messer Leon, "at the foot of Mount Sinai God crowned us with the Torah in its entirety: it contained all the sciences, natural sciences, logic, theology, law, politics, and it was here that the whole world slaked its thirst."[10] Messer Leon applied this general formula to rhetoric. For him, too, at the time of God's revelation to the prophets, "we studied and knew the Sciences and all of human discoveries through the Holy Torah, for all is contained therein, either in a latent or manifest form. All that the other peoples possessed was negligible by comparison. . . . It was only after we were deprived of the Presence of God, as a result of our sins, that Prophecy ceased and the wisdom of our sages disappeared, and we were no longer able to comprehend the perfect wholeness of the contents of the Torah. It is our fault if the process has been reversed: now only after we have learned all the sciences or at least part of them are our eyes opened and we realize that everything is already contained in the Torah. Then are we much amazed. How is it possible that we did not realize it from the very first? This is what has happened innumerable times! This is what happened in the case of rhetoric as well."[11] And so one sees Messer Leon concentrate his efforts to demonstrate that Psalm 45 is a perfect example of epideictic rhetoric, that the speech of Tekoa to King David (2 Samuel 14:1–20) is an example of judiciary rhetoric, and that "a good portion of what we find in the Bible in the form of commandments and admonitions belongs to the realm of deliberative oratory," in a word, that all of the Ciceronian rhetorical figures are already to be found in the text of the Bible, and that the Bible contains still others, not mentioned by Classical authors.[12]

The mentality of Messer Leon was not far removed from that of Poggio Bracciolini, the discoverer of Quintilian's treatise, or from that of Giannozzo Manetti, the perhaps overpraised Florentine orator. Like them, Messer Leon cultivated the ideals of eloquence in the service of high culture, its diffusion, and the exercise of authority and power in the bosom of society. Theirs was not, however, a rhetoric subversive of the old structures of scholastic culture. Messer Leon could not have imagined a culture any different from the one he had inherited from the Middle Ages. The majority of his works are commentaries on Aristotle in Averroës's translation. Furthermore, as we have seen, his rhetorical treatise inspired by Cicero and Quintilian also incorporates a considerable number of Averroistic texts. Did this represent a tension between scholastic and humanistic elements? Not at all. It represented an adjustment, rather, of the old structures to new exigencies, and consequently a tendency to perceive cultural identity as being in harmony with them, rather than in opposition. In other words, all of this is at one and the same time medieval and a hint of the beginnings of a changed mentality.

Heinrich Graetz in his day presented the figure of Messer Leon as an example of Italian-style humanist "liberalism," in contrast to the rabbinical "obscurantism" supposedly typical of Franco-German circles and represented in Italy by Judah Mintz and his followers.[13] This view is mistaken. As has been amply demonstrated, Messer Leon was an exemplary representative of the most rigorous Franco-German rabbinical tendencies, who took a violently polemical stand against the representatives of the more liberal local ritual tradition, based on the Code of Maimonides.

Another detail will perhaps help us add a further dimension to our description. In the course of what appears to be a completely personal polemic whose topic is unclear, an adversary of Messer Leon accused him of having simply translated from Latin to Hebrew the chief texts of his oeuvre, of which he was so proud. Messer Leon was particularly riled by such an accusation, seeing it as implying that he was nothing more than a Jew who had assimilated the alien culture. Messer Leon's reaction was violent, protesting the originality of his contribution. At this point, he added, significantly, that an accusation of that kind ought to have been considered nothing less than absurd in his own case. Where was it, if not in his debates with the Christians, that he had displayed the salient points of his scholarly personality?[14] In other words, the perception of Jewish identity as being in opposition to the Christian identity was for him a constant that the actual contents of his culture could never place in doubt. But that did imply that the contents themselves were susceptible to differing interpretations: bearing as they did a charge of ambiguity that was part of the roots of the general culture, they could be presented, particularly in a polemical context, as a flight from one's own specificity.

A RULE OF THUMB

IT SEEMS POSSIBLE to formulate a general rule: how adherence to the contents of the general culture was interpreted was a function of the observer's attitude. What for one man was the supreme expression of his identity, for another was exactly the opposite. This ambivalence could be exploited for purposes of propaganda, and this was what Messer Leon correctly recognized in his adversary's accusation. But, setting propaganda to one side, ambivalence also opened the way to contradictory opinions, depending on one's beliefs and ideology. The enlightened spirits of the nineteenth century, and their followers today, considered the phenomena described as clear signs of the abandonment of Jewishness. From my point of view, however, such an interpretation seems to be based on an ideological structure that assigns a negative valency to Jewish Otherness. From this kind of ideological stance, it goes without saying that any and every adherence to the culture of the Other can only be interpreted as negation of the Self. Even in the sixteenth century there were those who viewed general Renaissance culture as the opposite of Jewish culture. This was in particular the view of Christians conscious of their Christian identity. This explains why the Christian interlocutors of Azariah de' Rossi interpreted his tendency to introduce the methods of scientific criticism into Hebrew culture as a symptom of his imminent conversion to Christianity. De' Rossi himself, however, was of an altogether different opinion.[15]

THE CHARACTERISTICS OF JEWISH CULTURE

THE CHARACTERISTIC FEATURES of the culture elaborated by the Jews of Italy can at this point be summed up in a few specific traits: the sensitivity of Jewish culture to some of the forms and contents of Christian culture; the existence of a cultural relationship between Jews and Christians on the personal level as well as on the level of the learning they shared; and the selective adoption of forms and contents imported from outside as integral expressions of Jewish identity. The latter were perceived in a context of emulation, at times of genuine opposition to Christian society, as devices capable of expressing the cultural, and therefore human, superiority of the Jews. Why should one interpret this kind of participation in the mentality and general tendencies of the time as assimilation pure and simple? Why not see it as Jews' way of simply being men of their time? Or again, why claim that the Jews were *influenced* by the Renaissance, whereas Pico della Mirandola, Marsilio Ficino, or Cosimo de' Medici were its typical *representatives*? Why not say that Messer Leon, Elijah del Medigo, or Johannan Alemanno were just as much men of the Renaissance as their Christian contemporaries? In my opinion, this approach renders a better service to the general understanding of the Renaissance and of the mentality of its exponents than do current theories. Seen from this perspective, Jewish cultural production can upon occasion serve as a litmus test that helps distinguish among the elements of the Renaissance mentality those that were more universal from those that were rejected, precisely because they were peculiar to Christian Otherness, by those who were working toward a definition of Jewish cultural identity.

The attitude toward the symbiosis of the sacred and the profane exhibited by the medieval Jewish mentality, an attitude far from our modern sensibilities, may help us better understand the process of evolution touched off by the period we are studying. The condemnation of Immanuel of Rome's *Maḥbarot* is perhaps one of the most conspicuous signs of the changed mentality: the free-thinking audacity of this work angered devout readers in the centuries that followed to such an extent that Rabbi Joseph Caro forbade its reading in his ritual code *Shulḥan 'Arukh*, published for the first time in Venice in 1574. Up until that date, orthodox readers seem to have seen nothing strange in Immanuel's cultural promiscuity, though one cannot of course exclude the possibility of occasional idosyncratic opposition. Earlier in the sixteenth century, rabbis seated upon the chair of Moses had not been ashamed to borrow from the *Maḥbarot* some brilliant literary expression with which to adorn their own works. This was done, for example, by Samuel Archivolti, the rabbi from Padua, in the text of one of the letters cited in the previous chapter apropos of female education.[16] Texts that our modern point of view would classify as nothing less than pornographic are found side by side with others that we would classify as sacred. The work of Moses di Dattilo Rieti (Mosheh ben Yoav) is from this point of view even more exemplary than that of Immanuel of Rome of Joseph Zarfatti. Moses Rieti, not to be confused with the writer of the same name previously mentioned, lived in Florence in the first half of the sixteenth century. Among his poetic works, never published in their entirety, one finds sonnets on the immortality of the soul or on the study of the Talmud, alongside others that describe the joys of sexual union with a lovely companion of his youth. Boccaccio or Marguerite de Navarre would have acted no differently.

THE DIFFUSION OF THE KABBALAH

As was remarked earlier, the definition of Jewish identity made its restructuring in the direction of secularization or modernization particularly difficult. Given its extreme ambivalence, the operation called for a no less ambivalent agent. This role was filled, in my view, by the *Kabbalah*, which can be defined here as a system of thought and literary production strongly influenced by mystical tendencies. From the thirteenth century on, the Kabbalah enjoyed an extraordinarily widespread diffusion in the Christian West. Presented as an original interpretation, permeated with Neoplatonic ideas, of the Midrashic tradition, especially in its more speculative, cosmogonic, and theosophical elements, this system very quickly assumed a role antagonistic to that played by scholastic philosophy. Because of the crisis of scholasticism, from which European thought emerged profoundly renewed, the Kabbalah was given free rein among the Jews. The Kabbalah filled the gap left by scholasticism and affected every field, from intellectual activity to everyday religious practice. The reasons for its success seem to have resided, among other things, in its ambivalent nature, anthropocentric on the one hand, theocentric on the other. It was precisely this ambivalence that allowed it to act as an agent of modernity without breaking the links with the Middle Ages, to further the cause of secularization while claiming to be profoundly religious, to favor worldliness while presenting itself as clad in otherworldly mysticism.

Today we are fairly well informed as regards the penetration of the Kabbalah into the lives of the Jews of Italy. After an extended period of esoteric incubation, in which it was cultivated by a rather narrow circle of adepts, the Kabbalah emerged from seclusion in the sixteenth century and laid claim to a place of honor in Jewish society. The publication of the fundamental work of the Kabbalah, the *Book of Zohar*, printed in Mantua in 1558 and again in Cremona in 1560, was symptomatic of this emergence. Incidentally, its publication in two separate editions, each more than likely destined for a different audience outside of Italy, is further evidence of the cultural links between the Jews of Italy and those of other countries. Public teaching of the Kabbalah followed soon after; and after that the introduction of its themes and ideas into the rabbis' sermons. Finally came the *reformation* of religious ritual and prayers: the first steps in this direction took place in the last two decades of the sixteenth century, when they gave rise to a series of bitter polemics. Some of the changes in religious practices, such as the banning of the wearing of the

phylacteries (tefillin) on certain holidays (Ḥol ha-Moʾed), were so successful as to be universally adopted, despite the fact that the ban was in
open conflict with the provisions of all the codes on the subject of ritual
from the preceding period. The first prayer book revised and corrected
in the light of the *Book of Zohar* and the Kabbalah was published in 1587–
1588. Precisely because of its *innovative* nature, this new trend could only
develop outside traditional structures and could only lead to a total restructuring.

The first step was to affirm the superiority of the reforming truth of
the Kabbalah over all others. The result was a conviction of independence of previously codified individual decisions, and, in the last analysis,
of the entire heredity of the past. In this sense, adherence to the innovative categories of the Kabbalah was tantamount to cultivating the freedom of interpretation necessary if one were to pass from one worldview
to another. An analysis of a number of responsa on ritualistic topics by
Rabbi Menaḥem Azariah da Fano (1548–1620), one of the most influential personalities of his day, appears to confirm this general hypothesis.
But in my view it is above all its restructuring of the concepts of the space
and time of religious worship that gives the Kabbalah its revolutionary
role. Reference is made, above all, to the plethora of religious confraternities, whose activities went well beyond the practical needs they professed to serve. Mutual aid, works of charity, the study of sacred texts, all
assumed toward the end of the century a social character ever more influenced by kabbalistic practices. At the heart of the ritual of most of these
confraternities was by now the *Tikkun*, the public reading of texts drawn
for the most part from the *Book of Zohar*, which was supposed to accelerate
the restoration of the Divine Pleroma in all its integrity. Dozens of editions of books of *Tikkunim* were published. The Tikkun practiced in the
confraternities was a parasynagogal activity, ambivalent by its very nature:
public and exclusive at one and the same time, religious and yet always
performed outside the sacred space of the synagogue. The Tikkun also
permitted the introduction of a profane, we would say bourgeois, social
practice: the coffee break, which was motivated by the need to stay awake
into the night. The modern tendency to keep the religious and profane

spheres separate was thus covertly adopted by the Jews of the Renaissance, in the present case through the practice of the confraternities, which on the one hand made it possible to preserve the medieval symbiosis between the sacred and the profane, but on the other moved that symbiosis *outside* the sacred space of the synagogue, thereby leading to the separation within that space, too, of the two spheres.

The dates recorded above are highly indicative of the dynamics of the process, which represents a development typical of the second phase of the period. The Kabbalah in fact succeeded in assuming a determining role precisely at the end of the sixteenth century, thanks to the demographic concentration of the Jews. But there were certainly other and possibly more decisive reasons. One of these could have been the fact that during the course of the sixteenth century, both from the Jewish and the Christian points of view, the Kabbalah took on the character of an exclusively Jewish cultural expression. As such, it assumed in the last analysis a place of honor in the definition of Jewish identity.

CHRISTIAN HEBRAISTS

CHRISTIAN SCHOLARS soon lost the enormous interest they showed in the Kabbalah during the first phase of our period, at the time of the flourishing of humanistic studies. Christian humanists indeed showed a greater interest in the Kabbalah than they did in the contents of the other texts of the *Hebraica Veritas* to which they applied themselves in the context of their classicist ideals and their aspirations toward the renewal of culture and the expanding of the horizons of learning. The study of Hebrew texts was in line with a venerable Christian tradition, which held that the study of Hebrew was useful to perfect one's approach to biblical exegesis, as well as for a knowledge of the Talmud, to be used in the course of theological disputations. The first steps had been taken by men such as Roger Bacon, Nicholas of Lyra, Ramon Martì, and Ramon Lull: appeals for the reformation of customs and religious attitudes, and for independence in the approach to biblical texts, characterize the crisis of the Catholic Church in the Renaissance period and must have had a catalyzing effect on the revival of interest in Hebrew. Of course opposition, violent at times, to this tendency was by no means lacking. One need only think of Erasmus of Rotterdam, an outstanding example of the reforming spirit and the humanistic reading of the Bible. Erasmus was convinced that this whole cult of Hebrew would have no other outcome but to reinforce the Jews in their convictions, instead of causing Christianity to triumph. A number of Italian and foreign humanists were of a completely different persuasion: Poggio Bracciolini, Giannozzo Manetti, Pico della Mirandola, Egidio da Viterbo, the Medici pope Leo X, Domenico Grimani, Francesco Zorzi, and still others applied themselves without respite to the Hebrew texts, among which the texts of the Kabbalah enjoyed particular prestige.

In the course of the thirteenth century the distinction had been introduced between the current Hebrew theological tradition, considered to have been deliberately falsified, and that of the period before the refusal to recognize Christ (Prisca Theologia), the bearer of signs of truth. The texts of the Kabbalah might well form part of the latter, just like the Talmudic passages that Christian polemists based themselves on to demonstrate that the Hebrew tradition had in fact announced the coming of Christ. Nevertheless, it was the flowering of Neoplatonism coupled with the cult of Antiquity which determined the success of the Kabbalah. The acritical acceptance of the most recondite texts from the most disparate traditions—Hermetic, Zoroastrian, Pythagorean—and their use in a syncretist context, typical of certain ages of transition: all made a particular use of the Kabbalah possible.

The two greatest Christian thinkers to concern themselves with the Kabbalah were without a doubt Pico della Mirandola and Johannes Reuchlin. Pico was able to study the kabbalistic texts thanks to his Hebrew teachers, among them Johannan Alemanno. He approached the Averroistic texts in the same way, through the translation of another of his Jewish masters, Elijah del Medigo. Convinced that universal truth would finally be revealed through the convergence of Christian teachings with all of these ancient texts as well as other esoteric traditions considered authentic on account of their antiquity, Pico threw himself heart and soul into the attempt to demonstrate this convergence. His famous nine hundred theses, which he proposed to defend in public, are a little jewel of genius and ingenuousness. The Kabbalah has a place of honor in many of these theses. Pico died young, and it was Reuchlin, who had had occasion to reside in Florence in 1490 and who had been enchanted by the Platonic air he breathed there, who gathered his legacy and brought it to the attention of the reading public in two little books: *De verbo mirifico* and *De arte cabalistica*. Reuchlin raised the Kabbalah to the level of a Platonic philosophical science. For Reuchlin, the convergence of the Kabbalah with Christian dogma was a guarantee of the truth of both. Reuchlin's influence on the Jews is the best proof of his impact on the thought of the time. Some Jews, such as Todros ha-Kohen, almost certainly the brother of Joseph ha-Kohen, were so convinced of the truths expounded by Reuchlin that they made them the basis of their conversion to Christianity.[17] Others, terrorized by the danger that Reuchlin's ideas represented to the purity of Jewish faith, attempted to demonstrate their extraneousness to the kabbalistic tradition. Thus, for example, Mordecai Dato warned a correspondent who had inquired about the method to be followed in studying the *Book of Zohar* to be careful not to follow Reuchlin's example. By "bringing selection after selection [from the *Book of Zohar*] at random," claimed Dato, Reuchlin had erroneously tried to demonstrate the congruence between the Kabbalah and philosophy.[18] Christians, however, had nothing to fear, and they devoted themselves in considerable numbers to the study of what Reuchlin had expounded. Let it suffice to recall, among the better known, the influential French thinkers Jean Bodin and Jean Postel.

In order to learn Hebrew and to be in a position to read the texts of the Hebrew tradition, one had to obtain the books and above all to find a capable teacher. The best educated among the converted Jews were naturally those best cut out for this role: Flavius Mithridates, Paolo Riccio, and others placed their abilities at the service of Christian minds thirsting for knowledge. But most of all it was Jews who had remained faithful to their own religion who taught the sacred tongue to the Christians. In addition to Elijah del Medigo and Johannan Alemanno, we should also mention Elijah Levita, Elijah Menaḥem Ḥalfan, and Obadiah Sforno, who had the privilege of initiating Reuchlin himself. It was thus that a personal human contact began to be established, a contact whose importance should not be undervalued, as long as we do not jump to any false conclusions. This contact was not the *result* of a more favorable attitude toward the Jews. If anything, it was one of its *preliminary causes*. The Christians expected a certain service from the Jews: that they would supply them with arguments for the defense of Christian truth so they could conclude the process of appropriation of the Jewish Bible begun at the time of the Fathers of the Church. They were far from having given up the idea of exploiting the occasion of the intellectual encounter to add further Jewish conversions to the ultimate triumph of Christianity. The example of Giannozzo Manetti, who led his Jewish teacher to the baptismal font, is exemplary in this regard. The Jews in their turn could scarcely remain indifferent before this spectacle. Many forcefully opposed the idea that their coreligionists should render so dangerous a service to the Christians.

But it was not this opposition that separated the Jews from the Christians in the field of kabbalistic studies. It was rather the new direction taken by Christian learning as the seventeenth century approached that made this kind of speculation unacceptable, whereas the Kabbalah, now completely under the influence of Eastern thought, lost all contact with Western thought and became more and more the typical expression of a Jewish culture turned in upon itself. From one point of view, this was a disaster for Judaism in the Christian West; from another, it was its salvation.

THE ROLE OF THE KABBALAH
IN THE EVOLUTION OF JEWISH CULTURE

IT WAS A DISASTER, in that the tradition of the *entente cordiale* between Jewish and Christian thought was interrupted, with the result that the former became fossilized. In this sense it is difficult not to agree with the enlightened minds of the nineteenth century, who saw in the success of the Kabbalah one of the chief causes of the obscurantism that took over Jewish thought. There can be no doubt that men like Leone Modena, a fierce detractor of the Kabbalah, or his successor in Venice Simon Luzzatto, the author of the *Discourse on the Jews of Venice*, were fully cognizant of this danger, but impotent in the face of the general trend, which was given its tone from outside of Italy, especially from Safed. Nevertheless, given the particular conditions in which Western Judaism, and Italian Judaism in particular, found themselves, conditions, that is, of *exclusion* in every field of endeavor except the economic, the effect of the Kabbalah was to provide Jews with a mechanism to deny that exclusion on a level of *imaginaire*. Believing they could influence the process of cosmic becoming through kabbalistic practices, the Jews, convinced of their own truth, attributed to themselves an active and decisive influence over the course of history, even more active and decisive than that of the kings and princes who were deciding their immediate fate and their exclusion! In this sense, the Kabbalah paradoxically continued to play the role of mediator between exclusion and participation, which was indispensable if the link between the development of Jewish identity and that of the identity of the Other was not to be broken.

Somewhat less paradoxically perhaps, but in line with the tendency previously examined, the Kabbalah performed a mediating function between the Christian and Jewish worlds by providing the catalyst for the reinsertion of the New Christian converts into the Jewish context. The latter were for the most part of Iberian origin and educated in the bosom of Christian culture: in their case, philosophical speculations like Reuchlin's could serve as a bridge for them to return to Jewish thought. A particularly interesting example is provided by Abraham Kohen Herrera, who lived in Florence until about 1595, and who in his *Gate of Heaven* took the road of syncretism. This was one side of the coin. The other side was already presented above: the separation of the Jews from Western culture by means of the Kabbalah.

In conclusion, one is entitled to make a general statement: the course of Italian Jewish culture was determined by the need to define Jewish identity in opposition to that of the Christians, as the result of a specular reflection on the latter. The contacts with the Other described above, which have led others to different conclusions, were indispensable to that end. From this point of view, it would not be surprising if the beginning of the actual process of assimilation and the enfeeblement of the Jewish consciousness were paradoxically signaled by their enclosure in the ghetto. Contrary to what is usually affirmed, it was in fact precisely in the period following the one studied in these pages that the Jews little by little lost their chief source of strength, their consciousness of their own Otherness. In the course of a few generations, the Jews abandoned Hebrew as the language of group communication and cultural production. There is to my mind no more eloquent testimony to the reversal of the cultural trend. But that development belongs to a later period than the one under discussion here.

VI
COMMUNITY
INSTITUTIONS

THE SOURCES OF INSPIRATION
FOR COMMUNITY ORGANIZATION

THE JEWS IN THE CITIES naturally tended to organize themselves into a group. Community organization was achieved as the
result of an organic process of development, through mechanisms that
were set in motion whenever the number of coreligionists seemed sufficient to justify the creation of structured collective institutions. With the
exception of Rome and Sicily, where, as has already been seen, structures
inherited from the past continued to exist, this process took place during
the second phase of our period. Throughout the first phase, in most
places, the resident Jewish families were so few as to justify an embryonic
organization at best, a primitive association among heads of families designed to take care of their most immediate needs. It should be borne in
mind that in this period the official documents, and particularly the condotte, mentioned the Jews only as individuals. Formal evidence of the
transition from one phase to the next is provided by the collective mention of the Jews under the designation *Universitas Hebraeorum* or *Natione de
gli Hebrei*, found with increasing frequency in the documents drawn up
after the second decade of the sixteenth century on. The evolution was
no simple affair, and it was made more complex by the nature of the Jewish population residing in Italy at that time.

By and large, the Jewish community in Italy during the Renaissance
was no different from other such communities under the *ancien régime* and

may be described as a corporation with social, religious, and ethnic goals. As such, it constituted a sort of Jewish city within the Christian city, not because the Jews had obtained and established a degree of independence, but because they had always aspired to independence, despite the practical impossibility of achieving it. These Jewish communities lacked the political autonomy that alone could have guaranteed the independence of their institutions. They lacked the power of coercion necessary to impose the decisions of their leaders on all the members of the community. Consequently, they were completely dependent on the real masters of the political situation and all the more so since the latter, for reasons that will soon become evident, did not in the least favor the granting of independence. In spite of these limitations, Jewish communities were in the process of being organized more or less everywhere.

There were two sources that the communities drew upon for the elements necessary to define themselves at the organizational level. In the first place, there was their awareness of belonging to the Jewish people, with the attendant principle of strict adherence to Jewish law, including the best means of expressing the sovereign right of the collectivity to govern its own life as it saw fit. In second place came the inspiration provided by the institutional models in existence in the Italian cities, provided they did not appear to present a threat to the perception of Jewish identity in all its integrity. This no doubt explains the attraction exerted by the idealization of the political institutions of certain Italian cities, which were formulated at times in terms that were no less than mythical. Such, for example, were the myths of Venice and Florence, though the latter city proved on occasion quite prepared to draw the inspiration for some of its institutional reforms from the former. One should not be surprised, then, if the Jews too were fascinated by these models, surrounded as they were with a mythical aura. There is plenty of evidence to confirm this. Elijah Capsali, for instance, explained that the attraction exerted by Venice upon emigrants from Germany rested on the "greatness of Venice and her institutions, as well as on the perfection of her system of justice."[1] This is evidently an idiosyncratic formulation, from the Jewish point of view, of the chief constituent elements of the "myth of Venice." In the same period, Don Isaac Abravanel, abandoning the traditional Jewish predilection for a monarchy, saw in Venice the prototype of the ideal form of government,[2] whereas Johannan Alemanno praised the perfection of Florence under Lorenzo de' Medici.[3] These declarations of principle, however, did not signify total and unconditional allegiance to models external to the Jewish tradition. Otherwise, their allegiance to Jewish law, which the Jews reiterated on every possible occasion, would have had no real foundation. In fact, the process of Jews coming to self-awareness on the community level was not as simple as the schematic formulations and formal similarities might lead us to believe.

Generally speaking, the achievement of self-awareness in this area seems to have occurred in the same way as it did in other areas, that is to say, by the extremely complex route of imitation and rejection of the Other, which, in its turn, was by no means monolithic. In the present case, the Other was represented by the Christian majority, within the single city and in the country at large, as well as by the Jewish groups and individuals who were not part of the particular community, whether they resided in the same city or elsewhere. Reflection on the Other therefore implied further reflection on Christian political culture, as well as on the relationship between politics and religion, or rather, between the exercise of power and the religious conscience; but it also implied in addition reflection on the political culture of other Jewish groups, especially those of other national origins, who were the bearers of different customs, traditions, and concepts of the practice of public authority.

AN INITIAL PARADIGM: QUATTROCENTO FLORENCE

A SIGNIFICANT ILLUSTRATION of the competition between different elements in the initial phase of the constitution of a community is offered by the very city Johannan Alemanno praised for the perfection of her institutions: Florence. The Jews of Florence expressed their theoretical adherence to the Jewish law by seeking the opinion of the person who seemed best qualified to interpret it and accepting his decisions, whether he belonged to the Florentine collectivity or not. This is what occurred, for instance, when they called in Rabbi Joseph Colon to preside over the divorce ceremony of a Florentine couple, in consideration of the extraordinary prestige he enjoyed as an expert in Talmudic law. This, however, was far from implying that the Jews of Florence were incapable of handling the religious affairs of the group by themselves, and that, in the name of their obedience to Jewish law, they were ready to submit to any authoriy qualified to show them how to observe its precepts. Their sovereign right to choose the authority best qualified to decide the case in question was no less essential to them than their principled adherence to Jewish law. The choice made by the Jews of Florence, among whom there were a number of qualified rabbis, was therefore an expression of the will of the collectivity to *choose* freely the authority they were willing to submit to. Any attempt to exercise any authority whatsoever in the name of the duty to obey the law, without first securing an agreement in principle from the group, was doomed to failure. Judah Messer Leon, already encountered in the previous chapter, was to discover this to his cost. Without having been consulted, he presumed to address the Jews of Florence in the name of the law that he felt himself qualified to interpret, expecting to impose his opinion under pain of excommunication. Their reaction was violent. A rather more detailed analysis of this polemic will serve to bring to light further elements of the complex issue under examination.

One of the points on which Messer Leon claimed obedience had to do with the system of counting the minimum number of days that must elapse before a woman submitted to the purifying bath following her menstrual period. Messer Leon insisted on trying to impose a custom based on the Ashkenazi rite, more rigorous than that followed by the Florentines, who, being Italians, traditionally followed the opinion of Maimonides in these matters. Another point concerned the study of the Kabbalah, which Messer Leon viewed as second-rate Platonism, fraught with dangerous heretical temptations. Here are his words on the subject: "It is clear from the articles of Faith that anyone addressing his prayers to an intermediary between himself and the Creator is behaving in a false and evil manner. Shun, then, the tents of the Kabbalists, buried beneath the evil they do themselves by multiplying their invented attributes of God [a clear allusion to the *Sefiroth*], not hesitating in their ravings to attribute materiality, change, and multiplicity to the Creator, blessed may He be. They grope forward through the darkness of their misunderstanding of the purposes of the founders of their Doctrine, which, as far as I can see, is definitely in partial accord with the doctrine of the Platonists, a doctrine not of course without its sweetness."[4] In this passage, Messer Leon appealed rhetorically to various arguments to which the Jews of Florence ought to have shown themselves sensitive. The condemnation of the Kabbalah rested in fact on the insinuation that it resembled Christianity, because of certain Platonic elements. But a humanist like Messer Leon would certainly not have dared to openly denigrate Platonism in Florence during the very period when Marsilio Ficino was active there translating Plato. In typical humanist style, he preferred to accuse the Kabbalists of not understanding either Platonism or the Kabbalistic texts they believed in and of professing nothing more or less than pure Christianity! Clearly, for Messer Leon the worst possible accusation was that of being a Christian fellow traveler.

A third point of Messer Leon's attack concerned the philosophical commentary of Levi ben Gershon (Gersonides), which he also considered dangerously heretical. Once again, it was Messer Leon's intention to wean the Jews of Italy away from a text that had by now been on their library shelves for some time, as we know from the evidence of many inventories. On all three points, Messer Leon was claiming authority as a censor of customs and culture. His action, coupled with the reaction of the other people involved, can thus be viewed as paradigmatic of the perception of religiosity and culture on the part of a humanist intellectual with a clear idea of what the exercise of authority meant at the public level, as well as of the perception of the same phenomena on the part of the group over which that authority was intended to be exerted. In my opinion, this case would appear to refute the current clichés, according to which a rigorist attitude in questions of religious law went hand in hand with an aversion to culture in general and was frequently allied with the mysticism of the Kabbalists.

Further proof is provided, in this case by Guglielmo da Montalcino, himself a rabbi and a rich moneylender, one of the most influential members of the Florentine community. The model of this man's perception of religiosity and culture was exactly the same as Messer Leon's. Nevertheless, a different approach to the issues at hand led the two of them to diametrically opposed conclusions. It appears that Guglielmo was not indifferent to the seductions of the Kabbalah. Messer Leon's attack, therefore, touched his most profound religious convictions. Moreover, he found Messer Leon's rigorist attitude on questions of religious observance far from convincing. "Liberalism" in matters of observance, then, and mysticism, found themselves united in him in a structure that was the exact opposite of the *Weltanschauung* of Messer Leon. Perhaps this trait has something in common with that of Menaḥem Azariah da Fano examined in the preceding chapter. The same can be said for the reading of Gersonides' text, whose legitimacy was assured by a venerable tradition, as was the local custom with regard to menstruation. It is here that Guglielmo's answer to Messer Leon becomes particularly significant. By what right, asked Guglielmo, did Messer Leon think he could impose his opinions on the Jews of Florence? Did he think he was entitled by the dignity conferred upon him by the Emperor and the Pope in virtue of which he expected to be addressed as "Messer"? Absolutely not! Neither the Emperor nor the Pope had any authority in the territory to which Guglielmo belonged other than that freely recognized by its citizens. And the claims of a man whose honorific title had been conferred upon him by the Emperor and the Pope were even less binding. As far as Guglielmo was concerned, the only legitimate way to have one's authority recognized was by persuasion. All Messer Leon had to do, then, was to instruct a certain number of disciples in his principles. The latter would then convince people to follow the teachings of their Master. Notice the irony of these final words: Guglielmo was issuing a challenge to the master of Hebrew rhetoric in his own bailiwick. By the same token he was also expressing his allegiance to the culture of his times—those of Gian-nozzo Manetti—the culture of civic humanism, just as Messer Leon himself had done in his book of rhetoric. Moreover, just as Messer Leon had insinuated that adherence to the Kabbalah was a sure sign that the believer perceived Judaism in terms of Christianity, so Guglielmo let it be understood that his adversary's claim to impose his own authority de-rived from an idea of the exercise of power which was completely alien to the categories of Judaism, since this authority had in reality no other basis than that of a title conferred upon him by the Christians!

This detailed example suggests how a more general law might be for-mulated: the achievement of self-awareness at the community level took place through negation of the Other. This might be the power or reli-gion of the Christian Other, in a word, Christianity; but it also included those interpretations of Judaism which had not been freely chosen by the collectivity. Given this principle, there is nothing surprising about the fact that the Jews, living in a period like the Renaissance in which the civic values of government were idealized, formed within their own com-munities systems of institutional organization in keeping with the prin-ciples of Talmudic tradition and at the same time similar to those of the Italian cities. But one must be very careful not to take this similarity for pedestrian imitation.

ELEMENTS OF HETEROGENEITY

BEFORE PROCEEDING FURTHER, another element should be clarified. It has already been pointed out that the Jewish population residing in Italy in the period in question was somewhat heterogeneous in its origins. It would be quite inappropriate, however, to imagine the single Jewish communities of the time as an amalgam of heterogeneous groupings. On the contrary, particularly in the first phase, individual communities were made up of Jews who came on the whole from homo-geneous backgrounds. The differences between the different groups in rites and customs, cultural structures, and mentality were at times so rad-ical that for them to gather together under one roof would have been practically impossible. Throughout our entire first phase, it was difficult even to find Jews of differing cultural affiliations living together in the same place. The groups that settled in the North were made up almost exclusively of German Ashkenazi Jews, whereas those who lived in the regions around Rome were "Italian."

Those coming from France, French Ashkenazi in their affiliations, were naturally closer to their brethren of German or Austrian origin than they were to the "Italians"; but this does not explain their failure to produce communities of the "French" type. The true reason was their extreme poverty, which prevented them from taking part in the money traffic and acquiring a sense of independence like their "German" and "Italian" coreligionists. Despite their strong sense of a "French" cultural identity, for which there is much significant documentary evidence, they were compelled, except for a few exceptions that confirm the rule, to give up all thought of a grouping more in keeping with their desires and to disperse among the "Ashkenazi" and "Italian" Jews, taking positions in their service as salaried tutors or scribes. It is easy to understand why the "French" appear to have displayed a tendency to link up with the "Italians," especially those located in the center of the country or on the Adriatic coast, rather than with the "Germans," with whom they had greater affinities. The "Italians" were simply more affluent and therefore in a better position to offer them employment.

As for the Jews of Spanish or Portuguese origin, it has already been noted that they were relatively few in number in the first phase. It was not until the 1530s that their presence began to make itself felt at the local level in a few cities, as a result of the demographic changes outlined in chapter 1. In these cities, the "Portuguese" first of all and then the "Spanish" (including the "Levantine") organized themselves into separate communities, with a degree of separation from the others even more marked than that which had existed between "Italians" and "Germans" in the first phase. The profound difference between their respective economic activities, already mentioned in chapter 2, was no doubt one of the chief causes of this separation. As a result, first the "Portuguese" groups and then the "Spanish" were in a position to negotiate the terms of their settlement independently with the local authorities.

In the first phase, then, especially between the end of the fifteenth century and the beginning of the sixteenth, the "Italian" and "German" communities, made up essentially of moneylenders, formed more unified groups, particularly in their dealings with the Christian rulers. These communities were sometimes erroneously referred to as "German" in a generic sense. Later the "Spanish" and the "Portuguese" gave birth to separate communities, mostly made up of merchants. One must therefore be careful not to apply to the entire period the image evoked by Leone Modena when he declared that every Jewish community in Italy might be made up of several different communities.[5]

In the first place, then, two different types of heterogeneity combined to make the development of community organizations more complex: the heterogeneity resulting from cultural affiliation and that associated with the economic activities of the majority. Though they did not present an obstacle to group aggregation on levels other than that directly related to culture, such as contacts with the Christian authorities and the collection of the taxes necessary for the renewal of the condotta, they nevertheless lay at the root of a powerful dissociative tendency. Still other factors played an important role.

THE BEGINNINGS OF REGIONAL ORGANIZATION

THERE CAN BE LITTLE DOUBT that the community organization found its justification in the will of the Jews to survive as a group, in their collective awareness of the need to perpetuate their different social, religious, and ethnic identity. We find an extremely simple, and by that very token even more convincing, formulation of this idea on the first page of the volume that records the decisions handed down by the leaders of the Jewish community of Verona. In this text, dated 1539, we find summarily defined the goals to be pursued in the context of community organization: "to make provision for all dangers that may eventually threaten the community, and for matters of public utility, as well as for the individual misfortunes to which any member of the community may fall a victim."[6] The order of these three roles was not fortuitous; it was the expression of a scale of priorities: first of all, the defense of the group, then the promotion of its well-being, and finally the protection of the individual. It is not difficult to perceive the affinity between this formulation and the similar roles played by the Italian municipalities of the period. As previously stated, this affinity should not surprise us; nevertheless, it deserves to be further spelled out.

The first thing to note, however paradoxical it may seem, is that attempts to build organizations on a regional scale preceded efforts to create associations within the cities. The Jewish synods that met in Bologna in 1416, in Forlì in 1418, in Florence in 1428 or 1429, and in Tivoli and Ravenna in 1442–1443, were the first in a long series of meetings called together on a regional basis to decide matters of general public interest. Among these were the omnipresent problem of taxation, the question of appeals to the pope on political issues of general concern, and the stance to be taken on social problems relating to Jewish groups as a whole. Participating in the synod of Bologna were delegates from Rome, Padua, Ferrara, Bologna, and communities registered in the minutes as Romagna and Tuscany, though these are strictly speaking regions and not specific localities. At the Forlì synod they were joined by delegates from "Ancona," who are probably to be considered as representatives of an entire region, that of the March of Ancona which bears the city's name. In the same way, "Rome" probably also represented the whole of the Roman Campagna including its maritime region. In a sense, one may say that these men had not yet lost the awareness of belonging to a single overarching community, that of Rome, an awareness they manifested by calling themselves by the collective name of "Romaneschi." Their immediate problem was coming to terms with the situation of uncertainty created by the election of Pope Martin V at the end of the Great Western Schism and persuading the pope to publish another bull along the lines of the *Sicut Judaeis* bulls emanated by several of his predecessors. In addition, they had to support their brethren in Rome who found themselves saddled with the same community taxes as previously, even though the Jewish population had diminished considerably thanks to the exodus of the moneylenders, who had always been the wealthiest members of the community in any case. The texts of the resolutions adopted by these synods[7] are a clear indication that the sense of unity deriving from their common origin was still very much alive. It was precisely this sense that led the Jews to decide to make a contribution to the taxes imposed on the Roman community—like the long-standing levy on the "Agone and Testaccio" quarters, which the Jews of Rome paid so as to be spared the vexations to which they were habitually submitted during the celebration of the Roman Carnival—and to put together the necessary amount "according to the methods used in exacting the Roman tax" (ha-mas mi-Romi).

Little by little, as the Jewish population of the cities north of Rome expanded, the sense of a link with the Roman community grew weaker, giving rise to that of regional responsibility. We have in fact evidence of synods called together on a regional scale for the period preceding that of community organization in the proper sense of the term: for instance, the synods of the March of Ancona in c.1290, Rimini in 1399, and so on.[8] The regional framework survived even after local community organization began to take shape, as a consequence of the growth of the Jewish population in various cities, on a city by city basis. This later development was merely the logical outcome of the previous state of affairs and took place within the existing structures in response to changing needs. The only substantial difference was that the city communities took part in the regional councils by sending delegates chosen by their community assemblies, rather than individual envoys chosen on a personal basis. Furthermore, the principle of proportional representation had the natural effect of guaranteeing the larger cities, usually regional capitals, a position of marked prominence in the Regional Councils. A glance at the respective community registers clearly shows the leadership role played by the delegates from Casale in the Monferrato Council, or the delegates from the city of Padua in the Paduan area Council, and so on.

THE MODEL FOR THIS CONFIGURATION seems to have been quite similar to that of the Italian cities, which dominated the surrounding countryside or contado. In any case, in more general terms, nothing could be more natural than that the Italian cities should provide the Jewish communities with a complex of institutional models for their inspiration and formation. The first and most important of these community institutions was the General Assembly of all the enfranchised, in other words, of all taxpayers. We may see in this the equivalent of the General Assemblies of the city republics (sometimes known as *arenghi*), which provided their citizens in principle at least, with the opportunity to express their political will. The General Assembly was in theory the highest body of community governance, the body with the right to sanction communal ordinances, which corresponded to civic legislation. The community was basically identified with its General Assembly, and semantics helped obliterate any possible distinction, since the Hebrew word for community is *kehillah* and the term for General Assembly is *kahal*, which also means "the public, the population as a whole, the people." Classical Hebrew had no plural for the collective noun *kahal*, and therefore *kehilloth*, the plural of *kehillah*, was used as the plural of both. The innovatory distinction introduced by Oriental Jewish communities, who gave *kahal* the plural form *kehalim*, does not seem to have met with success in Italy, and a similar fate befell the artificial distinctions of lexicographers like Elia Levita, who claimed that *kehillah* was the Hebrew equivalent of *city*, whereas *kahal* stood for the *population of the city*.[9] The semantic confusion was further complicated by the shorthand practice of substituting words with their initial letters: *kk* could be interpreted either as *kahal kadosh* (holy public) or as *kehillah kedoshah* (holy community).

The General Assembly created functional organs upon which it conferred executive powers. These organs grew in complexity and number with the size of the population and its practical needs. The smaller communities limited themselves to nominating a couple of *parnassim* (plural of *parnas*), that is, leaders, who were usually sufficient to perform the necessary administrative functions and to represent the community before the local authorities. Larger communities produced a series of executive structures organized along more or less complex hierarchical lines, similar to those of the Italian cities: thus, in Mantua, Ferrara, or Venice we find first of all a Great Council (*Va'ad Gadol*), which can be compared to the Venetian institution of the same name, or, rather, to the Venetian Senate, then a Lesser Council (*Va'ad qatan*), similar to the *Collegio*, the steering committee of the Senate, and finally the parnassim, whom we may identify as the equivalent of the Procurators.

The larger communities also decided to form *special commissions*, with particular charges, such as assisting the poor, and the upkeep of the synagogue, the cemetery, and other community institutions. Middle-sized communities were satisfied with less elaborate systems: in Verona, for instance, where the Jewish population in the course of the sixteenth century did not exceed three or four hundred souls, the General Assembly, composed of thirty or so members, was content to elect an Executive Council of eleven members, in addition to two parnassim who held office for two months only.

The General Assemblies registered scrupulously of course in the Registers (*Pinkessim*, plural of *Pinkas*) what the powers of the executive councils were. Thus, also in Verona, the decisions of the Council of Eleven had to be unanimous or supported by a majority of at least seven, the Council could not dispense sums in excess of a certain ceiling decided ad hoc by the General Assembly, and so on. Incidentally, it is worth pointing out that the Registers of the Italian Jewish Communities of the Renaissance appear to be the oldest such documents to have survived intact. The Verona Register seems to be the oldest of them all: it contains decisions handed down as early as 1539. Today it is kept in the National Library in Jerusalem. A succinctly annotated edition of the Hebrew text, which is the oldest, was recently published by the University of Tel Aviv.[10] The Israeli National Academy of Sciences recently published in its entirety the oldest portion of the Register of Padua, still preserved in the archives of the Jewish community.[11] The Register of Casale Monferrato (which begins in 1590) has also survived intact, and we also have access to considerable fragments of others. Thanks to these documents, the historian of community institutions in Italy during the Renaissance period is in a fortunate position.

The similarities with Italian municipal structures are also evident in the various systems for the election of community leaders. Precisely like those of their Christian neighbors, these systems combined, in more or less complex ways, mechanisms designed to guarantee what today we would call the democratic process of the elections and the rotation of offices with others designed to protect the superiority of an aristocratic oligarchy based on socioeconomic preeminence. For example, it was up to a member drawn by lot by the incumbent Council to nominate a candidate; at that point, the Assembly cast its vote using black and white balls. The registers leave no doubt that the same relatively few persons succeeded one another over and over again at the helm of the community.

One should not forget that the exercise of power, however prestigious, was not in the least lucrative, indeed it might prove especially onerous. The parnassim, for example, like the members of the councils of the cities, were frequently called upon to answer personally for their decisions, pledging their private financial assets as security for the debts they contracted in the name of the community without previously obtaining a mandate, as might occur, for example, were they to decide on the spur of the moment to advance the sums necessary to liberate imprisoned coreligionists. It was therefore preferable, indeed practically indispensable, for the leaders to be among the wealthiest members of the community. Throughout the first phase of the Jewish settlement in Italy, the rich moneylenders also naturally played the role of community leaders. When, toward the end of the sixteenth century, the economic importance of the moneylenders suffered a decline, one of the consequences was the deterioration of their privileged position as leaders of the community. The prolonged polemics between the impoverished moneylenders, who refused to renounce the leadership, and the merchants, who sought their own share in power, provide proof of this fact. In Mantua, for instance, the conflict, which ended in a compromise, lasted for several decades. The documents regarding this community brought to light by Shlomo Simonsohn could be used to obtain a more detailed analysis of the changing socioeconomic profile of Italian Jewish society on the eve of the modern era.

TAXATION AND COMMUNITY SERVICES

THE SIMILARITY of Jewish community structures to those of the Italian cities naturally diminishes when we turn our attention to economic activities, the normative categories they imply, and their concrete expression in everyday life. These are comparable only in part. Both needed to draw up budgets based on similar conceptions of what a public administration considers it its duty to plan for. But the communities obviously did not have to provide for military expenditures, which made up the bulk of the Italian city budgets. The greater portion of community expenditures was made up instead of the sums that the Jews were compelled to pay at regular intervals for the renewal of the residence permit. In a certain sense, this expense was comparable to the military expenditures of the Italian cities: in both cases the item involved a vital necessity. The payment for the renewal of a condotta usually affected the population of an entire state. Decisions in this regard were therefore the responsibility of the Regional Council.

The tax was imposed according to a rudimentary system founded essentially on the conviction that the majority of the members of the community lived in fear of celestial retribution. First, the amount necessary was determined; then, the sum total of the assets possessed by all families above a certain minimum income was calculated, according to parameters that took into account the risk factor in the case of capital loaned out against collateral, the entity of which was confirmed by notarial act or by the debtor's signature; and finally, the tax share of each contributor was determined, as a percentage of the relative amount of his possessions. An interesting broadsheet printed in 1579 bears picturesque witness to the ceremonial aspect of tax collection in the duchy of Milan: three officials chosen by the Council prepared a preliminary list of heads of households to be taxed; these were invited by the leaders of the community to present themselves before the officials in order to confirm under oath the estimate of their respective possessions; two rabbis presided over the taking of the oath, though they did not have access to the figures involved; after the oath, the procedure was left in the hands of the political officials. The limited role of the rabbis provides further confirmation of the strictly religious esteem in which the rabbinical ministry was held, a phenomenon already remarked upon in chapter 4. As for the ceremony of the oath, it took place in the cemetery, a circumstance whose purpose does not have to be stressed in the present context. Once the oath had been administered, the calculation of the relative amount of tax payable, legal recourse in the case of disagreement, and the payment itself, could occur in any other location.[12]

This system of taxation concerned only the large sums necessary for extraordinary expenditures, and it was supplemented by another simpler method by which the services offered by the community were financed. This second system was decided on an individual basis, or, in cases where more than one community existed in the same city, community by community. In any case, all of the members of the community were taxed, except for the indigent. The tax was calculated "by couples," that is, by family groups, with widowers, widows, and bachelors above a certain age paying as "half couples." This system introduced a remarkably egalitarian factor among all members of the community, independent of their relative financial worth; its purpose was to observe a certain equality of responsibility as far as the services to which everyone was theoretically entitled were concerned; in other words, the essentially associative character of the group was thereby highlighted.

In the Jewish communities, as in the Italian cities, very few of these services were considered by the mentality of the period to be the province of the public administration. It would be an error to compare the services provided at the time with those that a modern state or community considers it its duty to provide. However, it must also be stressed that the number of services offered was far from negligible. The first duty of the community was to guarantee the cult of the synagogue, especially if there was no private synagogue capable of satisfying the needs of the group. It was a question of ensuring the proper functioning of the public synagogue, providing the necessary expenses for the cantor and the beadle (*shamash*), the purchase of wax candles for illumination, and so on. The community considered it its duty to engage a tutor for the children of the poor, who were unable to meet the expense of educating their children. The community also made provision for the employment of a notary (*sofer*) to draw up the acts; normally this role fell to the rabbi, whose duties we will return to immediately. The community was obviously responsible for providing a kosher butchery, so that its members could eat meat in conformity with the dietary laws, as well as other services of a religious nature, such as the ritual bath (*mikveh*), and the cemetery. With the institution of the ghetto, the community assumed additional responsibilities, such as street cleaning, which had previously been the responsibility of the public administration. This is not a sufficient reason, however, to see a substantial difference between communities before and after the ghetto: enclosure in the ghetto did not lead to an increased sense of group identity. Such a sense of identity would call for other criteria of measurement besides the need to collaborate on cleaning the streets!

Some of the functions assumed by modern communities were performed at the time by special confraternities. These confraternities, defined as voluntary organizations more or less religious in character, have rightly been recognized as one of the most typical forms of sociality in premodern Europe.[13] In the area of European Jewish society, the oldest known confraternities go back to thirteenth-century Spain. In Italy they began to flourish from the sixteenth century on. That century and the following witnessed a veritable proliferation of this form of social organization. The early appearance of this kind of institution in Spain, and the fact that the first phase of its spread to Italy coincided with the first quarter of the sixteenth century, which was, as was already seen, the period immediately preceding community organization, leads us to see in the confraternities an embryonic form of that organization. Initially created to meet urgent needs for social assistance, especially to provide for burial services, the first confraternities seem to have been a kind of elite club, whose members considered themselves, by reason of their relative wealth, automatically destined to be leaders of the tiny Jewish communities. The same people who claimed the title of representatives of these groups were the ones who were to form the governing core of the nascent communities. With the passage of time, once the structures of community organization had been laid down, the confraternities continued to assume the responsibility for a narrower gamut of public activities, in part out of inertia, as in the case of burial services, and in part because of the previously mentioned fact that the Jewish communities, whose reactions in this area paralleled those of the Italian cities, did not yet consider themselves obliged to take on these responsibilities themselves. The *Hevrat Talmud Torah* (Society for the Study of the Torah) provided in this early phase of its existence for one or more forms of public education; the *Hevrat Gemilut Hassadim* (Society for Beneficent Works) took care of charitable causes; and so on. The corresponding models in Christian society were the trade and professional guilds and the various *Scole*. Like the latter, in the course of time the Jewish confraternities came to represent centers of sociopolitical power and as such created problems of control for the organized communities, problems they resolved no differently than their Christian counterparts.

Instituted as an intermediate stage between the total absence of any form of community organization and the emergence of community structures, the confraternities continued to have an analogous mediating role in various other spheres, adapting themselves to changing needs. More than the emergence of community structures, what led to these changes were the transformations in the social profile of the Jewish communities, as well as the transformations in mentalities that occurred on the threshold of the modern era. The refinement of the "bourgeois" sensibility was a prime factor in the multiplication of needs of a social character. The result was a multiplication of the confraternities that, in the guise of meeting more or less essential needs for social assistance, acted in the last analysis as authentic social centers. Most noteworthy from this point of view was the appearance of the first youth confraternities, the precursors of modern youth movements, perfectly in keeping with the emergence in this period of a new sense of childhood. The ethnic heterogeneity of the Jewish population in the large communities led to a search for settings that would facilitate social integration alongside the more rigid traditional institutions, such as the synagogue and the Yeshivah, which tended instead to perpetuate differences. The vast majority of confraternities in fact admitted members of diverse ethnic origin. On this front too, then, the confraternities played a very important role as mediators, as will be further elaborated in our remarks on mentalities in the next chapter. For the moment, suffice it to stress the fact that the notion of an institutional community structure would not be complete without keeping in mind the complementary role played by the various confraternities.

COMMUNITY POWER AND THE RABBIS

IN CONTRAST to the Italian cities, Jewish communities had no means of imposing subordination and obedience upon their members: they were not in fact authorized to set up judicial magistracies with the power to pass judgment and promulgate sentences. This is where the cohesive power of the group showed its character, by recourse to the special resources of Talmudic law and tradition and employing the spiritual power of the rabbis in the context of community organizational structures. We have already seen that in theory the rabbinical title of Morenu ha-Rav ("our Lord and Master") implied a relationship of subordination between the Master and those who recognized his authority. The creation of the office of rabbi of the community was tantamount to a formal declaration on the part of the community, which reached its decisions in the General Assembly and recorded them in its Registers, that it considered itself subordinate from that moment on to the rabbi, Lord and Master of the entire community. What did this mean in practice? In principle, the subordination of the community to the rule of the rabbi was parallel to the nature of the relationship established in the field of education. The entire community felt itself elevated by the presence of the rabbi. Clearly, wherever the authority of the spiritual Masters was unquestioned, they were the universally recognized leaders, whether or not they held community office. The authority of the law was that of its qualified representatives. This was Judah Mintz's idea of authority, an idea he clearly expressed when, in 1506, in the Academy (Yeshivah) of Padua over which he presided, at the head of a large number of rabbis placed under his authority, he promulgated a series of ordinances concerning various sectors of Jewish social life. This text, which has already been referred to in chapter 4 and to which we will have occasion to return later, opens with the following preamble: "Given the impending need to establish ordinances according to our Law, and given the presence in Padua of a number of learned men and rabbis residing under the regime of the Serenissima, I, Judah Mintz, along with my other colleagues, have decided to promulgate the ordinances expounded in detail in what follows. . . ."[14] The fact that the contents of the majority of the ordinances published by Judah Mintz were accepted without hesitation by the Jews of Italy, who continued to take them as their inspiration down to the end of the century and even later, proves the old rabbi was not mistaken about the extent of his power. Nevertheless, as the cases of Guglielmo da Montalcino and Messer Leon show, things were never that simple. Messer Leon, who, it appears, had studied under the guidance of Judah Mintz and thought he could count on wielding the same kind of authority, soon found out how wrong he was.

This does not alter the fact that everyone agreed that the exercise of authority could only take place within a context of submission to the qualified representatives and interpreters of the law, in other words, to the rabbis. The problem was to ensure that such a context be created without giving rise to divisions within the community, and in such a way as to ensure both the exercise of sovereignty on the part of the public and the submission of the public to rabbinical authority. The ideal of course was to have a rabbi whose personality assured him of unchallenged charismatic authority. Unfortunately history offers only a few examples of the kind. Men like Judah Mintz, though even he was not spared criticism, represented an exception. It therefore became necessary to set up a system that would permit these two goals to be achieved without anyone being wronged. This was the purpose behind creating the office of community rabbi.

The primary duty of the official community rabbi was the teaching of the law. Its importance is clearly indicated in the formulas in which the General Assemblies set down the duties that the rabbis nominated by them agreed to perform before being invested with the office. These formulas repeat over and over again the same stereotyped phrases. Many have been discovered that go back to the very period in which community organization was beginning to take shape, that is, to the second quarter of the sixteenth century. They point out the need for public instruction and public cultural activities, and the corresponding responsibilities of the rabbi nominated: giving one public lesson per day, usually right after the morning service in the synagogue, supervising the work of the community tutors and periodically examining their level of competence. To these was occasionally added the obligation to perform the role of notary for the registration of public acts, in particular for recording in the community Registers the decisions adopted by the Assembly and its executive Councils. More than a rabbinical duty, however, the latter task usually constituted a means of rounding out his salary. The first and most important justification for the office of community rabbi was the need to provide the community with an instructional and cultural Master. It is not hard to see, however, that there was more at stake than just the *services* connected with education, since these services in themselves, however important, were not enough to bring the community to declare its submission to the will of the Master whom they themselves had chosen to nominate. It was not the community's need for a teacher that led to the institution of the community rabbi: the real reason was instead the need to ensure the proper functioning of community structures, which otherwise would have been quickly deprived of their authority.

Indeed, Jewish society had no more effective means of coercion than excommunication, and it has already been seen that this was the exclusive prerogative of the rabbis. The use of coercion was therefore destined to pass through their hands. The creation of community rabbis was, in other words, the method chosen to create as independent a power structure as possible. In fact, besides that of teaching, the most important duty of the rabbi was to place his rabbinical prerogative of excommunication at the service of the community. The rabbi agreed not to excommunicate without first obtaining the consensus of the community and, conversely, to excommunicate all those whom the leaders of the community decided to subject to this punishment.

There was of course more to this than the mere creation of an instrument of power. The inclusion of the rabbis in the institutional structure of the community was suggested instead by reasons that essentially had to do with the way the idea of leadership was interpreted. According to Talmudic law (T.B. *Baba Batra* 9a), any collective ordinance whatsoever is null and void if it is published without the preliminary approval of a person defined as "important" (*adam ḥashuv*), of a Master, that is, capable of exercising effective control over the decisions of the collectivity so as to prevent it deciding anything contrary to the law. This "important" person was supposed, in other words, to have a role comparable to our modern Constitutional Courts. The rabbi, upon his nomination as community rabbi, was raised to the rank of that "important" person required by the Talmud: without him, it would have been easy to prove the illegitimacy of any ordinance, particularly those important enough to warrant excommunication.

When a rabbi was elected to the prestigious position of Lord and Master of the community, the community thereby incorporated him into its organizational structure and became associated with him in their exercise of his rabbinical prerogatives. By declaring itself subject to the spiritual authority of its rabbi, the community actually reinforced its own institutional structure. This process was quickly perfected by prohibiting all those holding the title of rabbi from exercising their excommunicatory prerogative unless they had received a specific authorization from the official rabbi of the community. It seems unthinkable for the latter to authorize someone else to exercise a power that he himself could not wield without the assent of the leaders of the community. In any case we have found no evidence of such an occurrence. We must conclude that, by reinforcing still more the authority of the rabbi whom it nominated, the community further strengthened the vigor of its own institutional structure. The Congress of Delegates of the Communities of Italy, which met in Ferrara in 1554, definitively sanctioned this tendency when it promulgated the following ordinance: "Wherever there resides a rabbi, another rabbi residing outside of the city cannot publish a decree [of excommunication], unless he has obtained the consent of the rabbi of the city, or unless the latter has declared in writing or before witnesses that he prefers to have no part in the case. In a city where a rabbi nominated by the community or its leaders is in residence, another rabbi, even though he may live in the same city, cannot issue any sentence, written or oral, without the consent of the community rabbi. On the other hand, if an inhabitant of the city is involved in a dispute with the local rabbi, other rabbis may give opinions on the case provided they consider it just to do so."[15]

It should be stressed that, although the communities nominated the rabbis, the rabbis were *never* economically dependent upon them. The salaries they received for their services were practically insignificant. It should not be supposed, therefore, that by accepting the office the rabbi forfeited his independence. We should not see the rabbis as mere employees of the communities, at the beck and call of their employers. On the contrary, when the rabbi decided to abandon his office as a result of differences of opinion with community leaders, it was the latter who found themselves in an embarrassing position. If the reason for the difference was one of principle, the leaders would find themselves hard put to find another rabbi ready to do whatever it was that the resigning rabbi had refused to do. So far, only one such case has come to light. The rabbi of Padua Samuel Archivolti in 1585 found himself in disagreement with the leaders of his community and resigned. The leaders tried to get along without him, but it appears that their threats to excommunicate those who violated communal ordinances failed to achieve the desired result; an excommunication without a rabbi was apparently inconceivable. The leaders were obliged to give way, and the rabbi returned to his former position. It is a pity that the nature of the dispute is not known. When the difference had been resolved, it was decided to cancel all reference to it from the Registers, thereby condemning posterity to remain in the dark.

The sense of continuity in Talmudic law coupled with necessities of a practical nature thus determined the introduction of the rabbis into the organizational structures of the community, and this fact gave the latter a very special complexion. The symbiosis between the exercise of power and cultural activity, never without a conspicuously sacred character, would have given the community a singular quality comparable to that of an ecclesiastical government, were it not for the presence of another conspicuous component—the secular nature of the leadership. The governance of the community made it necessary to construct a very delicate and unstable balance between the rabbis' tendency to give a practical interpretation to their title of "Lord and Master" of the community, and the reluctance of the lay leadership to renounce their sovereignty. The foundation for such a construction was evidently the common sentiment of the unity of the law which all felt obliged to obey, and which was the cement that held the group together. As for the sources of instability, they may be traced back to the various cultural backgrounds that were the consequence of different ethnic origins, to the pressures of conflicting interests, and to human idiosyncrasies. All of the possible reasons for contesting the authority of the head of the Yeshivah were amplified here, since, unlike that of the head of the Yeshivah, the authority of the rabbi appointed by the community was not tacitly and implicitly recognized by all. The formal elevation of a rabbi to the rank of Lord and Master of the community by the General Assembly, however discreet, made it immediately imperative for those opposed to react. This was no doubt why, throughout the entire period, only small communities with a high degree of cultural and ethnic homogenity and social cohesion appointed a rabbi: Verona, Padua, Cremona, Casale Monferrato, and other communities with a population of from two to four hundred souls of similar origin, in the case in the communities cited and the others almost exclusively Ashkenazi.

In large communities, such as Mantua or Venice, which lacked a homogeneous population, it was impossible to agree on the choice of a rabbi acceptable to all. In these communities, the introduction of the rabbis into the institutional structures in a manner that would permit them to function had to take a more difficult and circuitous route. The process of actual "legislation," especially that accompanied by the threat of excommunication for the transgressor, was necessarily subordinated to preliminary agreement among *all those in possession of a rabbinical title*, or at least among those whom public opinion considered *the most representative* among the variegated local population.

The system became more effective as a result of the introduction of a distinction between ordinary rabbis and the "Most Excellent" (Eccellentissimi). The term "Eccellentissimi" is the Italian rendering—the translation is once again that of Elia Levita—of the Hebrew *Gaon* (plural *Geonim*), a term bearing venerable semantic associations with both knowledge and the exercise of ecumenical power. It should be added that, in deference to the tradition cited and to the inflation to which all titles are subject in the long run, the custom of prefacing the title of all qualified rabbis with the superlative "Eccellentissimo" is still in force in Italy. As was seen in chapter 4, the bestowal of rabbinical titles was the province of the rabbis. Nevertheless, it was not the rabbis who decided who had the right to the title "Eccellentissimo": this fell to public opinion, *outside of any institutional structure*, according to a complex of factors that took into account both learning and charisma. Thus it was that when for reasons of a fundamentally practical nature it was decided that only rabbis with the additional qualification of "Eccellentissimi" would be allowed to preside over the community legislative process in the place of the community rabbi who had failed to be nominated, all that public opinion could do was to acquiesce. In the large communities, all ordinances of any importance were sanctioned in the presence of the "Eccellentissimi," and it was to them collectively that people turned to pronounce the ban of excommunication. The model adopted by the large communities was therefore the same as that adopted by the small ones. It could be said to express in an even more significant way the equilibrium that the cohesive forces within the group had achieved, balancing against one another those reciprocally hostile forces that were a consequence of the pluralistic nature of the groups themselves.

ASPIRATIONS TOWARD JURISDICTIONAL INDEPENDENCE

WITH THE STRUCTURES DESCRIBED, the communities were theoretically in a position to develop a high degree of autonomy, but this was prevented in practice by the opposition of the Christian authorities. There can be no doubt that the responsibility is in part attributable to considerations of a vaguely "constitutional" nature, since it is clear that the more or less complete independence of the Jewish communities would have implied limiting the powers of the state in the exercise of its sovereignty. But considerations of religious psychology were also responsible, as well as upon occasion the direct influence of the ecclesiastical authorities. In fact, the Christian mentality of the time could never have permitted the Jews to exercise power independently: the Jews were condemned to perpetual servitude because they had failed to recognize Christ's divinity.

Christian opposition to the complete independence of the Jewish communities was manifested with extreme vigor in the most sensitive areas having to do with the exercise of power and made it its goal to eliminate any possibility of the community making totally independent use of coercion. In the first place, the publication of excommunications required preliminary authorization ad hoc from the Christian secular magistrates, who claimed the right to control Jewish community institutions down to the smallest details. The Christian authorities naturally did not oppose the publication of excommunications as long as these served their interests too. They did not oppose, for instance, the excommunications decreed to encourage people to pay their taxes, the better part of which went into the coffers of the state. As a rule, disturbers of morality and public order were also permitted to be excommunicated. In all these cases, the community acted as the representative of the Christian authorities. This was not the case, however, with excommunications meted out in order to compel the members of the community to obey ordinances in which the Christians could see no utility, all the more so for those that could be construed as contrary to Christian interests. An example are the ordinances designed to compel Jews to present themselves before Jewish community tribunals and accept the verdicts they handed down. Here, Christian rejection was strongly conditioned by the religious mentality and by the ecclesiastical instututions that fostered it.

It should not be forgotten that for Christian theology recognizing the validity of Jewish jurisdiction would have meant denying one of its fundamental principles, that of the supersession of the Old Testament. A ruler authorizing the exercise of Jewish jurisdiction in his territories would have been recognizing implicitly at the same time the validity of the sentences handed down according to the Old Testament, *quae habent vim obligandi ex veteris legis,* as Thomas Aquinas would have said.[16] This obstacle to Jewish autonomy was never removed from the path of the community. It is not surprising, then, if the opposition to the institution of Jewish tribunals was somehow proportional to the power of the Church and her institutions. In the States of the Church, Jewish tribunals were not permitted until their incorporation into the Kingdom of Italy and the abolition of the temporal power of the popes in 1870. In other states, the extant documentation offers numerous examples in which the relationship between local power structures and the institutions of the Church manifested itself in a wide variety of different ways far beyond the scope of the present work.

Communities could not help trying to take advantage of the fact that the local magistracies recognized the validity of the results of their arbitration. All of the Italian cities had incorported arbitration into their own jurisdictions, not only recognizing the validity of the outcome of arbitration, but also compelling recourse to arbitration rather than to the magistracy in cases such as those involving litigation between members of the same family or the same corporation. As for the Jews, who were never denied rights of citizenship according to Roman law, opinions handed down in arbitration according to Jewish law were explicitly recognized as valid.[17] As a result, communities attempted to substitute arbitration for jurisdiction.

A Jewish court in session, as shown in the opening page of the legal work Tur
Ḥoshen Mishpat, *copied in Mantua in 1535. Vatican, Biblioteca Apostolica,
Ms. Rossiana 555, f. 292ᵛ.*

Upon occasion the Jews were able to have included in the condotta
clauses obliging them to resolve their own litigation by recourse to the
arbitration of other Jews. Francesco II, Duke of Milan, sanctioned in
1533 in the condotta issued to the Jews residing in his duchy, under pain
of a 20 lira fine to be paid to the ducal exchequer, that "should a dispute
or civil controversy arise for any reason among the Jews, let two Jewish
Doctors [that is, two rabbis] be appointed, or two Jewish arbiters, who
will consider and judge the difference according to their own laws and
ordinances."[18] In addition, ordinances were issued which obliged the contending parties to nominate as arbiters in a dispute of some importance
the rabbi and the parnassim of the community, who thus came to represent a kind of de facto rabbinical tribunal. At times a detailed compromise was spelled out, so as to avoid all possibility of the sentence being
declared null and void on the basis of a supposed failure to conform with

its terms. Here also, despite the variety of local solutions, one is left with the impression that basically one is always dealing with the same phenomenon. In all these solutions the forces involved are quite clear: in addition to the Christian opposition, one recognizes the rabbis' determination to ensure that the institution of arbitration should remain in their hands, the insistence of the community that the system should work efficiently, and its greater or lesser success in persuading the Christian authorities to close one eye to the situation created de facto, and finally its greater or lesser success in convincing its members to practice self-discipline. All of these forces could not fail to conflict with the interests of given individuals or groups, so that in reality the road to autonomy proved to be paved with obstacles. The private interests of those who, out of simple self-interest or utilitarian considerations would have preferred the way of compromise to that of the strict application of the law, were opposed, for example, to the aspirations of the rabbis. Such private interests found themselves allied upon occasion with the general tendency of the parnassim, though no one would ever have admitted openly that they were opposed to the concentration of too many independent forces outside the control of the "secular" leadership.

The possibility of convincing the Christian authorities discreetly to ignore what was going on was evidently conditioned by a number of variables, such as the liberality of the government, the influence of the ecclesiastical authorities, and the ability of the Jews themselves to carry on their business with discretion. To this were also opposed the incidental interests of individuals for whom the application of the Jewish law would certainly have meant losing their case. Readiness to sacrifice oneself on the altar of self-discipline could hardly have been expected to be the norm. The case of the disguised institution of a rabbinical tribunal in Ferrara in 1575 provides a significant example. That year, the Jews of the "Italian" and "German" communities, taking advantage of a propitious moment (the "Portuguese" community had just obtained the privilege of judicial autonomy), managed to obtain authorization from the Duke of Ferrara to set up a "tribunal of three experts charged with overseeing the conduct of the Jews with regard to permitted and forbidden foodstuffs, as well as marriages and divorces, so as to avoid noise in the synagogue [that is, interrupting the prayers according to the ancient institution of *Bittul ha-Tamid*, which will be dealt with in more detail in the next chapter], by obliging the parties to choose arbitrators." The three experts, whose names were specified, were three rabbis, and the idea was evidently to create an institution that, under the pretext of supervising the proper religious conduct of the Jews, would in fact have acted as a genuine rabbinical tribunal. It was two Jews, Joseph and Samuel Levi, who submitted to the Duke their reservations, which were of a "constitutional" character, stressing the fact that in authorizing the creation of a rabbinical tribunal, the Duke was surrendering his sovereignty over a portion of his subjects, who in their turn were being deprived of part of their freedom.[19] One finds here an interesting mix of Thomas Aquinas's arguments, already recalled, and others that one can have no hesitation in defining as absolutely "modern." The upshot of the story is unclear: the fact remains that the "tribunal" of Ferrara, even in this camouflaged form, at the moment of its creation met with the opposition of a number of Jews.

This does not, however, alter the fact that the system, whatever its weaknesses, proved effective. Indirect confirmation is provided by the fact that almost all the histories of the Italian Jews continue to assert today that the Jews enjoyed complete autonomy, something that, as has been seen, is quite untrue. For this very reason, we must beware of descriptions that use the neutral term "rabbinical tribunal," a term that, in the absence of further specification, leads to a completely erroneous view of the reality. We must also beware of generalizations that, on the basis of documents that show how the Jews preferred upon occasion to have recourse to Christian rather than Jewish tribunals, might lead us to conclude a relaxation of the cohesive force of the group, according to some general tendency to give way to centrifugal forces and to opt for acculturation. In the circumstances described above, one is tempted instead to affirm the opposite: given the impossibility of resorting with complete independence to the use of excommunication, the degree of self-government achieved by the communities on the basis of their sense of self-discipline alone is absolutely remarkable. The incidence of recourse to Christian justice on the part of the Jews was relatively low compared with what the situation might have produced. All things considered, the aim of the communities was to set up an institutional structure calculated to justify as fully as possible their own characterization of themselves as a "city within the city."

It may be that some distortion on this score proceeds from the fact that all the evidence regarding these disputes concerns the communities' ruling classes. Among these classes it is only natural that we should find a higher degree of public responsibility. This is not a characteristic that applies to Jewish groups exclusively; still, among the latter, the high level of socioeconomic homogeneity was translated into a remarkable sense of collective public responsibility. Toward the end of the sixteenth century the radical change that took place also influenced the functioning of judiciary structures. The crisis in Jewish banking activities, the heterogeneity and socioeconomic polarization that was the result of the enormous increase in poverty, inevitably led to a comparative slackening in the degree of self-discipline. Contrary to what is usually affirmed, in the period of the ghetto, the centrifugal tendencies in the area of independent juridical administration increased, a feature analogous to a number of other developments that characterized the particular historical moment. It is one of history's many paradoxes that the slackening of the sense of self-discipline was partially offset by the change that took place in the attitude of the Christians vis-à-vis the "Jewish question," in the sense specified in our opening chapter. In the course of the seventeenth century, the institution of true rabbinical tribunals in Italy's Jewish communities was tolerated more or less everywhere, though their powers were considerably limited. But this phase in the evolution of community institutions lies outside the chronological scope of this book.

The situation so far described was apparently responsible for the downgrading of the status of the rabbi within the Jewish communities of Italy. Unable to perform the role of Head of the Rabbinical Tribunal (*Av Beth Din*), a role permitted his colleagues in states that did not oppose the functioning of Jewish justice, the Italian rabbi saw his authority somewhat curtailed. The responsibility for the breakdown of community institutions has been attributed by many scholars to the individualistic spirit of the Renaissance. It ought instead to be blamed on the practical impediments placed in the way of the Jewish communities. The multiplicity of states obviously contributed to this situation. How could respect for the decisions adopted by the rabbinical tribunal of one community be imposed on the members of another community, especially when the second community had its own learned rabbis whose opinion differed from that of the first tribunal? How could a man be obliged to respect the judgment of one tribunal rather than another? How could excommunications issued by rabbis residing in other states be prevented from conditioning the course of justice?

Most disputes among the Jews of the period had to do with this complexity. The recent blossoming of publications concerning the Jews in the Renaissance has brought to light a number of case histories that only serve to confirm this overall picture. Take for instance the dispute that in 1518–1521 opposed two rich moneylenders, Abraham Raphael Finzi of Bologna and Immanuel Norzi of Ferrara, when they decided to terminate their partnership and proceed to the division of their assets. It proved impossible to persuade the contending parties to submit to the decisions of any court of law. Finzi insisted that his case be tried in Bologna, Norzi would accept no other forum but Ferrara. The number of different responsa drawn up by the many rabbis who took part in the discussion is evidence both of their doctrinal abilities and of their complete inability to have one opinion accepted rather than another. During the dispute regarding the breaking off of the engagement between the rich widow Rosa da Montalcino, a resident of Chianciano, and Isaac Danuti of Pesaro (1534–1535), the eventual compromise was preceded by a number of discussions that took place among the rabbis of almost every city in Italy. The same is true of the refusal of Joseph Tamari, a Venetian doctor, to honor his promise, made in 1560, to grant the hand of his daughter to the young adventurer Samuel da Perugia, who went by the nickname of Venturozzo: their dispute, referred to by modern historians as the "Tamari-Venturozzo scandal," dragged on for years, reaching well beyond the confines of Italy. In this case, the complexity of the situation was exacerbated by the severity of the religious law, which meant that the slightest doubt regarding the woman's civil status was sufficient to make marriage practically impossible. Many further cases could be cited, but they would not modify the picture.

Be that as it may, the rabbis, having no authority beyond that deriving to them from their title, appear for the most part in the role of counselors, either to their community or to its individual members. This is the role in which the various defenders of one cause or another in the course of the disputes are to be seen. These men, who, as we know, frequently placed their learning in the service of some magnate, saw nothing wrong with assisting their patrons with legal advice. This is the only way to explain what is in my opinion a perfectly natural phenomenon, and which in no way justifies the ingenious theory of Isaiah Sonne, who saw it as a typical expression of the extreme individualism of the rabbis who, independent of the community establishment, were determined, in the service of their patrons, to totter the very foundations of community structures. Sonne's theory, whose influence shows no signs of abating, in part because of the continuing appeal of the classical semantics on which it is founded, in my opinion finds no justification in the documents that have been adduced to prove it, and still less in the new documentation recently brought to light. It is impossible to distinguish between a rabbi appointed by the community and one of the ones Sonne dubs, somewhat contemptuously, "itinerant." Community rabbis were not dependent on the community leaders any more than the "itinerant" rabbis, supposedly ready to bend the law to any interpretation the defense of their patrons' interests might require, were dependent on their patrons. This does not mean one should close one's eyes to the corruption and bad faith of humankind, of whom we should expect no more in Italy in the Renaissance than we do at other times and places. Judah Sommo, for instance, painted a picturesque portrait of corruption and bad faith in his comedy *Tzaḥuth bediḥuta de-kiddushin*, in which he describes the behavior of an astute rabbi in the service of a deceitful dowry-hunter. Examples of this kind could easily be multiplied.

Communities tried, of course, to limit as far as possible the improper use of rabbinical prerogative by the publication of ordinances at the local and intercommunitary level. It was forbidden, for example, to import excommunications from outside the community. The ordinance published by the representatives of the communities gathered in Ferrara in 1554, recalled in detail above, is simply one of many, though perhaps the most complex: an examination of its formulation permits one to discern the reflection of the multiplicity of possible situations.

Success could evidently never be total. All things considered, however, one cannot help being impressed by the fact that the communities succeeded in maintaining such an independent administration of justice, despite the fragility of the basis on which it rested. In fact the communities evinced qualities that were paradigmatically modern: forced to organize along largely voluntary lines long before the Emancipation of European Jewry, they found themselves obliged to cope with conceptual problems similar to those the Jews of the modern period have had to come to terms with. The communities were compelled above all to face the problem of identity on the level of group organization in such a way as to establish a delicate balance between their perception of their independence and diversity and at the same time of their belonging to a complex variety of more general contexts and structures—those of their Other Jewish coreligionists as well as those of the Christian society around them.

PART THREE
STRUCTURES OF
MENTALITY

VII
TIME AND SPACE

ECCLESIA AND SYNAGOGA

T HE MENTALITY OF THE JEWS over time is one aspect of
Jewish history that has so far received comparatively little attention.
The following observations will therefore have a purely preliminary character. We will begin by investigating the categories of time and space,
the first and most general categories in our perception of the world
around us. On one level these categories were naturally perceived by the
Jews in a way quite similar to that of their Christian neighbors. Their
Jewish religion, however, conferred upon them certain characteristics
that meant that their perception was in the last analysis profoundly different. This is one feature of their perception of the world that the available information regarding the history of the Jews permits us to study in
a fairly detailed manner.

The time of the quotidian was a slow, uniform time, measured by the
devotional practices of the synagogue, themselves closely bound up with
the rhythms of nature: morning prayers at the start of the day, evening
and night prayers in a single sequence at the end of the day. To adapt
Jacques Le Goff's felicitous phrase, we can speak, *mutatis mutandis*, of a
"time of the synagogue," not unlike the medieval Christian's *"time of the
church."* The relationship between the two, however, must also take into
account what *opposes* the Christian *Ecclesia* to the Jewish *Synagoga*, and must

Exterior and interior of the Levantine synagogue, which was built in 1538.

therefore be seen in terms of specularity or opposition, which must also be extended to their respective perceptions of space. *Ecclesia* and *Synagoga* are, in other words, primarily perceived in terms of their three-dimensional representations, as occupying two sacred spaces opposed by their very natures. It comes as no surprise, then, to find the same similarity and opposition equally evident in a whole series of concrete expressions of social activity.

Leone Modena gives us an idea of how a sixteenth-century Jew would have described the sacred space of the Synagogue?[1]

They make their Synagogues, or Schools, as they call them, sometimes small, sometimes large, sometimes on the ground level, sometimes on an upper story, sometimes freestanding, sometimes part of a house, the best way they can, not being free to build tall or sumptuous buildings. The inside walls are white or panelled with wood or with wooden benchbacks, with verses or sayings written around the walls reminding them to concentrate on their prayers. And all around there are benches to sit in, some of which have little cupboards in which to keep books, prayer shawls and other objects. Above are many lamps, chandeliers and lights, oil or candle, to light the place up. By the doors a box or casket in

Interior of the Ashkenazi synagogue, which was built in 1529.

which whoever wishes may put money to be given as alms for the poor. On the
eastern side is placed an Ark or repository, which they call *Aron*, in imitation
of the Ark of the Covenant, which formerly stood in the Temple, and in which
the Pentateuch, or the first five books of Moses, is kept, written by hand with the
greatest diligence on parchment with specially prepared ink in capital letters
known as Merubaad [i.e., square] letters. . . . In the middle, or at one end, there
is a sort of narrow aisle or a little wooden altar, raised up slightly to rest the book
on when they read, or to lean on while preaching a sermon, or for other purposes.
There is a separate space above or to one side with wooden screens for the
women, who can pray and see what is going on, but cannot be seen by the men or
mix with them, so as not to turn the mind aside from its prayers towards some
sinful thought. . . . There are one, two, six, ten or more of these Synagogues in
each Town, depending on how many Jews there are living there, so that they can
all be accommodated, and also according to the variety of their place of origin,
Levantine, German or Italian, because they are more different in their prayers
than in anything else, and each nation insists on doing things its own way.

In this description, the contrasts with the Christian church are no less
striking than the similarities. First of all, the decor and the cult objects.

Leone seems particularly concerned to stress the *light* that fills the interior of the synagogue. We are immediately led to contrast this brightness with the semidarkness of the Christian church. A comparison with the Jewish banks, described by the author of the *Book of the Moneylender and the Borrower*, quoted in chapter 1, renders this image even more eloquent. The mere sequence of the paragraphs in Leone's description brings out the close relationship between the luminosity of the inside of the synagogue and the restrictive regulations that governed its external architecture. The inhibition deriving from the turning inwards was, in a sense, the natural consequence of these restrictions, whereas the stress on artificial illumination corresponded to the effort invested in the aspiration to separate artificially the actual space from its natural context, in other words, a symbolic visual expression of the totality of the Jewish experience in the very bosom of Christianity.

It is certainly no accident that Leone should insist on the decor of the Holy Ark and the scroll of the Torah! Any study of medieval Jewish symbolism, however superficial, would confirm the fact that the Torah was seen in opposition to Christ (the Logos) and that the Torah scroll was a cult object opposed to the Crucifix, the chief visual symbol of the Christian church.

Other points to which attention should be drawn are the separation of the male from the female space and the absence from the Jewish liturgical function of the figure of the priest. These two details appear to concern two completely different aspects, and yet they are intimately related. From Leone's point of view, the first stresses the *natural differentiation* within the congregation present at the service, whereas the second underscores the absence of an *artificial differentiation* of roles among believers in the sight of God. In the image Leone had of the Christian church this opposition must have been attenuated if not inverted. The same goes for the attention he devotes to the multitude of different Jewish rites existing within a single Jewish community: this variety invites comparison with the Catholic Church's refusal, particularly in Leone's day, to recognize the legitimacy of different forms of Christianity.

THE CONTRAST between the Synagogue and the Church certainly
does not stop with the details brought out in Leone Modena's text.
Others can easily be added. People gathered in the synagogue, as they did
in the church, to address their prayers to God, but, contrarily to the
church, people gathered in the synagogue for a whole gamut of activities,
for the most part of a "profane" nature, that had nothing to do with
prayer. Sacred and profane were mingled in the synagogue in a way in
which they had not been mingled in the church for some time. This is
directly related to Leone's point about the multiplicity of rites. For the
synagogue is a symbol of diversity within the civic space, whereas the
church no longer performs that function except on the parochial level,
that is to say at a level that brings in the specific problems of the diversity
among citizens differently *equal* to each other. We might formulate a general law: the proportion of the "profane" mingled with the "sacred" in
the place of worship is directly proportional to the degree of cultural and
socioeconomic diversity that is a consequence of religious diversity. This
is by no means a unique phenomenon: we encounter it in all expressions
of religious separatism, in the earliest Protestant communities, for example, which are from the typological point of view very similar to the
Jewish communities. The profane activities that took place in the synagogue all derived from the Jews' perception of their cultural and socioeconomic diversity, a "total" diversity that was a consequence of the religious diversity of which the synagogue was the symbol. These
observations should be added to those made in chapter 5 apropos of the
symbiosis between sacred and profane in the field of cultural production.

The synagogue was in fact a general group meeting place. When the
authorities wished to communicate something to the Jews, they would
attach a notice to the doors of the synagogue. The Jews gathered in the
synagogue just as their neighbors gathered in the Piazza dell'Arengo or
in front of the Palazzo della Signoria or the Commune. The synagogue
was "neutral" ground, where friends and rivals, rich and poor, weak and

powerful sat side by side. The synagogue was the embodiment of the abstract idea of the "public." Some people went so far as to confuse the semantics of the synagogue with the semantics of the public, especially the Jews of Iberian origin, for whom the word "synagogue" was a synonym for "public" (*kahal*).

People gathered in the synagogue, then, not only to pray but also to engage in a series of profane or semiprofane activities of concern to the entire community. As a result, the time of the synagogue was further characterized by a mingling of the sacred and the profane. The time of prayer was never isolated: it was first of all closely linked with the time of collective study for all members of the community (whereas, as was already seen in chapter 2, the study activity of particular groups took place outside the synagogue, in the space known as the Yeshivah). This reinforced the sacred component of collective study, which in its turn tended to be transformed from a cultural activity to a cult activity. In the second phase of our period, this transformation really did in fact take place, through the agency of the Kabbalah, previously discussed in chapter 5. We will return to this point in a moment.

The times of the administration of law and justice were also mingled with the time of prayer. Wherever there existed community "tribunals," within the limits outlined in the preceding chapter, they invariably met in the synagogue, right after morning prayers and the study period. This was also the scene of the ceremonies associated with the application of Jewish law, in which it is difficult to draw a clear-cut distinction between religious, civil, and even penal law. It was in the synagogue therefore that interested parties received their divorce documents, or where the *ḥalitzah* (barefoot) ceremony, required to free a widow whose husband had died without leaving heirs from the obligation to marry his brother, according to the biblical custom of levirate, was performed. Given the special conditions of the Italian communities, in which, as we have seen, the administration of justice labored under severe restrictions, the times of justice and the times of prayer continued to be linked far longer than they did elsewhere, thanks also to the existence of an ancient institution, typical of a situation characterized by the absence of administrative and judiciary structures with the power of coercion: the institution known as *Bittul ha-Tamid* or *'Ikkuv Tefillah*, "the interruption of prayers."

What this amounted to was as follows: any individual who thought he had been offended in some way, and who had exhausted all the means at his disposal for obtaining justice, had the right to interrupt public prayers by striking the *Tevah* with his hand: the prayer could not continue until the group had ensured that a process had been set in motion designed to see justice done. Failing that, the interrupted prayer had in practice to be canceled for the rest of the day. One does not have to insist on the psychological and social impact of such a gesture. The persistence of this institution throughout the entire period offers a paradigmatic example of the way every activity undertaken outside of the synagogue, even the most profane, could be subsequently projected into its interior, thereby influencing the way the time and space of the sacred was interpreted.

The rhythm of the activities of the synagogue, moreover, was also projected outside the synagogue, mingling in its turn with that of profane activities. Think for instance of the picturesque figure of the beadle (*shammash*) patrolling the *street of the Jews* and summoning them to interrupt their business and to proceed to take part in evening prayers or some other ceremony taking place in the synagogue. Or even better, think of the community ordinances that took the hours of services in the synagogue as their temporal parameters. The Verona Registers, for example, provide reliable evidence of the fact that in that community banking business hours were arranged taking into consideration the times set aside for prayer.

On the level of quotidian everyday activities, then, we encounter a perception of the categories of collective time opposed to that of the Christians: Jewish collective time, measured according to the parameters of the synagogue, was strongly laced with secular elements, not because of any lack of religiosity, but rather, on the contrary, as a consequence of the elementary fact that all these elements concerned their group diversity, essentially defined by their diversity of religion.

To this same order belong additional elements of a specular conception of space and time. The rhythm of the week, of the year, of the whole of life was, for Jews as well as Christians, marked by days and events fraught with religious significance: the weekly day of rest, days of collective celebration or mourning, events impinging on family life — birth, the passage to adulthood, marriage, death. The Jews, however, abstained from servile work on Saturdays, the Christians on Sundays; Jewish feast days were not the same as Christian feast days, and there were even mechanisms in existence to ensure against overlap; family events also took a different course.

Holy days were so numerous among Christians that for a long time Jews found themselves compelled to produce formal justification for their failure to observe the precept of the Mishnah which forbids engaging in economic activity on Gentile feast days. From this difference in sacred days there derived a clear-cut opposition between the perception of scared versus profane time in the two camps. This automatically influenced the perception of differences between the two groups at every level. The Jews recited the differences every week in the ceremony of the *havdalah*, the ancient rite of transition between holidays and work days. In the formula used by Jews of Italian origin, God was blessed for having "distinguished between sacred and profane, light and darkness, Jews and Gentiles, the Sabbath and the six working days." This perception of difference may have an excessively subtle ring to our ears, even for those among us who are strict observers of religious interdictions: part of the responsibility for this sense of excessive subtlety should probably be attributed to the institution of the "weekend," which includes both Saturday and Sunday, thereby putting both Jews and Christians in the same festive context, but an even more telling factor is the attenuation of the public aspects of the feast day, which is a specific instance of the attenuation of everything having to do with religious expression.

THE STRUCTURAL CONTRAST between the Jews and their Christian neighbors regarding the degree of the profane intermingled with the sacred on working days is also projected in a singular fashion onto the feast days, but in the opposite sense. Feast days feature a massive invasion of the sacred into the area of the profane. As was to be expected, this admixture primarily occurred in public and, consequently, chiefly in the synagogue. The men spent practically their entire day there. First of all, prayers on feast days lasted considerably longer than on normal days. The prayer formularies of the Italian Jews contain a vast range of liturgical poetic compositions (*piyyutim*), arranged according to the varying circumstances of the day, covering all of the year's sabbaths and other feasts, to be *added* to the regular texts. The Sabbaths on which there were no prayers to be added were few and far between, especially in the larger communities. There are additional prayers for the four Sabbaths before Passover, for the one before Pentecost and the Day of Atonement, and so on, without neglecting of course the other feast days. There were also added prayers for days in which a bridegroom was in attendance in the synagogue during the week of his marriage or the week before, or a father in the week in which his child was born. This is one of the most typical characteristics of the Italian rite, evidence of a millenary tradition dating back to the religious practices in force in Palestine in the early centuries of the Common Era. But of equal concern from the present point of view is the fact that these texts constituted a substantial addition to the basic liturgy already scheduled to be recited, all the more so since these were the bravura pieces preferred by the cantors, desirous of exhibiting their musical talents and giving satisfaction to the other members of the congregation on feast days. Then came the reading of the weekly passages from the Torah and from the Prophets, the rabbi's sermon, which, since it was forbidden to eat before the services, to avoid the congregation having to fast for most of the day, was sometimes postponed until the afternoon and given during evening prayers, especially in the short days of winter. All of this without counting the possibility that some kind of public study period might be added, by no means a rare occurrence when the days grew longer.

It does not require much imagination to realize that at this rate there would not be much time left outside of the synagogue. And even that time was devoted for the most part to the ritual meals. Religious custom imposed the consumption of at least three meals on the Sabbath, two of which had to be consumed on Saturday while it was still daylight. To fit into the three or at most four remaining hours of a winter day two festive meals, accompanied by ritual chants and discussion of the weekly passage from the Torah, was next to impossible. The solution they came up with was quite ingenious: in winter a single meal was consumed, ritually divided into two—at a certain point, they simply declared the first meal over, recited the blessing, washed their hands, as ritual required, before the "second meal," and began all over again. Needless to say, this custom came in for considerable criticism for those who saw in it a mere pretext for shirking religious duties.

We could go on adding to these examples of the overlapping of sacred and profane time, accompanied by the consciousness of a sense of cultural identity opposed to that of the Christian world. It should come as no surprise to learn that for many centuries there existed among Jews no such tension as that so acutely identified by Jacques Le Goff between the "time of the church" and the "time of the merchants," a tension that the Catholic West succeeded in eliminating only at the end of a long process of secularization of thought, by drastically isolating the first from the second. Nor should we be surprised to find a much less violent contrast than among their Christian neighbors between "carnival time" and "normal time," though the tendency to distinguish the two naturally existed among Jews too. This had nothing to do with the greater respect for religious and moral values that Jewish apologetics has always invoked in this connection: instead it was simply a natural consequence of the attenuated contrast between sacred and profane time stressed above. The rigorous attitude of the ritualists could not fail to take advantage of this fact to insist on the prohibition of anything that might have contributed to aggravating the contrast by introducing out of the ordinary everyday behavior. What was at stake does not appear to have been the legitimacy of celebrating in itself, but rather the practice of putting on masks and disguises on the day of Purim and dancing with other men's wives. Perhaps another reason why it did not occur to them that everything forbidden during the remainder of the year might be permitted during Carnival was that they did not make an absolutely antithetical distinction of the sacred and the profane in everyday life.

This should suffice to establish a kind of general rule. The secular "time of the synagogue" was in harmony with the "time of the merchants," the bankers and all those who worked, and in contrast to the "time of the church." The "time of the church" was of course in contrast to the time of the merchants, the bankers, and all those who worked. This is a trait of the Jewish mentality of the period worth elaborating on.

THE EVOLUTION OF THE PERCEPTION OF SPACE AND TIME

THE TRANSITION TO THE MODERN era marks a radical change. The process was identical to the one that led, by a different route, to the restructuring and redefining of the opposition between Jews and Christians, and hence to a new collective self-awareness, and, as a consequence, to an altered perception, among other things, of the category of time. As a result of the general secularization of thought, the Jewish perception of time naturally tended to become more uniform with that of their Christian neighbors. The result was a restructuring of the "time of the synagogue," which became less and less secular from this point on, and therefore more closely in line with the "time of the church." This transformation cannot be studied without taking into consideration the parallel transformation in the perception of space to which it is so closely connected. We mentioned above the other trait typical of the perception of the synagogal space, and saw how the latter was imbued with powerful secular elements, which led to its being opposed to the Christian ecclesiastical space, in an opposition that was simply one more particular aspect of the more general opposition between *Ecclesia* and *Syn-*

agoga. Here again, it comes as anything but a surprise when, in due course of time, one encounters, again as a consequence of the secularization of Western thought, another change parallel to that in the perception of the times of the synagogue. A rapid glance will clarify the traits characteristic of premodern times.

It is common knowledge that the removal of the restrictions regulating the building of synagogues was translated, in the modern era, into an architectural tendency to build monumental synagogues, more and more similar to Christian churches. One might be tempted to see in this a manifestation pure and simple of the tendency to assimilate. From the point of view suggested here, however, we must see in it something more. If what is involved is assimilation, then it is first and foremost assimilation of the general categories that caused Judaism to be seen as limited to the area of religious practices and not as a global condition informing all sectors of existence. There is nothing unusual, then, in the fact that the delimitation of the Jewish space, after a lengthy period in which the notion of collective identity underwent a progressive restructuring, had the predictable result of emphasizing its sacred aspect, erasing the secular elements previously discussed, thereby transforming the synagogue into a kind of Jewish cathedral. In fact the synagogue becomes more and more a place where people assemble to turn in prayer to God. Profane activities have to be transferred to another venue. There is surely no need to pause to examine in detail what has become for us an everyday reality.

One of the most tangible signs that such a process of transformation was under way may be perceived in the tendency to insist, from the sixteenth century on, that the synagogue be decorated in a way previously unheard of. The contrast between Jews and Christians on the level of their social and cultural self-perception, in addition to the juridical interdictions based upon never abrogated Roman law, naturally did not permit this tendency to manifest itself outside the specifically Jewish space; it therefore found extraordinary expression within that space. It was not a case of the unexpected discovery of an artistic sensibility hitherto in abeyance: one has only to recall the many Jewish art objects and illuminated manuscripts produced before the sixteenth century. From that moment on, however, the quantity and the quality of the decoration of the public synagogal space became remarkably different from the decoration of private Jewish space, leading to a much more pronounced distinction between the two than had existed in the past. It is nonetheless practically impossible to draw a clear dividing line between the two spaces, given that it was usually still difficult to say where one began and the other ended: synagogues were still located next door to the private apartments in the same building, and in many cases were not more than unusually large rooms in one of these apartments. The most extraordinary examples of synagogal art go back in any case to this period of transition, and may still be seen, for example, in the beautiful synagogues of the Venice ghetto, recently restored and opened up to the public, or the synagogue from Conegliano Veneto, which was moved to Jerusalem where it has been restored and is used as a place of worship by a community of Italian-rite Jews, as well as a public museum.

In the course of the transition to the modern era, this tendency gained in intensity and in degree of exteriorization. One has only to think of the synagogues built during the nineteenth century or in the initial decades of the twentieth: majestic, grandiose, competing architecturally with the Christian churches—a competition unthinkable of course in premodern times. All that had been suffocated and repressed by legal prohibitions, cribbed and confined to the space of mythic imagination, exploded in a clamorous exhibition of monumentality, magnificence, and outward-looking urban embellishment. One might label it a vigorous assertion of the presence of Jewish difference, corresponding to a need for self-expression. Perhaps those who speak of an awareness of the danger threatening that diversity from within and the concomitant necessity of defending it by insistently proclaiming its essential vigor on the outside are not entirely wrong. Other traits parallel to the ones already mentioned could easily be pointed out, all bearing witness to the same transformation of the synagogal space into a space increasingly devoid of the secular elements that had once characterized it in premodern times. The role of the rabbi, for instance, came to more closely approximate that of the priest or the pastor, moving further and further away from that of doctor of Jewish law, president of the tribunal, master of jurisprudence; increasingly detached from the public of which he had once been an integral part; increasingly less representative of the general public opinion of which he had once been the symbol. What one encounters here then is another set of expressions of the same transformation, that of the synagogue from a tendentially secular space to a religious space, a Sanctuary, a Temple, in which people gather almost exclusively in order to pray, a space from which all of the secularly oriented activities discussed above have been removed. A general conclusion may therefore be drawn. The space of the "secular" synagogue corresponded to the time of the "secular" synagogue: both underwent parallel transformations, and the synagogal space, as it gained in sacredness and became separated from the profane space, became more and more similar to the space of the Christian church.

So far we have only spoken of the sacred space. To the change in perception of that space, however, corresponds a parallel change in the perception of the existential space in its entirety. Chapter 1 already described how the Jewish space gradually became less dispersed in the new situation imposed on account of the pressures imposed by those in power, as well as by the force of economic circumstances. After abandoning the majority of Italian cities, the Jews directly affected joined up with their other coreligionists elsewhere, though still preferring the remaining cities to the countryside. As it lost in the area of its diffusion, the Jewish space gained in concentration. The institution of the ghetto brought this process to a head. Seen from outside, the phenomenon can certainly be considered as an individual case typical of all of the attempts to separate and segregate supposedly anomalous, and therefore dangerous, groups, in the name of the health of the Christian body politic as it restructured itself on the eve of the modern period, along the lines illustrated by Michel Foucault in his *Madness and Civilization*. The tendency to exclude the Other became more and more pronounced and reached its outer limits, until the absurdity of the process and the need for change became self-evident. Seen from within, the process is analogous: the perception of an abnormally defined existential space, which tended *in loco* toward zero and toward the infinite, was not destroyed by the Jews' demographic concentration and still less by the institution of the ghetto. On the contrary, these developments caused it to become exaggerated. The tendency toward restriction *in loco* is obvious and all the more noticeable in that it corresponds to a moment of urban expansion on the part of the Italian cities, whose growth was particularly intense in the course of the sixteenth century. The dilation of the external space was in its turn a consequence of the more general dilation of space produced by the new geographical discoveries and by the large-scale revolution in the demographic distribution of the Jews following their exodus from the Iberian peninsula. The sense of enclosure must have been suffocating.

Another contributing factor in the perception of the categories of space and time must have been the fact that the perception of group homogeneity was also affected, especially in the second half of the sixteenth century, by the arrival of the newcomers, from East and West, for the most part merchants. It was not only that they brought with them a different conception of time, in their case a genuine "time of the merchants." It involved a whole range of behaviors, customs, and habits. Different religious rites made it necessary to increase the number of synagogues in the cities, which constituted another element of disruption of the status quo. It was mentioned earlier that, similarly to the division of Christians into parishes, the various synagogues served mostly to stress the idea of differentiation *within* the group, rather than their difference with reference to what lay outside, the latter difference being in any case already vigorously proclaimed and corroborated by enclosure within the ghetto. This multiplication took place just about everywhere: it was strikingly evident in Venice, Ferrara, Ancona, cities, that is, whose attraction for the Levantine merchants was especially powerful. It was less evident, even at times completely absent, in other cities. It is true that the phenomenon of differentiation according to rite was not entirely new: Jews of Italian origin had become accustomed in the past to coexisting with coreligionists of Franco-German origin. It has already been seen that when the government referred to "German" Jews in Venice, it was really referring to Jews of either Ashkenazi or Italian origin, in other words, all the Jews who settled in Venice (and were incorporated into the moneylending charter) when the more numerous Ashkenazi were setting the tone. But the restructuring mechanism did not depend on a single dynamic element: the restructuring of the notion of time should not be interpreted therefore merely as a consequence of the increased presence of Levantine merchants. Jewish time was also affected by Jewish demographic concentration, which increased the possibilities for collective activities, thereby compressing the time available, disrupting its uniformity and slowness, and at the same time enriching it in dynamic variety. Wherever a number of different factors combined, the phenomenon acquired an appreciable degree of acceleration. If restructuring occurred more rapidly in Venice than in Mantua, this was certainly no accident.

THE ROLE OF THE KABBALAH AND THE CONFRATERNITIES

THE MECHANISMS governing the restructuring of time and space in the Jewish consciousness are still inadequately understood. They are no doubt the quite complex result of combinations of events such as those just mentioned with gradual changes of mentality, which it is difficult to put one's finger on precisely, but which are nevertheless somehow epiphenomenally discernible. Among the long-range changes, one is particularly significant for our argument: the transformation of the practice, study, and uses of the Kabbalah from esoteric to exoteric, and its resulting spread through all levels of the Jewish social body. This transformation was the high point in a tendency already immanent in the Kabbalah since its first appearance in the thirteenth century: the humanization of the worldview. In this connection, the spread of the Kabbalah must be seen in the context of the more general evolution of Jewish thought from the Middle Ages to the modern era. The topic deserves more detailed discussion than can be devoted to it here. To capture one significant aspect, one need only think of the magical elements in the Kabbalah and their different degrees of expression—from the theurgy implicit in the conscious practice of religious precepts down to the out-and-out magical and clandestine practices of which the popular use of the term "cabala" (Fr. *cabale*, etc.) is a symptom.

There can be no doubt that kabbalistic practice played a central role in the restructuring of space and time in the social reality of West European Jews, and the case of Italy is highly paradigmatic, since the peninsula was in fact the fertile soil for the transmission of the Kabbalah to the rest of Europe after the sixteenth century, the point of contact between Safed and the West, through the men who sailed in and out of Venice and the printing presses in operation there. As far as the main events are concerned, the process was a very simple one: the study of kabbalistic texts became mixed with the study of other traditional texts within the synagogue. Toward the end of our period, study activity was transferred to the confraternities. Thus it was that the detachment of this profane element from the synagogue took place, further encouraging the latter's sacralization. For example, in Venice at the close of the sixteenth century, as a result of the fervent promotion of Rabbi Menaḥem Azariah da Fano, the study of the Kabbalah was introduced into the Italian synagogue from 1575 on. This marks the first phase of the transformation: the rest followed gradually along the general lines described above. From the point of view proposed in chapter 6, this would constitute yet another example of the mediating role played by the confraternities—an extension, in other words, of strictly social mediation to activities more properly speaking of a sociocultural nature, and from this level to that of mental attitudes. Study meetings organized by the confraternities were in fact less formal and rigid in nature than those organized by the synagogue. It was therefore easier to include, along with the conventional subjects of study, in particular the Talmud and the ritual Codes, not only other less conventional subjects, especially the Kabbalah, but also certain specific types of more profane activity. In other words, the restructuring of the relationship between sacred and profane was more easily effected in the space of the confraternities than in that of the synagogue. In the same category, one may include the introduction of the use of coffee not only for the purpose of staying awake during the vigils required by certain ritually sacred activities that took place in the confraternity, but also its use as a socially profane interlude between two different times of prayer.

In this way, chiefly through the activities of the confraternities, the divorce between sacred space and profane activity, and therefore between the time of the synagogue and profane time, became a fait accompli. Jewish time suffered the same fate, though in a more nuanced fashion, at least so long as the observance of religious precepts remained categorical. But Jewish time too began to be perceived less and less as opposed to Christian time, as the opposition itself became more and more confined to religious practices. Even the latter became weakened when religious observance waned, leading ultimately to the complete dissolution of the sense of Jewish difference with regard to the categories of time and space. And since these are the categories essential to any act of self-awareness in the context of the world around us, the result was the uneasy search for a new definition of Jewish identity, a search that is still going on today.

VIII
SOUNDS AND
SILENCE

THE REALITY OF SILENCE

I F, A S W E H A V E S E E N, Jewish otherness conditioned the spatial and temporal universe, it also conditioned the universe of sound. The Jewish world presented itself in the first place as more silent than the surrounding Christian world. In one sense, this was a consequence of the uniqueness of the demographic pattern and of the economic activities of the Jews, to say nothing of the influence of the latter on the Jewish perception of space. The differences between the two phases of our period, although not entirely absent, are, from this point of view, more subtle. It has already been observed that, in the context of extreme dispersion that characterized the first phase, Jewish space appeared formless, tending either toward zero or toward infinity. The Jews, isolated in hundreds of towns and villages, could not be aware of themselves as participants in a common Jewish space, except for the space that transcended their individual places of residence, a space in which social relationships could be kept up only by correspondence. This was as true of the smaller as it was of the larger cities. Four or five families, however numerous, were obviously insufficient to create a specifically Jewish space, even though they might live in the same neighborhood or in the same street; and, in any case, it has already been seen that cases of this kind were few and far between. In such a state of affairs, *silence* (to be understood of course in a relative, not a literal sense) remained the essential distinguishing feature of the Jewish condition. On occasion this silence was imposed from without, at other times it was self-chosen. When imposed, its imposition was due to the fact that the Jews did not belong in Christian society, and hence to the reduction of verbal communication with Christians to the minimum strictly necessary, the presence of Jews in such minimal numbers being incapable of providing a viable alternative. The slim evidence for purely social contacts between Jews and Christians, as in the case of the games of chance in which both participated, does not affect the nature of these conclusions. But the Jews' silence was also chosen, in the more general context of the Jewish tendency to cancel their presence, whereas their Christian neighbors tended to underline and exaggerate it, given that from the Christian point of view that presence was something abnormal. It may be added that the inclination to choose silence was just one more manifestation of the more general propensity on the part of the Jews to elide and conceal their presence, while at the same time seeking, unconsciously and paradoxically, to be as fully integrated as possible in a society determined to exclude them and with which, in any case, they had very little in common.

THE IMPORTANCE OF LETTER WRITING

ONE OF THE CHIEF CONSEQUENCES of this situation was the flourishing of the epistolary genre, which became one of the most frequent forms of expression in Renaissance Jewish literature. The letter, *sermo absentium*, served only to exaggerate the perception of the social universe in terms of silence rather than of sound, since writing almost completely replaced actual meeting and conversation. This assertion should, however, be qualified somewhat, bearing in mind that as yet the divorce between "reading" and the sonorities of the voice, typical of the modern age, had not yet occurred. It was still customary, among both Jews and Christians, to read aloud rather than silently. But this form of sonority was nonetheless different from that of conversation. In a certain sense it amounted to replacing the natural sounds of conversation with a surrogate. However that may be, the result was the tendency to make letter writing one of the pillars of primary education. Children were habituated to write a letter a day to their fathers, even when they lived under the same roof. It was the custom to write letters to one's relatives, to one's friends, to everybody. They wrote about everything—whom they had met the day before (the occasion was usually a religious holiday), whom they expected to meet the next day, noteworthy events, ideas they had gotten from something they had read, and, naturally, about the business of the moment. For the modern historian these letters are a gold mine. The recent publication of several epistolary collections has provided the historian with a rich seam to exploit, notwithstanding the inevitable stereotyped formulas encountered in many of the letters. The mentality of these bored individuals, frequently isolated in villages so small that cities like Venice or Ferrara seemed to them enormous metropolises, is unveiled before our eyes in these epistolary exchanges, whose purpose was to maintain contact with relatives and friends residing sometimes no more than a few kilometers away, but difficult to meet because of the slowness, danger, and cost of transportation and the primitive state of the ways of communication.

The fact that they expressed themselves preferably through written correspondence naturally led to the accentuation of agreements and disagreements, to say nothing of the ceremonious literary decorum carried to exaggerated lengths in the literary models transmitted by the complex medieval tradition, models that the change in mentality that took place in the Renaissance does not appear to have substantially modified. It was common to indulge in poetic diction, in puns, in complex wordplay, in other words in the literarily elaborated epistolary form, which required a great deal of attention to write, as well as to appreciate its nuances. A letter could be so complex and difficult upon occasion as to require a second letter to permit the reader to penetrate its meaning. And often, the more trivial the subject matter, the more complex the literary treatment. Contemplating today the dimensions of this correspondence, we occasionally have the impression that we are dealing with a collection of compulsive graphomaniacs!

The changes that occurred in the second phase of the period did not have a revolutionary effect on the Jew's perception of his exclusion and alienation from Christian space. On the contrary, though he many have been given more opportunity to converse with his Jewish neighbors in the ghetto, in the extremely stifling atmosphere provoked by the imposition of segregation and exacerbated by the urbanistic expansion of the sixteenth century, his sense of isolation and estrangement from Christian space could not help being reinforced. Despite the deafening noise of the crowd, packed together and sealed off in the most limited of spaces, or rather because of it, a silence partly metaphorical, but in part indubitably real, remained characteristic of the Jewish condition. It was, in any case, imposed by contrast: the need for intimacy made it necessary, the need not to expose oneself, so much the more because to expose oneself was a risky business. A young tutor, writing toward the end of the sixteenth century to reassure his addressee of his discretion in a certain affair, declared simply: "You may be sure, my lord, that I shall be careful not to speak to anyone about it, as is only natural in any case, *given the fact that I am a Jew.*"[1]

Throughout the period the letter composed in Hebrew remains the chief means of communication, especially for individuals with a certain cultural affinity. In spite of the opportunities offered by demographic concentration for the development of oral communication, *writing* remained the indisputed queen of the field, to be dethroned only at a later date as a result of the decline in the knowledge of Hebrew. The use of writing in the place of oral discourse is one component to be related to the features of the culture of their Christian neighbors. Jewish rhetoric found expression, then, above all in writing, in the literary production examined briefly in chapter 5. From the present point of view, it could be called a rhetoric of silence, despite the fact that it was often produced against the background of the overwhelming din of the stifling overpopulated ghettos. A rabbi active in the first half of the seventeenth century, a period that saw a truly extraordinary literary flowering, gives us a rather picturesque insight: when he attempted to define the essence of the spiritual creativity of the ghetto, the only activity to come to his mind was *writing*, to which he dedicated several fine pages in the introduction to the bulky collection of his sermons, comparing it to the industry of the ants, who never steal from their fellows, but store up one by one the grains of cereal they have gathered.² The association of ideas probably contains a reference to the densely packed demographic structure of the ghetto.

THE ABSENCE OF DIALOGUE BETWEEN JEWS AND CHRISTIANS

THE SUGGESTION that silence be considered as the distinguishing feature of the Jewish condition should not be understood as an affirmation that Jews did not speak at all! They did speak, at times to excess, *when they had someone to speak to*, or, to put it more precisely, to converse with, which is not exactly the same thing, since conversation implies a mental affinity, a common meeting ground at the cultural level, an identity of interests that is not normally separate from the other levels of existential structure. It is true that at times the encounter at the cultural level conditioned the other levels, creating affinities of interest where there had previously only been disagreement—no one will deny that in every conflict among nations the role of the intellectual is to create a bridge. Nevertheless it is also true that this bridge is not opened up automatically wherever there are intellectuals, that it takes courage, indeed audacity, to construct it, and that as a rule it is only the best of minds who make its construction their business. These two propositions are not mutually exclusive; indeed there is no contradiction between them. On the contrary, it is the truth of the latter assertion which keeps the torch of hope burning in times of conflict, which are unfortunately the rule.

Simone Luzzatto, reflecting on the tendency toward reciprocal cultural detachment between the Jews and Christians of his time, came to sad conclusions regarding the future of his people, subject as they were to the good will of others. In Luzzatto's opinion, in the situation in which the Jews found themselves at the time, "having no other form of freedom apart from the employment of their minds in studies and learning, they should devote themselves to these things with every waking thought and effort, holding for certain that the unity of dogma, the protection vouchsafed to them by Princes, and the conservation they have for so long enjoyed amid so many oppressions, are the fruit of the virtue and doctrine of a few in their midst, who have won credit and authority with the Rulers, and, since they lack any other opportunity to aspire to the grace and favor of the great, they should hold it for certain that, if they cease to appreciate learning and esteem among the virtuous, they will fall into some notable decline, and into a more despised oppression than they ever suffered in the past."[3]

For Luzzatto, evidently, there was no other hope beyond the spiritual affinity among the members of the elite who made up the "Republic of Letters," enlightened and liberal, in whose bosom the dialogue between Christians and Jews was still possible. He was surely right. Never, either in the Middle Ages or in the Modern Era, was the dialogue between rivals possible outside of an encounter on an intellectual plane. It is nonetheless clear that, as Simone Luzzatto rightly observed, in the case of men divided by a conflict, this encounter was a necessary condition, but not of itself sufficient to set in motion the process of reconciliation and mutual understanding: for this one had to work, since it certainly would not occur spontaneously. Indeed, the opposite was usually the case. During the Renaissance, encounter and dialogue were not the result of an understanding, which would have implied the elimination of the fundamental opposition between Jews and Christians; instead, they were the product of the intellectual tendencies of a very limited group of individuals, interested for the most part in procuring certain texts, and certainly not in laying the bases for a dialogue. On the other hand, it is also true that it was these very men who kept the dialogue itself alive. In any case, dialogue was the exception rather than the rule. The rule, as stated above, was the absence of dialogue between Jews and Christians. This is the sense in which one must understand the characteristic trait of silence proper to the Jewish condition: as an absence of conversation or dialogue with all those outside the Jewish space, which frequently led to the complete suppression of the word, especially when the Jewish space tended toward zero. We have already seen how the Jewish space showed a marked component of religiosity, a natural consequence of the very definition of Jewish otherness. We have also pointed out how, likewise as a natural consequence, in the sacred space *par excellence*, the synagogue, the elements were reversed because of the introduction of a strong component of the profane. It will come as no surprise, then, if after what has been said apropos of the sacred, one finds a parallel inversion of the characteristic of silence at the level of the quotidian.

A PHENOMENOLOGY OF SOUND

RATHER THAN BY SILENCE, which was so typical of the atmosphere surrounding Christian ecclesiastical services, the liturgical activity of the Jews was characterized by its loudness. To the eyes of Christian observers, this could only be a cause for scandal. All of the many available witnesses, dating back to the earliest period, agree upon this point. Prayers were recited out loud, the more important sections were recited in unison, the poetical compositions of the liturgy (piyyutim) had refrains that the entire congregation recited along with the officiant. For a visitor entering the synagogue, nothing was more typical than this noise that defined beyond the shadow of a doubt the group's identity. Outside the synagogue, but still within the compressed space of the ghetto, the demographic density could only accentuate the characteristic noisiness. It was, we maintain, a noisiness altogether different from the noise that met one's ears in the Christian space.

First of all, the language: Italian of course, but an Italian quite different from the Italian heard outside the ghetto. A cultural tradition, whose historical precedents and precise significance are still the object of discussion by linguists, left perceptible traces in the form of a specific dialect of Italian deformed and enriched at the same time. It was *deformed* because traditional elementary education, which prescribed the study of the Bible with a word-for-word Italian translation of the original Hebrew made for an inevitable deformation of the vocabulary of Italian and even more of its syntax. The consequence was a somewhat ridiculous fashion of speaking Italian, with transpositions of gender from masculine and feminine and vice versa, in accordance with Hebrew usage, and phrases that were nothing more than literal translations of the original Hebrew idiomatic expressions. It was, however, at the same time a language in a sense *enriched*, since it incorporated Hebrew words not easily translated into Italian, and above all denigratory words used to designate Christians and Christian practices, words obviously that the others were not supposed to understand: *To'evah*, which in Hebrew means "abomination," referred to the Church; *davar* ("word") was used to convey to one's interlocutor that he had better *keep silent* — which, after all that has been said, should come as no surprise. The numerous Judeo-Italian texts that have come down to us have preserved the flavor of this picturesque language. It is also found at times in the translations of legal documents originally in Hebrew prepared for the use of Christian magistrates.

Jews of French, Spanish, or German origin naturally enriched this deformed dialect still more, introducing words and idiomatic expressions from the countries from which they came. It is worth mentioning that the first literary monuments in Yiddish come from Italy. Venetian and Mantuan printers published the first volumes in Yiddish, destined no doubt for other European markets, but some of the Jews of Italy were certainly capable of appreciating them. Perhaps they did not speak the same variety of Yiddish as their brethren in Prague, since they would tend to interpolate words in Italian and Hebrew, just as they mingled Hebrew and Yiddish words with their Italian. There is much evidence of the persistence of this additional linguistic contamination at all levels. In short, a Christian would have no trouble recognizing a Jew by his manner of talking. So much is confirmed, for instance, in a completely natural way, by one of the witnesses who testified at the trial of those accused of having murdered little Simon of Trent.

Jews could also be recognized by their characteristic names: Abramuzio, Aleuzio, Dattilo, Consiglio, to cite but a few, could only be Jews — their names in fact were nothing more than translations or adaptations, along typical lines, of biblical or postbiblical names into Italian. *Consiglio* (Counsel), for instance, rendered the Hebrew *Yekutiel*, one of the traditional appellatives of Moses, the master of counselor of history. The men, however, retained their Hebrew appellatives in the context of the liturgy, where they were all called by name to read the Torah. This explains why the women had more "Italianized" names than the men, though this did not prevent many female names being typically Jewish in their formation: Virtuosa (Virtuous), Ricca (Rich), and so on.

In conclusion, it may safely be affirmed that the Jew was conscious of his own presence in society in terms of very definite otherness from the point of view of noise and silence as well as of time and space. The proposition remains valid not only for hearing, but also, as will now be seen, for the other senses.

IX
COLORS, TASTES,
AND ODORS

COLORS

THE SENSORY PERCEPTION of Jewish otherness, as was observed in passing in chapter 3, was very much alive at the visual as well as the auditory level. In the Jewish space, especially in the ghettos, dark colors—black, grey, green, blue—were dominant. The metaphorical significance attached to the conscious adoption of these colors has already been discussed in the light of medieval symbolism, where they stood for the choice of placing oneself on an inferior level with respect to others, the only viable option in a social order imposed by the Other. We have also observed the impression of quasi-monastic austerity created by such a state of affairs, an austerity encouraged by the sumptuary laws through a complex of ideological principles designed to make a virtue out of necessity and to represent inferiority as superiority—superiority, to be sure, of a moral and religious order.

Color symbolism was added to other elements already present as part of the observance of the religious law and its detailed tenets: the requirement that both men and women keep their heads covered, for example. It is true that Leone Modena, for instance, dared to remove his hat in the extreme heat of summer, whereas Jewish women in the Renaissance attempted, for the first time, it seems, in Jewish history, to transform the observance of the religious law into observance of the laws of fashion by wearing wigs to cover their heads. Still, this does not alter the fact that the reaction to Leone's behavior and the discussion over the use of wigs only confirmed the universally accepted rule, that is, that people's heads should be covered as a token of religious devotion. Governments, naturally, insisted that Jews be distinguished by their dress, the general rule being that yellow, sometimes red, headgear was obligatory, which contributed to the general impression of uniformity. The Jewish group appeared in the eyes of the others with a uniform, compact, monolithic aspect, which made the Christians feel threatened and reinforced their fear—the fear of the Jew. The yellow headgear worn by Jewish women was moreover the same as that worn by prostitutes, with the resulting assimilation of the former to the latter as far as their social perception was concerned. The contrast between the dark dull colors of their clothes and the red or yellow of their headgear served only to exacerbate the visual perception of Jewish otherness in terms of moral degradation as well as an evil power to be feared, to be kept at arm's length, not to be trusted. Be that as it may, even in places where they were exempted from the obligation to wear the discriminatory badge, the wearing of some form of head covering remained typical of the Jews. It is true that in this case the component of contrast heightened by the clash of the colors was absent: as a result, however, the impression of uniformity was heightened. The available illustrations appear to testify to a practically stereotyped form of headgear, very similar to the monk's hood, which it is difficult not to see as yet another, extremely eloquent, expression of forced introversion and closedness. In a word, a Christian whose path crossed that of a Jew, even outside the ghetto, was not as a rule in doubt as to his identity.

It was impossible for all of this not to have profound consequences for Jewish self-perception. Only very rarely was a Jew able to sublimate frustration into pride. In the course of a controversy between Jews of different classes, for instance, a rabbi advised his coreligionists to appear before their Christian rulers displaying in full view the yellow badge, so as to underscore the substantial unity of the Jews above and beyond political divisions, "because the Jews are comparable to the monastic orders and religious communities," he declared.[1] It would be wrong, however, to conclude that this attitude reflects the view of the majority. On the contrary, especially in the first phase, more characterized than the second by the aspiration toward integration into the general social context, the majority tendency was to seek exemption from the obligation to wear the badge. Those who enjoyed greater influence with the Christian rulers were as a rule the ones who were successful—a few famous doctors, wealthy moneylenders, and so on. We have already dwelt at length in chapter 3 on the mediating role between Jewish and Christian society played by these exceptions. This did not prevent them, from the point of view of the present argument, from being exceptions. The exception proves the rule, and the rule was that of the visual *definition* of Jewish difference within the Christian space.

TASTES AND ODORS

THE SAME HOLDS GOOD at the level of tastes and odors, especially those associated with eating habits. There was not a great variety of foodstuffs, and the Jews cooked and ate for the most part like their Christian neighbors. Bread first of all, since bread was still at the time the essential basis of nourishment, but also pasta, wheat, barley, and even Indian corn, once it had made its appearance in Europe toward the end of our period. Then came what they ate with the bread, a fairly limited assortment: greens as a rule, but also cheese, butter, eggs, and less frequently fish and meat. The poorer one was, of course, the more one's diet was made up of starchy foods and the less of proteins. Both meat and fish were usually preserved by salting—only the richest and above all the sickly could permit themselves fresh food products. Even though the topic has not yet been thoroughly studied, it is easy to imagine how many diseases, particularly of the circulation, were provoked by the excessive use of salt for food conservation. The prevalence of starchy and salty food products also led to a fairly high consumption of wine. Rich and poor drank wine rather than water. The result, for the Jews of Italy, was an extremely liberal attitude as far as the consumption of wine produced by non-Jews was concerned. Though in theory forbidden, almost all the Jews of Italy considered it permitted in practice. A controversy on this issue, which broke out toward the end of the sixteenth century in the context of the more general transformation of religious attitudes, served to point out that differences of opinion among individuals derived not so much from their ethnic origins as from their individual character traits.

At the time, despite the substantial similarity with the nutritional customs of their neighbors, it was possible to observe precise features of Jewish difference. We have in mind the specificity of the smells, whose strength and pungency were of course heightened by the shut-in nature of the ghettos, and whose diversity derived from the ritual norms imposed by religious custom on Jewish cuisine: the total lack of the mixture of animal fat and milk products, otherwise so characteristic of Mediterranean cooking, then even more than today. An entire dossier could be assembled on the topic of diet. What has been said so far, however, provides a sufficient basis for affirming that, generally speaking, Jewish difference was very readily perceived within the Christian space, thanks to a series of conspicuous elements of distinction. This perception did not necessarily entail a sense of contrast or tension with regard to the other set of features that they shared with the overall mentality of the period. This is a rule that will soon be confirmed at the level of attitudes and behaviors governing daily life in the miniscule Jewish community.

THE DAYS OF LIFE

BIRTH

A SON was certainly considered more valuable than a daughter. A tradition dating back for several millennia, whose weight is still felt today, did not leave room for any other way of thinking. Traditionally, the parents of a female child were consoled with the reassurance that "a female firstborn is a good omen for the male children to come." The father recorded the birth of his children in the place where things worthy of record were recorded, on a blank sheet or on the inside of the binding of a book, usually a Bible or a prayer book. Births were diligently recorded, not omitting the exact time of delivery: this was essential if the astronomical influences on which the health and the very life of the child depended were to be calculated. In recording the birth of a daughter, the father also wrote down the wish he hoped would come true one day: his daughter fully grown, no longer in her father's house, a wife and the happy mother of male offspring!

The birth of a daughter, however, like that of a son, was observed by hanging over the crib an amulet, made of silver if the family was rich enough to afford it, with the inscription *Shaddai*, one of the names of Almighty God. Once this was done, there was no further reason to fear the female demon Lilith, who was supposed to steal newborn children, and against whom special amulets were hung in the four corners of the infant's room. At the end of the first month, after the mother had visited the synagogue for the first time since her delivery, the Cantor blessed the little girl and gave her her name; Leone Modena underlines the fact that the name had to meet with the father's approval!' And that was that. The newborn girl was thus set on the slow road to learning what it meant to be born a woman in the society in which she had seen the light of day.

For little boys things were very different. From the moment of birth, the family's only concern was the circumcision, which was supposed to take place on the eighth day, unless the child were ailing. The circumcising Master was chosen and, if he was not a resident of the same town, a circumstance far from rare, especially in the first phase of our period, he was immediately sent a letter inviting him to set off on his journey. Next the two godfathers and the godmother were chosen, usually relatives, but sometimes just friends or people with whom the family had a business relationship. To be named a godfather was a sign of honor and respect on the parents' part. An acceptance showed that the gesture was appreciated. The least that could be expected of the godparents was a present, concrete evidence of the reciprocal affection binding the two parties. There was nothing unusual about choosing godparents who lived outside the city, to whom letters had therefore to be sent. The shortness of the time available made it essential to act quickly. If one was not to fall back on a form letter, the letter had to be prepared in advance, since there was no time to think of everything according to the correct etiquette under the pressure of events. If a little girl was born instead of a boy, there was nothing for it but to put the letter away in a drawer and wait for another opportunity!

First and foremost, circumcision compelled people to travel, highlighting the difference between the Jewish social space and that of their neighbors. This removal, which corresponded to something similar among the upper classes of Christian society, in other words among the nobility, was merely one more detail in a set of symbolic gestures, all bearing the same sense. The circumcision ceremony took place in the synagogue, which meant that the entire congregation took part. Through the religious ceremony, a social identity was confirmed; yet, the role of

A circumcision scene shown in a Hebrew manuscript of North Italian provenance, second half of the fifteenth century. Parma, Biblioteca Palatina, Ms. 3596, f. 268. Courtesy of Dr. Giulio Busi.

the synagogue was thus very different from that of the Christian church, since, as was seen in an earlier chapter, its role was more that of a social than a sacred place. At the same time, however, the synagogue was a sacred space by definition, the symbol of Jewish difference in the face of Christian society. The newborn child was received therefore into a sacred space within the city, isolated from its physical environment, but open to the outside, that is, to what lay beyond the city walls; in communication, then, with another environment, that of Jewry at large.

It was only in a period closer to our own, when, as was seen, the synagogue came to be characterized more in terms of its sacred than of its social function, that the ceremony was transferred to an inner space, that is, to the parents' private dwelling, another detail in harmony with what we pointed out in our preceding chapters. It is difficult to establish with precision the exact period in which this transformation took place. Michel de Montaigne wrote as early as 1580 that "as for circumcision, it is performed in private homes, in the child's own room, which is the most comfortable and best lighted."[2] It is true that the ceremony he happened to observe "took place in the entrance hall," but this was because "the bedroom was inconvenient." The present state of research does not authorize us to say whether Montaigne was one of the first to testify to the transferral of the ceremony away from the synagogue, since Leone Modena for his part writes that in his day, in other words in the first quarter of the seventeenth century, circumcisions were still performed in the synagogue.[3] We must not let ourselves be taken in in this regard by the evidence of circumcisions that took place in the presence of Christians, such as that observed by Montaigne, or even in a Christian household, like that described by Abraham Farissol.[4] Without excluding the possibility that part of this evidence was due to special circumstances difficult to trace and determine, suffice it to insist that the notion of a closed space is not incompatible with observation on the part of someone not organically associated with it, nor with the fact that the exhibition was directed toward the outside, as probably occurred with some frequency in our period. On the contrary: one is tempted to assert that the greater the tendency toward mental closure, in which there are strong hints of parochial sentiments, such as national pride, the more conspicuous the presence of manifestations of an exhibitionistic nature.

In any case, Montaigne had the opportunity to observe and to report in detail on what he saw. His report is not without interest. When Leone Modena came to describe the ceremony, he had very few supplementary details to add. For circumcision in the synagogue, one must of course make the necessary adjustments, which will be immediately evident. Let us read Montaigne's description, then:

The godfather sits on a table, placing a cushion on his knees; the godmother brings him the child, and then withdraws. The child is all swaddled, according to our custom; the godfather holds him out with his legs hanging down, and then the assistants, and the one who is to perform the operation, begin to chant, and the chant accompanies everything they do, though the whole thing lasts less than a quarter of an hour. The minister may also be someone who is not a rabbi, anyone there among them, anyone who wishes to be called to this task, since they consider it a great blessing to be frequently involved in it: they even pay to be invited, one offering an article of clothing, another something else useful for the child, and they believe that a man who has circumcised up to a certain number known to them, has the privilege that when he dies the parts of his mouth will never be eaten by the worms. On the table where the godfather sits, all the instruments used in the performance of the operation are laid out in order. Besides this, a man holds in his hands a carafe full of wine and a glass. There is also a brazier on the ground, at which the minister first warms his hands, then, seeing the child safely held in place by the godfather, with his head towards the latter, he takes hold of the child's member and with one hand he pulls on the skin at the tip, while with the other he pushes in the glans and the member. At the inner extremity of the skin which he holds still away from the glans, he places a silver instrument which holds the skin in place and ensures that in cutting it no harm is done to the glans or to the member. After which, with a knife he cuts the skin, which is immediately buried in the earth gathered in a basin which is among the other objects which form the panoply of this mystery. The minister then proceeds to use his fingernails to take hold of a certain membrane which covers the glans and to tear it off forcibly, pushing it back behind the glans. It appears that this involves a considerable effort and some pain. Nonetheless, they do not consider it in the least dangerous and the wound invariably heals in four or five days. The crying of the child is the same as one of our children held at baptism. As soon as the glans is thus uncovered, wine is quickly offered to the minister, who takes a little in his mouth and then proceeds to suck the bleeding glans of the child, then he spits out the blood, repeating the operation as many as three times. This completed, he is handed a screw of paper containing a red powder that they call dragon's blood, and with it he powders the wound. Then he wraps the child's member with specially prepared bandages. Having done this, he is handed a glassful of wine, which, on account of certain prayers that he recites, is said to be of benediction. He takes a sip, then he dips his finger in it and makes the child suck it three times. The same glass, exactly as it is, is then sent to the mother and the other women who are waiting in another room so they can drink what is left of the wine. Then a third personage takes a round object riddled with holes, like one of our civet boxes, and holds it first to the minister's nose, then to the child's, and lastly to the godfather's: they believe in fact that scents fortify and clear the mind making it more suited to devotion.

Montaigne was a very attentive observer. If he had been told it would have been better to begin his description on the previous day, he would certainly have done so with no less skill. He would have described the night before the circumcision, which was spent as a vigil designed to protect the child from evil spirits through prayer and study. The vigil was also a social occasion, especially for the women who gathered around the mother in their specifically female space. Social, cultural, and religious elements were so entwined together that it would be difficult to disentangle the various components without the aid of a cultural anthropological study that still remains to be done. Next, Montaigne would have attended the morning liturgical service in the synagogue, which would certainly have led him to notice further clues to the exceptional nature of the day. These signs would have been so clear that nobody would have been surprised by the omission of those portions of the prayers that are normally omitted only on feast days. Even those who had not yet heard about the event would have realized what was about to occur when they saw the two armchairs set up inside the synagogue: one for the godfather (instead of the table Montaigne saw), who would have sat on it holding the child by the knees throughout the entire operation, and the other, far more richly decorated, for the prophet Elijah, an invisible guest at all circumcisions, zealous defender of the alliance between God and His people, as he demonstrated on Mount Carmel (see 1 Kings 3), and hence defender *par excellence* of whomever respects the Covenant. A symbol of the Jews' desire to stress their faithful orthodoxy in the face of a world seen as idolatrous, and a symbol therefore of the essential Jewish Difference, imposed from the very moment he is received into the bosom of the Jewish people, examples of Elijah's chair can be admired in Jewish museums throughout the world, all of them authentic works of art, remarkably delicate in their workmanship.

One symbol followed another in a mystical sequence, to which the customs of the Kabbalists, openly adopted during our period, could only add further mystery. Indeed, Montaigne defined what he had had the opportunity to see and to describe as a *mystery*, conscious as he was of not having been able to follow, and therefore understand, all the details. And even though we know more than Montaigne, it would be difficult to give a synthetic explanation of all the symbols, given that a serious anthropological study, as previously remarked, has still to be undertaken. Let us stick to the most significant: the use of the right hand, the fact that the operation took place over a basin full of water, the burying of the prepuce in a pot of earth, the wine, the glass of benediction which ended the sacred ceremony — its contents tasted by the same mouth that had sucked the blood of circumcision, then placed upon the blood itself, and finally the dipping of the finger of the hand that had performed the operation and its placing upon the mouth of the infant while pronouncing the verse of Ezekiel (16:40) *Et dixit tibi in sanguine tuo vive, in sanguine tuo vive*. All these gestures are typical of a rite of passage, concluded naturally with a sacramental banquet, whose social dimension was underscored by the stress placed on the ostentation of luxury, against which the community ordinances never ceased to thunder.

Finally, it should not escape us that the rite was essentially masculine in nature: performed upon the male member, in the presence of men only, gathered around the father, while the mother was far from the scene, surrounded by the other women. The godmother, usually the wife of the godfather, was the one who mediated between the two male and female spaces. Even during the wake, and even when it took place in a private home, the male space was kept rigorously apart from the female

Jewish wedding ceremony as depicted in the legal work Tur Hoshen Mishpat, *copied in Mantua in 1535. Vatican, Biblioteca Apostolica, Ms. Rossiana 555, f. 220ᵛ.*

space. Montaigne found nothing to take exception to in this circumstance: his view of the world was in no way different from that of the Jews he was observing. Just as we saw Leone Modena remark in passing that the name of the daughter should be "to the father's liking," in the same way Montaigne wrote simply, "As in our own case, it is the father who gives a name to the child." This was an important aspect of a bygone mentality, according to which inequality among persons was the natural state of affairs, making it equally natural to consider the Other as either an inferior or a superior: everyone in his own place, men with respect to women, the rich with respect to the poor, the powerful with respect to the weak, Christians with respect to Jews. Through the act of circumcision, the infant Jewish male took his proper place in society.

THERE WAS NO YOUTH or adolescence as we understand it in the premodern world. We have already witnessed the efforts that were made in the education of young people in order to make them into adults in the shortest possible space of time. The brevity of life expectancy made it more possible that a young person would end up an orphan and have to look out for him or herself, if not also for younger siblings. This stress on adulthood formed a curious contrast with the practically total submission to paternal authority that was difficult to escape even at a fairly advanced age. This authority was paramount especially as long as father and children lived under the same roof. It is true that children were frequently emancipated and even granted their independence: strictly speaking, someone who had been exonerated under a special notorial deed was no longer subject to paternal authority. It does not appear, however, that formal emancipation was necessarily the prelude to leaving home and living independently. It was often more of a precautionary measure intended to safeguard the family patrimony from the dangers that might stem from the enterprises of one of its members operating on his own, or, alternatively, to distinguish between the earnings of the latter and those of the rest of the family. An example of the first type may be provided by the emancipation of Leone Modena's prodigal son.

The identification of the idea of the *family* with that of the household must have had a more metaphorical sense for Jews than for Christians, for whom it took the concrete shape of the family dwelling or *palazzo*, with the family coat of arms over the main entrance. It was nevertheless an idea based on the *name* of the family, which was of course the father's name. And here one finds another feature of the general mentality that contributed to the great importance given to male offspring who would bear the family name, even when they were legally recognized natural children. The family spirit was chiefly expressed in the hierarchical relationship obtaining between fathers and children and between siblings and other male family members. The figure of the father was considerably enhanced as a consequence. Although disputes between siblings were not at all rare, between fathers and children they seem to have been very exceptional.

Family dignity and prestige were based as much upon socioeconomic importance as upon the memory of the *greatness* proper to its lineage, such as might be the case for the *"four* families deported to Rome by Titus at the time of the destruction of the Temple" mentioned in our second chapter. One of the most characteristic and decisive factors on which the greatness of an individual—the pride of the family for all subsequent generations—was based seems to have been the extent to which that greatness was recognized and remarked upon by his Christian neighbors. This appears to have been more than a simple reflection of the fact that the role of community and group leader, a role that called for a prestigious name and matching wealth, was exercised particularly as a representative of the Jews before Christian rulers.

The memory of past greatness was tied to the family name. One had to be particularly careful then not to dishonor that name, to show oneself worthy of it. In case of necessity—an economic disaster, for example—it was thought right to transfer the onus of one's obligations onto public shoulders, advancing the claim, the right even, to financial assistance on the part of the community. It was to be supposed in fact that the latter had a stake in seeing that the bearers of illustrious names not be forced to suffer the shame of poverty.

The persistence of paternal authority was thus reinforced by the general mentality, which attached fundamental importance to the family name, in other words, to the name of the father. This principle of unshakable continuity remained valid in spite of the children's adulthood, and came on top of others, thereby helping to obliterate the traces of many important changes that occurred in the life of the males: we have already remarked on the lack of a rite of passage to the age of majority, which religious practice had fixed at the age of thirteen years and a day for male children and twelve years and a day for females. Even during the time when a son was far from home receiving his education (see chapter 4), paternal authority was continually nourished by the requirement that

the young man write his father a detailed daily letter, crammed with pro-
testations of devout submission, often simulated no doubt, but no less
influential in fostering a certain mental attitude.

And this is how the figure of the female also takes shape, as a powerless
silent underling. As a rule, before being emancipated, the groom would
bring his young bride under his father's roof, whereupon the father immediately extended his authority over her as well. From that moment on,
the bride ceased to all intents and purposes to be a part of the family into
which she had been born, her father's wish at the time of her birth. If
everything went according to plan, and if she had brought with her a
dowry befitting the social status of her husband, the marriage might seal
an alliance whose first implicit purpose was to consolidate the position of
the family of the groom's father, and in the second place, as a reflection
of the first, that of the father of the bride.

Marriage fitted into the rigid patriarchal system, with very little regard
for the age of the couple, though the available information on this latter
point is not really sufficient. Some couples married very young, others
later. The daughter of the famous kabbalistic rabbi Menaḥem Azariah da
Fano married at thirty, but this was assuredly not the rule. The fact that
marriage was above all tied to the creation of family connections led to
the stipulation of "engagements" between very young people. In order to
grasp the characteristic features of this mechanism, one need only recall
the engagements among kings and princes, which reached the limits of
absurdity with promises of matrimony between babes in arms a few
months old. Nothing of that sort, of course, took place among the Jews.
Still, it was considered perfectly natural for parents to draw up marriage
contracts when the children were thirteen or fourteen years old.

Even more than through a study of the marriageable age, one can understand how the mentality of the period conceived the relationship between family ties and the socioeconomic position of the *Household* by examining the attitude of Jewish society toward the dowry and its
introduction into the patrimony of the husband's family. It goes without
saying that a large dowry was a sign of the wealth, and therefore of the
economic importance, of the bride's family. A dowry, however, must also

be matched to the importance of the family one wanted one's daughter to marry into. Those who were unable to afford it had perforce to resign themselves to marrying someone with a lesser "title of nobility." This was a first source of energy which made it possible to keep alive a social dynamic otherwise condemned. But it was also another reason not to be too overjoyed at the birth of a daughter. Dante might have affirmed that the Jews feared the birth of a daughter more than his coreligionists (see *Paradiso*, XV, 103–105), since the Jews did not have the option of shutting their daughters up in a convent, a stratagem the Christian father might occasionally find salutary. The more daughters one had, the more dowries one had to provide for, which could be a risky business for the maintenance of the family's wealth. The selfsame risk, from the husband's family's point of view, was run if the sum of the "counter-dowries" turned out to be high. This "counter-dowry" was prescribed by Jewish law and was an amount specified in the marriage contract, to be paid, along with the dowry, to the woman in case of divorce or on her husband's death should she decide to abandon his *Household*. The structure of society could have found itself threatened by these customs in the same way as it was threatened by the bankruptcies of the rich. The very existence of the community could be placed in peril, given the fact that it depended on the payments made by the rich to the local government. This was a good reason to decide to reduce the amount of the dowry and the counter-dowry, as was being done in any case by the Italian cities themselves. If at the beginning of the sixteenth century the Venetian Senate passed a law limiting dowries to 3,000 ducats, the figures mentioned in the Jewish ordinances in the same geographical region must clearly have been lower. In 1506 Rabbi Judah Mintz ordered that the counter-dowry never be higher than 150 percent of the dowry, and that the total amount stipulated in the nuptial contract never be less than 100 ducats. As was the case in Christian circles, Jewish documents also attest to a close correspondence between legislation and practice. This has to be remembered whenever one is tempted to interpret the figures contained in these nuptial agreements as parameters by which to judge the relative wealth of the families. Their stereotypical uniformity must clearly be due more to the force of public ordinances than to any alleged uniformity of socioeconomic conditions. The study of parental wills in favor of daughters, a study that remains to be undertaken in a systematic fashion, would no doubt add significant details to this general picture.

It is worth pointing out that, once a woman was married, as the bearer of a dowry that in the case of divorce would have to be returned to her personally, with the counter-dowry into the bargain, she paradoxically ended up, in theory at least, in a position of greater strength than her husband, who continued to live in the shadow of his father. The specific weight of the bearer of a dowry tended in a certain sense to balance out the weakness of her position as a woman. A natural consequence of this state of affairs was the importance of the dowry, more from the woman's than from the man's point of view, to the success of the marriage. Be that as it may, another consequence was the meticulous recording in the wedding contract of everything the woman brought with her as part of her dowry. Furthermore, the presents brought by the guests on the bride's side were recorded separately from those on the side of the groom. Should the marriage end in divorce, each of the parties would have the right to his or her own! In this regard the documentary sources are extremely rich. In fact, the realization that disputes over the dowry question were so relatively frequent affords for the time being no more than a glimpse of the extent and complexity of a problem that to date has received only superficial attention and which is further complicated by the contrast between the provisions of Jewish law and those of the secular city legislatures. It is worth insisting on an important fact: as far as the right of the daughter to her dowry was concerned, or the obligation of setting the amount of the dowry according to the actual value of the father's wealth, or the exclusion of daughters from further access to the family wealth through the institution of the dowry, the custom that governed the decisions of both Jews and Christians on these points found justification in the provisions of Talmudic law and of Roman law, respectively.

In any case, in our period nobody married for love. Opportunities to meet and to get to know each other in private, so natural in our day, were practically nonexistent. "Practically," because occasionally opportunities of the kind did occur, at private parties, for instance, when it came time to dance. Even the intransigent rabbi Judah Mintz consented to allow bachelors to dance with marriageable girls, under the vigilant eyes of their parents of course. But, even if the possibility of a love story was not out of the question, nothing could be done without parental consent. The tendency to protect family wealth from attempts on the part of the poorer classes to take advantage of the theoretical possibilities offered by social mobility found institutional expression in the ordinances promulgated by Judah Mintz and his College of Rabbis. Whoever dared to marry without the consent of the girl's parents would be excommunicated. Of course there was no dearth of attempts to circumvent the obstacle on the part of poor lovers or of dowry hunters. The rule nevertheless remained that of parentally arranged marriages, subordinated to strategies of alliances among families, in the name of the "class" solidarity already glimpsed in Judah Mintz's ordinance. Our documents confirm the existence of a matrimonial policy among great families like the da Pisas, the del Bancos, the da Rietis, the da Fanos, and others. However, it was only to be expected that this policy should find itself curbed by the facts of a particular case: rich parents with an unattractive, strange, or otherwise problematic daughter clearly could not expect to make the match they might have hoped for. In the Renaissance some things were not all that different from the way they are today!

Wedding ceremonies were another expression of the mentality of the persons and of their time. In the first place, one notes the same awareness of the difference between Jewish and Christian social space found in the case of circumcision. The bride did not live as a rule in the same city as her husband: all the arrangements, therefore, had to be made by correspondence. The same went for the guests. There was no particular hurry. There was all the time in the world to make preparations without forgetting a single detail. Between the formal promise, which may be considered the equivalent of our modern engagement, and the marriage ceremony, months, sometimes even years, would go by. Throughout this period the fiancé paid visits to his future wife, bringing her presents con-

sonant with the dignity of her family and following the rituals consecrated by scrupulously observed traditions. Jews of Italian origin were accustomed to sending a fruit basket (of silver or porcelain, according to
one's means) containing fruit, accompanied by a stereotyped message:
"*Kallah* [bride], how do you like what your husband sends you?"

Should the promise be rescinded, this exchange of presents between
the fiancés could sometimes be transformed into tragedy. On account of
a detail of Talmudic law, by which a woman is considered formally married if and when her husband-to-be has given her an object of worth, at
the same time pronouncing the ritual formula "Behold thee consecrated
according to the law of Moses and of Israel," once the promise of marriage was rescinded some families would claim that the gifts presented to
the fiancée had been preceded by the solemn formula, and that the
woman was therefore bound forever by the marriage bond and that only
divorce could release her. Obtaining a divorce was no easy matter. First
of all, the decision to request it was the man's privilege, something he was
not always prepared to do: the temptation to use his position of strength
to his own advantage was too strong. Furthermore, once divorced, a
woman lost a great deal of her "value" on the marriage market. Quite
apart from the fact that henceforth people would always refer to her as a
divorced woman, marriage with a *Kohen* (descendant of a priestly lineage)
was forbidden. There is abundant evidence concerning disputes, frequently virulent, that arose in similar circumstances.

Once the couple was engaged, and once the standard presents had
been exchanged, all that remained was to wait for the great day. Here
again correspondence played an important part. The young husband-to-
be would write his fiancée and her parents, whom he began to address as
father- and mother-in-law, as well as her brothers and sisters. But he was
not the only one to spend so much time writing. The invitations had to
be sent out, to each according to his rank: the invitations were flowery
epistles full of elaborate literary expressions and veiled references to biblical verses that everyone knew by heart. It was no easy task. If one was to
convince people to attend the ceremony, one had to put on the pressure
discreetly, to flatter, at times to beg. What was being asked in fact was

considerably more than attending a wedding party. Those who had to come a long way had better start making preparations early: if they set off for the occasion, they had to be prepared to stay the whole seven days of the festivities and usually more, since they would plan to arrive on Friday before the wedding so as to be present at the solemn ceremony in honor of the groom celebrated next Saturday in the synagogue. To be a member of a wedding that took place away from one's own place of residence meant leaving one's own functions and one's own business for several days. What was involved was no negligible demonstration of group solidarity.

All these people coming from a distance for such an event served merely to reinforce the special features of Jewish space emphasized above in the discussion of circumcision. The local Jewish social space, compressed and closed off within the city, became, so to speak, exceptionally distended and enlarged in order to represent the true Jewish space, open and projected toward the outside, substantially detached from its immediate physical surroundings. The climax of this representation came with the entry of the bride into the city, like a princess followed by a train that everyone strove to make as impressive as possible, to the point that it became necessary to introduce curbing legislation, with which the various sumptuary laws abound. The local representatives gathered in the synod of Forlì in 1418, for example, decreed among other things "that when a bride-to-be arrives on horseback from another city, she may be escorted through the city she has come to by no more than ten mounted Jews and four on foot. Should she arrive by boat, no more than twelve Jewish men or women may accompany her to the wedding house." Further on, the order is given that "no Jew . . . may invite to the nuptial banquet more than twenty men, ten women and five children, whether inhabitants of the city or from outside. There is however no limit on the number of close relatives, down to the degree of cousins born of brothers and sisters, who may be invited." Ten men on horseback escorting the bride and entering in procession through the gates of a large city, such as Bologna, Ferrara, or Mantua, whose walls were only a few thousand meters in circumference, must certainly have provided quite an impressive spectacle, and even more so in the case of small urban centers like Montagnana or Este. One may also add the music, the lighted torches, and the flowers. The delegates to the synod were right in fearing the reactions of the Christians. All we needed was for these Jews to come riding into town like royalty! And although the Jews repeated in the words of tradition that the newlyweds were like a king and queen, the metaphor would not have made much impression on the hostile natives! One can get a better idea of the meaning in demographic terms of the number of guests at the wedding, bearing in mind all of our previous reservations, when we recall that in this period in many cities the total population did not exceed five thousand people, while the Jewish population was less than one hundred.

The wedding was celebrated in the synagogue. Italian Jews have jealously preserved this tradition down to the present. In this connection, one should bear in mind what was said earlier about circumcision. In the public sacred space, taken all together, the symbolic acts that made up the ceremony could only signify the blending of the public, the private and the national. The breaking of the wine glass, a propitiatory gesture to ensure fertility, was also associated with the national tragedy of the destruction of the Temple, which it was one's duty never to forget, even in the moments of greatest joy. It was not unusual for nuptial contracts to be decorated with miniatures representing the Temple and scenes of pastoral life in the Holy Land—scenes of other times and other places. In any case the very text of one of the seven nuptial benedictions was calculated to transport elsewhere the imagination of someone reflecting on the meaning of the words "Blessed art Thou, O Lord, who causeth Zion to rejoice with all her children." The rite was performed in one place, but it could, as it were, be transferred to another, placed on an imaginary level, detached from the concrete circumstance of its local physical context, adding a further dimension to the image of Jewish space described above.

There is no need to dwell on the details of the ceremony or on what followed. Jewish folklore blended perfectly with local lore to produce a rich and varied range of traditions that still await analysis from an anthropological point of view. Still, the fact that the ordinance prescribed the presence of at least ten men should not escape us. The text of the ordinance, drawn up for the first time in Italy by Judah Mintz and the members of his College, left no doubt as to its intentions: to ensure the presence of the public as a guarantee of the regularity of the deed. The ten men were necessary, according to the original formula, in a case where the parents of the bride were not present, to serve as proxies and protectors of the girl and of her family's interests. Later, the presence of the ten men was transformed into a habit. In this one may observe another trait characteristic of the blending of the public and the private in the solemnizing of a contract that affected the very identity of the group.

The elements we summarized in these pages are in perfect accord with those pointed out in the preceding chapter. Here too Jewish difference found expression, without any of that tension between centrifugal and centripetal forces that many historians have imagined, in one fairly typical set of factors connoting difference, coupled with another equally typical set suggesting similarity to the Other, the result of their belonging to the same historical context.

XI
DEATH AS THE
MIRROR OF LIFE

THE "GOOD DEATH" AS DESCRIBED BY CONTEMPORARIES

THE STUDY OF EVOLVING ATTITUDES toward death has
been especially favored by historical scholarship in the last few decades. Of all the specific aspects that have been brought to light, Philippe
Ariès, a pioneer in the field, has pointed above all the public dimension
that characterized the occasion in the premodern period, in marked contrast to today's way of death, dominated instead by the aseptic solitude
of the hospital: "People always died in public."[1] Death, the ultimate rite
of passage, involved a ritual fraught with meaning. As we study the ritual
of death among Jews, it is only natural to expect to find elements analogous to those prevailing in Christian society and that the various details
should fit into the general pattern traced in our preceding chapters. In
this, as in other cases, however, the study of Jewish society is considerably
less developed than that of Christian society. The few observations that
follow, therefore, should be considered strictly preliminary, awaiting a
more detailed and far-reaching study.

The ritual is a good place to begin. In his slender volume *Historia de'*
riti hebraici (*A History of Jewish Rites*) Leone Modena briefly describes its
principal features, as they had become crystallized by the first half of the
seventeenth century:

When someone fears he may die, he has ten or more people called in, among
whom is a rabbi, and if he does not want so many, he calls in as many as he

pleases. In their presence, he makes a general confession in the manner described above and then prays to God asking that he be made well, and, if it be God's will that his life come to an end, that God accept his soul, and that death be the purification of his sins, and, if he seeks the rabbi's advice or wishes to say something to him in secret, he does so, then he asks God's forgiveness and the forgiveness of all those he may have offended, and if he has children and family, he calls them to his bedside and gives them his blessing, or if he has a father or a mother, he asks for their blessing, and finally, if he has not yet made a will and put order among his goods and property, he makes such dispositions as he sees fit. . . .

As the sick man approaches the moment of death, when he is seen to be in imminent danger, he is never left alone; there is someone at his bedside day and night, and it is considered a good work to be present when the soul leaves the body of the dying man, especially if he is a learned and good man, according to Psalm 49: *Non videbit interitum, cum viderit sapientes morientes, etc.* And whoever is present when he breathes his last, tears some portion of his garment, as an ancient tradition. . . .

When he has given up the ghost, his body is placed on the floor, wrapped in a sheet, with his face covered and a wax candle at his head. Shortly afterwards they get ready to make him a pair of cloth breeches, and someone is called in to sew them, and it is usually women who go to be charitable, and the body is washed carefully in hot water with camomile and dried rose petals in it, and he is dressed in a good shirt and the breeches, with his square fringed shawl called a Tallith, and with a white cap on his head, and, a coffin having been made to his measurements, he is placed inside it, with a white cloth underneath and over him, and, if he is a leader of the community, they often make him a pointed coffin, and, if he is a rabbi, they place many books on his coffin, which is borne out of the house draped in black.

All the people gather, and since they consider it a very meritorious action to accompany the dead and carry them to their graves, everyone puts a shoulder under the coffin and, spreading the weight in this way, they carry him along. In some places it is the custom to carry lighted torches behind the coffin and to chant lamentations, while in others this is not the case, and the relatives go after the bier weeping and wailing.

Thus he is taken to the place of burial, which is a field set aside for that purpose and called by them *Bet Ahiam* [*Ahaim*], which signifies House of the Living, the dead being called living on account of the soul, and, when he has been set down, if the dead man is a person of regard, someone makes a sermon of his praises, then a special prayer is said which begins with the words of Deuteronomy 32: *Dei perfecta sunt opera, & omnes viae ejus judicia, etc.* After the words *Zidduch addim* [*Addin*] have been pronounced, a sack of earth is placed under his head, the coffin lid is nailed down, he is carried to the grave, which is a hole dug to his

Tombstones of two Sephardi Jews buried in the Lido cemetery of Venice. (1) David Franco, 1549. (2) Samuel Franco, 1629.

measurements, close by the graves of his other dead relatives. In some places it is the custom, having laid the coffin down on the ground, for ten people to turn the coffin around seven times, saying a prayer for the soul of the dead man, though other places do not do this. And the dead man's relatives tear the garments, then they lower him into the grave and cover him with earth, each one throwing a shovelful or a handful of dirt until he is covered. . . .

This is the custom in most places; though in some there are minor differences.[2]

Anyone who has witnessed a modern Jewish funeral will have no difficulty recognizing in this description many details that are still common practice. But, before pausing to consider a few of these details, it may be useful to compare this description with another account, unique among the documents of the time, the description of the ceremony that actually took place, more than a hundred years before Leone Modena's *Rites* were composed, on the occasion of the death of Rabbi Judah Mintz, the head of the Paduan Yeshivah (1509). It comes to us from the pen of Elijah Capsali, who, as was pointed out in chapter 4, was at that time a student in the Yeshivah. Here it is:

Shortly before dying, he sent for all the rabbis of Padua, among them my teacher Rabbi Isserlein, and these brave men of Israel gathered around his bed. Then he bid them persevere in the study of the Torah and in the observance of its precepts, and he commanded that the Master (the rabbi) be the one to show them the way to follow and the works they should accomplish. Then in their presence he conferred rabbinical ordination upon Rabbi Isserlein and ordered them to do him honor. He laid his hand upon him, blessed him and commanded him saying: "Now I am dying. May the Lord be with you. Do not allow the book of the Law of Moses to be removed from your mouths." Rabbi Abba Shaul [del Medigo] and I also were there to receive his blessing. After which, his son Rabbi Abraham Mintz approached, with his own children. The dying man had them come next to him on the bed, placed his hands upon their heads, kissed them and embraced them. When he had finished blessing his descendants, he composed his feet upon the bed and died, passing away on a Friday night at the ninth hour. He was ninety-eight years old. . . .

The next day, Saturday, after evening prayers, the notables of Padua gathered in the Great Synagogue, to discuss how best to honor that great man in accordance with the obligation to pronounce funeral homilies for learned men and heads of Yeshivot. It was decided that the whole community, adults and children, would fast the following day, the day of his burial. It was also decided to close all banks and to abstain from work so that everyone could come to pay homage to the deceased. It was further decided to dismantle the gates and the wooden stalls around the Yeshivah, on which the members of the Yeshivah rested during their discussions, to construct the coffin, which all of the rabbis and notables would then carry on their shoulders, as well as to keep torches burning all around while the funeral homilies were being delivered. All of this was decided by those in charge [i.e., the leaders of the community] with the acquiescence of Rabbi Abraham Mintz.

The following day, Sunday, leaving the synagogue, the entire congregation made its way to his house, where there was a large courtyard with a large room in it. The rabbis and notables stepped to the fore, raised up the deceased, and carried him on their shoulders to the room in the courtyard, whose walls had been draped in black. A black cloth was also spread over the benches. The body was laid on a raised bench. All around were other benches, on which the books he had used during his lifetime were arranged. Alongside his pillow a *Sefer Torah* was placed, in a new case. Next to the books stacked around the bier, Rabbi Abraham Mintz, his children, and another son of the deceased rabbi, God rest his soul, took their places. They were wrapped in their *Taletoth* [i.e., ritual shawls] and bowed down in sign of mourning. Then the whole congregation took their places all around the room, which was packed from one end to the other. Then forty great torches, or lamps as they are called, made of white wax, each one worth a Rhenish groat, the equivalent of nine *marcelli*, were taken out and distributed to the rabbis, the notables, and the most distinguished young men of the Yeshivah. They lined up in pairs, in order of their importance. I too, the least of them all, received a torch and was paired off with Rabbi Judah del Medigo, the son of Rabbi Elijah of blessed memory. We all stood thus around the bier and then we lit them. My master Rabbi Isserlein got up onto a special podium and delivered a homily until noon. Then we extinguished the torches. The leaders of the community then stepped forward and picked up the bier, which was wrapped in black serge. During the procession the bearers were changed, so that all the students of the Yeshivah and the notables of the community participated in his transportation, from which everyone else not considered worthy was excluded. When we arrived at the cemetery, we lit the torches again, and other funeral homilies were pronounced. Rabbi Hirtzen then came forward, recited the prayer, and raised up a great lamentation. A *Sefer Torah* was then lowered into the grave, in a new case so that it would keep for a long time, at the end where the deceased's head was to lay, then he too was laid in the tomb, while those present raised their voices high in lamentation. Whereupon we put out our torches and accompanied the deceased's children and the other members of his family to the room draped in black we spoke of earlier. There everyone took their places, and until evening came on funeral homilies on the text "This for Judah" [the name of the deceased rabbi; see Deuteronomy 33:7] were delivered. All of these honors were done to the above-mentioned deceased by the notables and rabbis of Padua.[3]

The main differences between the description of Leone Modena and that of Elijah Capsali come from the fact that the first is intended as a generically typical account, whereas the second is concerned with the exceptional case of an extraordinary man. Indeed, if the ceremony here described by Capsali had not been viewed by him as something out of the ordinary, he would not have felt the need to go into so many details. Nevertheless, precisely because of its unusual nature, his description is an invaluable complement to that supplied by Leone Modena and can be used for comparison and confirmation. If we take away or attenuate those elements of Capsali's account characteristic of the funeral of a great public figure and add in those elements of normal practice that he neglects to mention, it is reasonable to suppose that the resulting account will be fairly close to that of the death of an ordinary individual. In this sense, the peculiar features stressed by Capsali also fit into the general pattern, so that the "good death" of Rabbi Mintz can be read as an extreme case of the ideals held in common by the people of the time.

RITUAL AND SYMBOLISM

THE FIRST THING to be observed is the preponderance of symbolism in the ceremony. More tenuously alluded to in Leone Modena's account, it is developed to the fullest extent in the account of the death of the Paduan rabbi. Judah Mintz was a man invested with public responsibility, even before he was a family man; his quitting the stage throws strong emphasis on this dimension. One must make an effort to discern in this text those elements which even today tend to be present in the case of the deaths of outstanding personages and to observe how the ideal society of the day is reflected. It may appear natural then that in this instance community should take precedence over family, and in terms of community, leadership over everything else. Equally natural is the fact that in the spiritual testament designed for public consumption the concern for continuity in leadership should have pride of place. The *kind of leader* required, however, about which Judah Mintz had not the slightest doubt, is absolutely typical of the specific historical context of his generation. Indeed, if one bears in mind what was said in preceding chapters, one can affirm that at that very moment the model was undergoing a process of rapid transformation. The model indicated by Mintz is therefore doubly important. For the dying rabbi in fact the true undisputed and exclusive leader could only be someone ordained as a rabbi. This idea is underlined by the act of ordination conferred on the most gifted of the younger generation, Isserlein. This act, introduced in such a way and at such a time, is clearly designed to represent symbolically the welding of the Chain of Tradition as far was the exercise of authority within the Jewish society was concerned.

An analogous role in the context is played by the blessing of the entire community, which reproduces symbolically the blessing conferred by Jacob upon his children. As we saw also from Leone Modena's text, every head of a family repeated on his deathbed the deathbed blessing of Jacob called Israel (see Genesis 58–59), the ideal father of the Jewish nation, echoing as far as possible the gestures taken from the biblical passage that everyone, or almost everyone, knew by heart and which they had heard elaborated upon in innumerable sermons in the synagogue. Capsali's text stressed Judah Mintz's singular manner of interpreting the symbolism and semantics of the passage: what in the Bible in fact was a purely family context is here transformed into a decidedly public one. In other words, it appears that the death of the leader reproduces the death of the patriarch not only and not so much in the typology of *imitatio*, postponed for the most part to the final act, as in the affirmation of the essential unity of Jewish society beyond space and time, a *single family*, as it were, patriarchal in character, whose *pater familias* is none other than its rabbi-leader.

From this point of view, the biological family disappears practically into the background. And yet there is a notable effort to carve out a minimum of privacy in the midst of all the public aspects (the gathering of the family on the bed, the silent benediction of his children and grandchildren in contrast to the public blessing recited aloud), without however excluding the public from the scene. Without wishing to read more into the text than is really there, it almost seems, perfectly in line with other similar changes that have been pointed out in the Renaissance mentality, that the idea of the need to keep separate the public and private domains makes a first, timid appearance. Unless our interpretation is mistaken, this is all the more noteworthy in that in the present case it is reasonable to maintain (even according to the categories of our modern mentality) that the dying man really "belongs" more to the public domain than to his own family.

Neither Capsali nor Modena mentioned what in that period was universal practice, the custom, that is, of reciting on the point of death the biblical verse *"Hear ye Israel, the Lord is our God, the Lord is One"* (Deuteronomy 6:4). Capsali probably disregarded it because he thought it superfluous to insist on so obvious a point. As for Modena, perhaps he preferred not to mention a practice that might have given offense to the Christian reader, for whom his book was intended. However that may be, in a very ancient *midrash* (T. B. Pesaḥin 56*a*), read, reread, and interpreted countless times, that same verse is intimately associated with the paradigmatic death of Jacob. According to the *midrash*, the sons of the Patriarch themselves are claimed to have pronounced the verse as a token of reassurance for the dying man that the continuity of the tradition of the faith would not be interrupted by his death. In the course of time, the meaning of the verse had been enriched by a millenary historical experience, thus coming to reflect the gesture of defiance of all those who had been victims or martyrs of the persecutions undergone for having refused to abjure their faith, at least since the time of the crusades. It was also a reflection of the polemical attitude implicit in the defense of the difference rooted in the singularity of the faith in the One God, an attitude all the more polemical in the context of the Western world, where the Unity of the God of the Jews had always been opposed by them to the Trinity of the Christian God. The verse, in other words, represented the quintessence of the awareness of Jewish difference. Recited on the point of death, by the dying man and the others present, the declaration of the Unity of God introduced into the rite of passage the dimension of history, which unites past and future. This was most salutary from the psychological point of view, at a time when the sense of the nullity of the present was felt in all its terrible concreteness.

The moment of passing was accompanied by many ritual details crystallized by a centuries-old tradition, enormously more conservative in the case of death than in any other segment of human religious experience. In the premodern period this conservatism was thrown into still greater relief by the dimension of publicness that we have been observing. The "collective memory" of those present was subsumed, then as now at moments of the kind, into the competence of the one who, by virtue of some institutional affiliation, was called to direct the rite (rabbis, representatives of funeral confraternities, and the like), whose job it was to ensure the repetition of time-honored gestures, whose significance or appropriateness no one present had, under the circumstances, any desire to question. Someone would suggest that the eyes of the deceased be immediately closed; someone else would point out that, if the son were present, this duty was his; others took care to cover the dead man's face; yet others suggested he be laid out at once on the ground; and last, someone would take it upon himself to throw out the window the water contained in the pots in the house, only to be followed in this right away by the neighbors, who thus spread the news without speaking a word; and so on.

Most of these details were obviously marked by the characteristic Jewish "difference." In some, however, one may recognize the imprint of similar Christian usages, more typical of the common mentality than of any discordance in religious beliefs. Among the latter, the dying man's confession on the point of death, which had become institutionalized more or less everywhere in the course of the Middle Ages, should be particularly mentioned. Leone Modena recorded it diligently at the head of his schematic outline, underlining, however, one or two details. In the first place there was the presence of the rabbi. The latter is not at all indispensable in the Jewish rite, whereas the Christian rite cannot be performed without the presence of the priest. The symbol of the social mediation between the sacred and the profane, as well as of the conceptual mediation between heaven and earth, the presence of the man of religion served, in the case of this particular rite of passage, to facilitate the transition from life to death. Second, Modena underlines the institutionalization of the public nature of the rite through the custom of gathering at the dying man's bedside ten men, the minimum number necessary for the performance of the most important religious functions (*minyan*). This custom too had become established during the Middle Ages. In this connection, however, Modena added a consideration that must have had its roots in a widespread attitude: "And if he does not want so many, he calls in as many as he pleases," thus registering in his own way the progress made by the sense of privacy in the mentality of the period, in contrast with the public aspects, so rooted in medieval ritual. A similar phenomenon was noted earlier apropos of the death of Judah Mintz.

P ASSING OVER the many minor ritualistic details that accompanied and followed the moment of death, let us concentrate our attention on the funeral, the chief concern of the majority of the survivors, once they had made sure that the body of the deceased, in observation of the canons of religious propriety, would not be left unattended. The funeral, the very last of the ceremonies in which the deceased and the community to which he belonged were to participate actively, takes us back to the public aspect of death which in this service, by its very nature more public than the ritual of passage, was accentuated to the maximum. In the protocols of the funeral the structure and ideals of the society were clearly reflected. The rituals of precedence, so evident in the account of Judah Mintz's funeral, reflected the social position of the participants. One can say without the shadow of a doubt that in this instance the protocol of relative precedence exactly reproduced the seating arrangements of the synagogue and the Yeshivah, just as the protocol of Christian processions reproduced the sociopolitical hierarchy of the city. Anyone considered unworthy was excluded outright from the ceremony. It was not a matter of the practical impossibility of having everyone participate in the final homage to a venerated Master: in a community that numbered barely one hundred adults it would not have been difficult to admit everyone to the bearing of the corpse. But this was not done. As the *numerus clausus* of the forty torchbearers was defined, so too those chosen to transport the corpse took turns one after the other, rigid control being kept over who was eligible to do so. The criterion was one of sociocultural prominence, not one of age. Whereas, therefore, a callow youth like Elijah Capsali was called to take a leading role, old men of low social extraction took a back seat. From this point of view one should not miss a very important detail: women were absent from the ceremony, even the women of the Mintz household. A social event *par excellence*, the funeral rite was still an exclusively male affair.

The detail of the torches also throws into relief the tendency to give the public ceremony an appearance similar to that of analogous Christian ceremonies. In the case of Judah Mintz, there were those who did not hesitate to criticize this practice.[4] But the criticism was not heeded. In the interpretation of the use of the torches, which had in the event a two-fold purpose, the practical one of providing light and a secondary role of public affirmation, it was probably thought preferable to see a means of expressing more efficaciously the symbolism of light, associated from time immemorial with the idea of the ongoing life of the soul (Proverbs 20:27), as opposed to the darkness of corporal death. The still widespread custom of keeping lights lit in similar circumstances gives us some idea of the power of this symbolism. In any case, what seems to have been an innovation in Judah Mintz's day appears as a solidly established practice in the following period. The same goes for the black funeral decorations, considered noteworthy, perhaps extraordinary, by Capsali, but mentioned by Modena as standard practice. In this case, too, it appears that color symbolism, which instinctively linked black with seriousness and solemnity, and which, as was mentioned earlier, also received ideological formulation in the conventions of the day, turned out to carry more weight than the arguments of those who took exception to the practice, seeing in it too strong a resemblance to Christian customs.

CLUES TO AN EVOLUTION

MOST OF WHAT HAS BEEN DESCRIBED so far constitutes what are customarily defined as "the constants of long duration," from which it is quite difficult to derive clues as to the further development of a mentality. One was nevertheless able to point in passing to one or two indications. Evolution is best perceived, however, if one directs one's gaze to the effects of mortuary rites on the institutional structures of Jewish society. The dialectical tension between the traditional tendency of medieval civilization, which privileged the public and therefore visual aspects, and the encroaching modern culture, which, in cases such as these, emphasized above all the private aspects, removing them from public curiosity and observation, was gradually resolved in the exercise of institutional control. This was perfectly coherent with the overall development of community institutions we spoke of in chapter 6, though in a completely peculiar and noteworthy way. The institutional control of funeral ritual was delegated in general terms to the confraternities, which, in this instance, broadened the range of the functions they had performed in the phase preceding the consolidation of the communities. In that period, in fact, these associations were called upon to discharge responsibilities that, in the absence of an organized community, no other body could have performed. Even after the community became established in the course of the sixteenth century, rarely did it take upon itself the responsibilities that traditional practice attributes to the confraternities. In some cases, in Ferrara for example, even the cemetery continued for a very long time to be the property of a confraternity rather than that of the community. The institutional and sociological model can no doubt be compared with that of the voluntary organizations operating in various parts of the world, where for some reason the framework of central authority is weak. In this case, however, it seems that there was more to it than that. More than a merely conservative tendency, the persisting vigor of the confraternities in this specific area seems to attest to a change in the role they played, not dissimilar in any case from what occurred in other sectors too. Brought into being to respond to the need for public organization in the precommunity phase, that is, to mediate between the present lack of a community organization and its emergence, the confraternities now found themselves fulfilling a mediating role of an entirely different order, in a certain sense the opposite of their former role. They served to facilitate the mediation between the public and the private spheres in a period in which the need for a separation between the two was particularly felt. In other words, the funeral ritual continued to fall to the competence of the confraternities, a tradition still valid in most Jewish communities, thus acquiring a private dimension that the public nature of the ritual tended to annul. It is true that under exceptional circumstances, in which the need to demonstrate the social unity of a heterogeneous community was especially felt, a ceremony could be orchestrated in which all of the city's confraternities took part. This happened, for example, on the occasion of the funeral of Rabbi Samuel Aboab in

Venice in 1694. But such events were rare, exceptions that confirm the rule.

FUNERAL ORATORY

A COMPARABLE EVOLUTION OF MENTALITY is illustrated by the practice of funeral oratory. A very ancient tradition, accepted under Talmudic norms as a form of religious duty, the funeral sermon was of course also widespread among the Jews of Italy in our period. Both Capsali and Modena took regular note of the practice in their accounts. A public activity designed to bolster the cultural values of the community, the funeral sermon naturally served to reinforce the public dimension of the rite of passage, removing the deceased so to speak from the limited space of his own family and placing him at the center of the entire community space. In this connection too we may say that the degree of that removal had to be proportional to the specific weight attributed to the deceased in the defense of the ideals the society held dear, according to the same criteria that informed the orchestration of the "good death" of the rabbi Judah Mintz, and on the basis of which it was decided "if the dead man is a person of regard," as Leone Modena wrote. This being the case, it is not surprising that almost all the funeral sermons that have come down to us (a dozen in printed form, in addition to an unspecified number unpublished) are in honor of rabbis. Indeed, it was sometimes considered natural to deliver funeral orations in honor of some extraordinary personality who had not really been a member of the community. Sermons of this kind were pronounced, for instance, in Italy in memory of Rabbi Joseph Caro, the author of the ritual code *Shulḥan 'Arukh*, later adopted by almost all the Jewish communities in the world, who died at Safed in 1573. In this way, that sense of dilation of the local Jewish space referred to in chapter 7 found further expression, going so far as to include the entire *oikoumene* and to signify the national unity of the diaspora. In the same way, it was found desirable to extend the time devoted to delivering sermons of the kind well beyond the day of the funeral: from the documents at our disposal, indeed, it appears that this time included the whole week, sometimes even the month, of the mourning period. The demographic dispersion described in the first chapter of this book, combined with sanitary considerations, no doubt contributed to this phenomenon: if, as was to be expected, one wanted people from other geographical areas to be present at the funeral sermon, one had no choice but to schedule the most important speech allowing time to communicate the news to the mourners and time for them to reach the place where the sermon was being given. Thus, for example, a funeral sermon in honor of Rabbi Menaḥem Azariah da Fano (who died and was buried in Mantua) was delivered by Rabbi Samuel Portaleone in Lugo in the presence of one of the deceased's sons several days after the funeral, on the fast of the ninth of Av (celebrated that year on Sunday the tenth of Av).[5] In this instance the choice of the day of the funeral sermon was probably partly influenced by the coincidence with the date commemorating the destruction of the Temple. In these funeral sermons, the association of the figure of the rabbi and that of the Ark of the Covenant was not at all rare.[6] It appears in fact that the greater part of the printed sermons that have survived were delivered some days after the burial.

These funeral sermons also serve to delineate other typical aspects of the worldview of the people of the time. Absolutely noteworthy, for instance, is the progress made in this period by the idea of the usefulness of the sermon for the living, especially in inducing them to repent and to act according to justice, as the example of the deceased, or the very idea of death and divine justice, should have suggested: a position at odds with the conclusion that had emerged from the Talmudic discussion of the issue (see T.B. *Sanhedrin*, 46b), for which the funeral sermon was to be considered chiefly in the light of its "usefulness" for the deceased. The phenomenon may therefore be interpreted as part of the more generalized expression of that love for life implicit in the new sense of death that developed in this period. Perhaps one may also see evidence of a tendency on the part of the rabbinical establishment to "take advantage" of the situation in order to mold society in the light of its own life ideals, in a manner similar to that of the Catholic Church at the time of the

Counter-Reformation. And finally a connection may be suggested with the growth of pietistic tendencies in the religious circles of the time, in perfect accord with other kindred phenomena. The funeral oration, however, also had links with the humanistic tradition. The long sermon delivered by Rabbi Hirtzen before the bier of Judah Mintz, which lasted five hours, cannot help calling to mind the much praised oration of Giannozzo Manetti on the occasion of the death of a certain illustrious Florentine.[7]

Along the same lines, it is not surprising to find in Jewish wills of the period, recently brought to light by scholars and studied in the light of similar studies conducted on Christian wills, a set of attitudes quite comparable to the attitudes revealed in the latter: stereotypical professions of faith, whose conventionality is probably exacerbated by the inertial force of the notorial formulas of the day, more or less equally stereotypical provisions of a devout character — distributions of alms, bequests in favor of public (religious or pious) institutions, and so on. In the intentions of someone preparing to leave behind the environment in which he had spent his entire life, all of these formalities bore witness to the position he aspired to maintain for as long as possible in the minds of those who survived him (as seems to be the universal tendency in every time and place), as well as to the idea he had of life in general and of religion in particular, let alone of the instrumental role attributed to religious practices in ensuring the best possible destiny in the world beyond (which the Jews of course imagined in an altogether different fashion from the Christians). Even though there does not appear at first sight to be a great difference between the stereotypical formulas of the fifteenth century[8] and those of the seventeenth,[9] it seems reasonable to expect that a systematic study of a representative number of wills will make it possible to ascertain to what extent and in what form they reflect the overall evolution of the mentality, along with the other aspects alluded to briefly here. From what has so far been discovered, it seems in any case to be fairly clear that in this area too the general rule seen in the preceding chapters holds good: as far as attitudes toward death went, Jewish tendencies and behaviors were modeled on those of their Christian counterparts, so long as these did not represent a challenge to their religious identity, and so long as the Christian authorities did not step in to prevent it.

A curious example of such prevention has to do with the use of black drapery. From the sumptuary point of view, much as is the case to this day in Italy and elsewhere, the custom was intended to draw attention to the social prominence of the deceased and in particular of his family. The solemnity of which the black drapery was the expression was also the expression of social affirmation, not essentially different from the public ceremony of the funeral. In the logic of the period, which forbade the Jews any form of social affirmation, it was not therefore entirely unreasonable that they should seek and on occasion obtain special permission to wear mourning.[10] The exceptionality of the privilege granted to the few clearly reflected the sense of the norm, which continued to be that of exclusion or at the least marginalization, a condition which led on the part of the Jews to a corresponding aspiration to overcome that exclusion, without being compelled to renounce their own spiritual identity.

THE JEWISH CEMETERY

THIS BECOMES EVEN CLEARER from the study of the problems surrounding Jewish places of burial. The Jews' perception of their religious otherness called for the absolute separateness of their burial places, an idea in which the Christians fully concurred. If, however, the need for such a distinction was a shared sentiment, the manner of conceiving the means to effect it was quite different. A first radical difference sprang from the way the Jews perceived their religion, and the ritual norms that followed. In the eyes of the Jews, Christians seemed in fact to idealize the image of the dead god, and therefore not to take a negative attitude toward death; indeed they went so far as to attribute sanctity to the relics of the dead. For the Jews, however, the exact contrary was true — in part because they adhered to the biblical idea of the impurity of death (see, for example, Numbers 19), meticulously formulated case by case in postbiblical and Talmudic ritual norms, in part precisely as a result of their programmatic opposition in principle to what seemed to them the cardinal idea of Christianity. The Jews therefore insisted, often quite vociferously, on the contrast between the "dead God" of the Christians and their own "living God." One of the chief reasons for the idea of impurity associated with Christian places of worship came from the fact that they contained relics and saints' tombs, as well as the tombs of famous people buried *ad sanctos*. This explains not only why there was no burial of Jews *ad sanctos*, or in the vicinity of the synagogue, but also the immanent tendency to keep the cemetery far away from the populated area, so as to separate in the most concrete possible way the purity of life from the impurity of death.

There was another reason the Jews preferred to keep the cemetery away from the populated area. They wished to avoid as far as possible the exposure of their funeral rites to the eyes of the Christians. The latter in fact not only took every opportunity for mockery, making the rites the basis of popular comic theatrical spectacles, such as the well-known Roman *"giudiate,"* but, what was worse, they not infrequently disrupted the funeral ceremony, interrupting it with loud derisive comments. There were times when a police escort was needed to ensure safe burial, and often enough even this was insufficient: the funeral procession was thus compelled to abandon the bier and run away if they valued their skins.

The Jew's preference coincided with a similar Christian tendency to want to keep Jewish graves as far away as possible from their own built-up areas. For the Christians, granting the Jews the "privilege" of having their own cemetery, giving them, that is, the opportunity to acquire a piece of land for this purpose, was anything but self-evident. It was not at all rare in fact for it to be denied. Under these circumstances, it is easy to understand one of the motivations for settlement referred to in passing in chapter 1, the fact that the possibility of having a cemetery of their own was one of the first things to be considered when deciding where to settle. Should that possibility be denied, they were compelled to transport their dead to the cemetery of the nearest Jewish community, a circumstance that, given the prevailing conditions of transportation, could turn out to be extremely difficult and bothersome, particularly in the summer months, as well as hazardous. Rabbi Azriel Diena, for instance, records that when he lived at Pavia where there was no Jewish cemetery, the dead had to be transported to Cremona or some other neighboring town, such as Voghera, "thereby bringing grief and mockery upon the dead."[11] At Cremona the funeral epigraph of a Jew who died at Brescello and was transported to the cemetery of Cremona following his own express wishes can still be seen.[12] In any case, just as they were not too ready to make life easy for the Jews in their cities, so the Christians were loath to make it easy for them to pay their final respects to their dead. In a word, the Jewish tendency to keep to themselves combined with the Christian tendency to marginalize them, with the result that the social separation that sprang from the difference in religions was projected into the field of death: "Thus, while the Christians choose their final dwelling place *intra muros* [within the walls], in their churches and in the adjacent cemeteries, the Jews tend to be assigned a distant and suburban place of burial."[13]

Moreover, considerations of a practical nature made it desirable that the cemetery not be too far from the populated area. In the first place, closeness was advisable if some form of surveillance was to be effective and prevent as far as possible the profanation of the tombs by wrong-doers. The obsession with profanation survives even to this day in the collective memory of the Italian Jews and finds expression in some peculiar local customs, such as that by which the Jews of Ferrara imprint four Hebrew letters on the earth covering fresh graves with a special mold. Although it is not clear whether or not they have any specific meaning, they nevertheless make it possible to tell immediately whether the earth has been disturbed. Even more than the need for surveillance, closeness was promoted by the very mentality of the period, for the separation between the world of the living and the world of the dead was by no means as clear as it is today. Like the Christians, the Jews too visited the cemetery much more often than is the custom today. They went to speak with the dead, to feel them near, to seek their advice (which they gave to the living in their dreams), to have a concrete sense of the presence of death from which to draw inspiration to behave in consequence.

From this point of view, as the natural extension of the society of the living, the cemeteries had to reproduce visibly and effectively the characteristics of the latter. The inscriptions and emblems on the tombstones had to transmit successfully to visitors, to the members, that is, of the society of the living, a sense of the social prominence of the family of the dead person rather than of the greatness of the dead person himself or herself who lay beneath the stone. What are today merely sad monuments from a distant chapter of our history were then tangible projections into the cemetery space of features characteristic of the social space of the Jewish community.

The cemeteries of the Jews, then, convey quite effectively the sense of the Jewish condition in Christian territory. They were the expression of a mentality formed as a mirror image of the Other, even though at times in open opposition to it, a mentality that though separate, shared the same mind-set and was therefore intent on reproducing in miniature the same social world, of which the cemetery too was an integral part. *Extra moenia* [outside the city walls], distant but not too distant, even though today they may be in the downtown area on account of subsequent urban sprawl, many Jewish cemeteries are still in existence: in Padua, Venice, Ferrara, Mantua. There one can see, "photographed" in stone, the grandeur of the rabbis, the "nobility" of the Spanish and the Portuguese. The segregated cemetery of the Portuguese in Ferrara is a concrete demonstration of the group separatism of the Iberian Jews, along the lines discussed in chapters 1 and 6. In the gradual substitution of Italian or Spanish for Hebrew in the epitaphs, the cultural transformation we spoke of in chapter 5 also becomes a tangible reality. In the form and content of the epitaphs we can grasp a sense of the cultural sensibility of the times in which the deceased lived. Various documentary projects, including photographs, are under way in this field, and it is to be hoped that a systematic analysis of the available data will in the near future help us flesh out considerably these very general observations of ours.

To conclude, in Jewish society, too, all the features typical of the social transformation set in motion by the passage from the Middle Ages to the Renaissance and thence to the post-Renaissance period are clearly present. The ritual of death continues to be an essentially public event, in accordance with time-honored medieval tradition. Typical expressions of sliding and change are, however, very clearly visible. Among these, we have noted the gradual increase in the weight given to the actions of the man on the point of death, a phenomenon that, as we know, was one of the most typical clues to the increased importance the Renaissance attached to life. We have also noticed signs of a slow transformation of the context of death from being exclusively pertinent to the public sphere to ever more pertinent to the private sphere. We have noted in particular how among Jews, too, the accent on the relationship between the dying man and his family gradually changed as well as the part they played in the overall ritual. However, we have noted the constant preoccupation of those in power to extend their control, or rather their paternalistic domination, which in the preceding period seems to have been limited to the public manifestations of the ritual itself, to this field too.

Alongside the general characteristics common to everyone at the time, we have observed the ones that are more specifically Jewish, conditioned, that is, by the diversity of the Jew and his culture on the two principal levels implied by that diversity: first, that of the contents of the ritual, eminently religious in nature, and therefore marked by the Jewish ethos, rigidly opposed to and exclusive of the Christian one; and second, that of the repressive attitude adopted by Christian society with regard to the tendencies cultivated by Jewish society insofar as it was a product of its own time and place. In other words, the observation of Jewish society of the period from the point of view of the rituals of death exemplifies and confirms the picture presented in the preceding chapters: like his life, the death of the Jew leaves us with the sense of a presence in the local sociocultural context transfigured by a pronounced element of "absence."

AFTERWORD

THIS BOOK has proposed a portrait of the history of the Jews in Italy based on the accounts contained in a number of previous works, without which this book could scarcely have been written, but from which it takes a by no means negligible distance. The patient reader who has followed me thus far certainly has the right to the opinion that, rather than having proven my case, I have simply suggested a new way of reading the sources. It is true that I have offered elsewhere a more detailed demonstration of some of the arguments set forth in the present synthesis; be that as it may, I myself would be the first to admit that we are only at the start of the journey. Many important themes, and among them those that delight the historians of today, have been left to one side, since the relevant historical research is still in an initial, not to say embryonic, stage of development. Problems such as the image of childhood, of women, of work, of play, of sickness and death, and, why not, of the imagery linked with the important issue of the contrast between the world of reality and the dream of a return to the Holy Land, not to mention many others, have been touched upon only in passing. These are all topics that cry out for detailed treatment, and that treatment does not appear to be just around the corner. The little I have been able to suggest will, however, have served its purpose if I have convinced the reader that the history of the Jews in Italy during the Renaissance is in no way the history of a gradual assimilation followed by a new wave of anti-Semitism, that anti-Semitism was not the reason these Jews refused to assimilate, that the logical outcome of their perception of their Jewish identity in terms of difference/otherness was not necessarily a centripetal dynamic of refusal to participate in the context of the time. The two elements were instead reciprocally complementary, without that complementarity giving rise to alienation, or indeed any other form of tension, except for the dialectic tensions of coexistence. The task that I set myself was to show how it is also possible to read the history of the Jews of the Renaissance in a modern perspective — that of the complex question of the definition of an identity in the context of a nascent awareness of the Self as organically interrelated with the Other, without for all that becoming confused with the Other, and still less annihilated by it. I am not sure I have succeeded; but I would be satisfied at least to have planted a seed of doubt.

NOTES

PREFACE

1. See, for example, Hava Tirosh-Rothschild, "Jewish Culture in Renaissance Italy: A Methodological Survey," *Italia, Studi e ricerche sulla storia, la cultura e la letteratura degli ebrei d'Italia* IX (1990), 63–96.

INTRODUCTION

1. Jacob Burckhardt, *The Civilization of the Renaissance in Italy.* 2 vols. (New York, 1958). For the classic revisionist view, see Wallace K. Ferguson, *The Renaissance in Historical Thought: Five Centuries of Interpretation* (Cambridge, 1948).

2. Cecil Roth, *The Jews in the Renaissance* (Philadelphia, 1977 [first printing, 1959]), 15.

3. Cecil Roth, "The Jews in the Middle Ages," *Cambridge Medieval History* (Cambridge, 1932), 1: 649.

4. Cecil Roth, *The History of the Jews of Italy* (Philadelphia, 1946).

5. Moses Avigdor Shulvass, *The Jews in the World of the Renaissance* (Leiden, 1973).

6. Giuseppe Calasso, "Le forme del potere, classi e gerarchie sociali," in *Storia d'Italia,* ed. Ruggero Romano and Corrado Vivanti (Turin, 1972), 1: 450.

CHAPTER I
THE LAWS OF TOPODEMOGRAPHIC DISTRIBUTION

1. The chronicle (in Hebrew) was published by M. A. Shulvass in *Hebrew Union College Annual* 22 (1949).

2. Bernardino da Feltre, *Le prediche volgari* II, 375, quoted according to Vittorino Meneghin, *Bernardino da Feltre e i Monti di Pietà* (Vicenza, 1974), 127.

3. Léon Poliakov, *Les banchieri juifs et le Saint Siège du XIIIe au XVIIe siècle* (Paris, 1965), 205. [English translation by Miriam Kochan: *Jewish Bankers and the Holy See, from the Thirteenth to the Seventeenth Century* (London, 1977), 148.]

4. Johannes Hofer, *Giovanni da Capestrano. Una vita spesa nella lotta per la riforma della Chiesa* (L'Aquila, 1955), 529–530, n. 240 (also cited by Léon Poliakov, *Les banchieri juifs*).

5. P. Alberto Ghinato, O.F.M., *Studi e documenti intorno ai primitivi Monti di Pietà*, vol. II: *I primordi del Monte di Pietà di Terni (1464–1489)* (Rome, 1959), 27, n. 1.

6. Vittorino Meneghin, *Bernardino da Feltre*, 424.

7. See Umberto Cassuto, *Gli Ebrei a Firenze nell'età del Rinascimento* (Florence, 1918 [reprinted 1965]), 68–73.

8. "Orribile et grave peccatum esse in toto populo Amerino, tam usurae quam etiam excommunicationis, vigore capitulorum iam factorum cum Ebreis." Cited in P. Alberto Ghinato, O.F.M., *Monte di Pietà e monti frumentari di Amelia. Origine e antichi statuti* (Rome, 1956), 19.

9. Bernardino da Siena, Sermon XLIII, as quoted by Léon Poliakov, *Les banchieri juifs*, 199 [English translation, p. 142].

10. Vittorino Meneghin, *Bernardino da Feltre*, 25.

11. Bernardino da Siena, *Opera omnia iussa et auctoritate R.mi P. Augustini Sépinski* (Florence, 1956), passim, but see, for example, III: 298; IV: 203, 244, 249, 256, 392, 402.

12. Johannes Hofer, *Giovanni da Capestrano*, 467.

13. Ibid., 528.

14. Umberto Cassuto, *Gli Ebrei a Firenze*, 56–60, where references can be found to the various chronicles.

15. Fausta Casolini, *Bernardino da Feltre* (Milano, 1939), 60 (quoted by Léon Poliakov, *Les banchieri juifs*, 206).

16. Cf. Cecil Roth, *Jews in the Renaissance*, 15 [first printing, p. 7].

17. The document was recently republished in Solomon Grayzel, *The Church and the Jews in the XIIIth Century*, vol. II: *1254–1314*, ed. and arranged, with additional notes by Kenneth R. Stow (New York and Detroit, 1989), 54–55.

18. Brian Pullan, *A History of Early Renaissance Italy* (London, 1973), 52.

19. These figures are taken from Anthony Molho, *Florentine Public Finances in the Early Renaissance, 1400–1433* (Cambridge, Mass., 1971).

20. See Umberto Cassuto, *Gli Ebrei a Firenze*, 68–73.

21. William M. Bowsky, *The Finance of the Commune of Siena, 1287–1355* (Oxford, 1970), 205–209.

22. Ariel Toaff, *Gli Ebrei a Perugia* (Perugia, 1975), 17.

23. Léon Poliakov, *Les banchieri juifs*, 222 [English translation, 160].

24. Leone Modena, *She'elot u-Teshuvot Zikney Yehudah* [*Responsa of the Elders of Judah*], ed. S. Simonsohn (Jerusalem, 1955), 139, n. 88.

25. S. Simonsohn, *The Jews in the Duchy of Milan* (Jerusalem, 1982), 2: 1045.

26. Léon Poliakov, *Les banchieri juifs*, 274 [English translation, 202].

27. R. Mueller, "Pratiques économiques et groupes sociaux," *AESC* 30 (1975), 1285.

28. Speech of the Doge Tommaso Mocenigo at the Signoria, April 1423, Archivio di Stato, Venice, *Bilanci Generali*, Series II, t. 1, 81 (Venice, 1912). Cited by Philippe Braunstein and Robert Delort, *Venise, portrait historique d'une cité* (Paris, 1971), 123–124.

29. Marin Sanudo, *I diarii* (Venice, 1879–1902; [reprinted Bologna, 1969]), vol. 28, cols. 62–64. [The translator thanks Linda Carroll and Gianna Gardenal for their help in interpreting the elliptical syntax and erratic punctuation of the graphomaniac — 58 stout double-columned tomes! — Sanudo's idiosyncratic Venetian dialect notes. This discussion is referred to and portions of Sanudo's text translated in Brian Pullan, *Rich and Poor in Renaissance Venice: The Social Institutions of a Catholic State, to 1620* (Cambridge, Mass., 1971), 493–495.]

30. Marin Sanudo, *I diarii*, vol. 28, col. 363.

31. Cecil Roth, *History of the Jews in Venice* (Philadelphia, 1930), 29.

32. Marin Sanudo, *I diarii*.

33. The full text of the epistle is quoted by Emanuel Rodocanachi, *Le Saint Siège et les Juifs. Le ghetto à Rome* (Paris, 1891 [reprinted Bologna, 1972]), 315–319.

34. Ariel Toaff, *Gli Ebrei a Perugia*, 63.

35. Cecil Roth, *Venice*, 29. Léon Poliakov, *Les banchieri juifs*, 274–275 [English translation, 203].

36. Joseph Colon, *Responsa* (Venice, 1519), no. 192. My interpretation differs from that of Léon Poliakov, *Les banchieri juifs*, 201 [English translation, 145].

37. Leone Modena, *Historia de' riti hebraici* [*A History of Jewish Rites*] (Venice, 1678 [reprinted Bologna, 1979]), 44.

38. Anonymous chronicle published by M. A. Shulvass.

39. Cherubino Ghirardacci, *Della Historia di Bologna*, Parte Terza, a cura di Albano Sorbelli (Città di Castello, 1915; part 3 in the series published by Lodovico Muratori: *Rerum Italicarum Scriptores: Raccolta degli Storici Italiani dal Cinquecento al Millecinquecento*, vol. 33, 1), 40.

40. Vittorino Meneghin, *Bernardino da Feltre*, 71.

41. C. Piana, "Il beato Marco da Bologna e il suo convento di S. Paolo in Monte nel Quattrocento," *Atti e Memorie della Deputazione di Storia Patria per le Province di Romagna* n.s. 22 (1971), 153; Rossella Rinaldi, "Un inventario di beni dell'anno 1503: Abramo Sforno e la sua attività di prestatore," *Il Carrobbio* 9 (1983), 315.

42. Vittorino Meneghin, *Bernardino da Feltre*, 126.

43. *The Book of the Moneylender and the Borrower*, 2: 1–2. This work, whose importance was correctly stressed by Léon Poliakov, was composed earlier than Poliakov himself believed. Its author seems to have been Maestro Kaufmann, the father-in-law of the famous R. Judah Mintz, whom we will have occasion to mention in subsequent chapters. A manuscript version of the work, today in the Ginzburg Collection in Moscow (Ms. 722), was copied in 1501 by Meshullam Cusi, the son of Moses Jacob. It was published by A. N. Z. Roth, *Hebrew Union College Annual* 26 (1955), 39–74 of the Hebrew text. A French translation is provided by Léon Poliakov, *Les banchieri juifs*, 310–328. The English translation of Poliakov's work does not include the appendix in which the document is included.

44. I. Sonne, *Mi-Pavlo ha revi'i 'ad Pius ha-ḥamishi* [*From Paul IV to Pius V. A Jewish Chronicle of the Sixteenth Century*] (Jerusalem, 1954), 15.

45. Simone Luzzatto, *Discorso circa il stato de gl'hebrei, et in particolar dimoranti nell'inclita città di Venezia* [*Discourse on the State of the Jews, in Particular Those Dwelling in the Noble City of Venice*] (Venice, 1638).

CHAPTER II
TRADES AND PROFESSIONS

1. S. D. Goitein, *A Mediterranean Society: The Jewish Communities of the Arab World as Portrayed in the Documents of the Cairo Geniza*, 5 vols. (Berkeley, Los Angeles, London, 1967–1988).

2. Bartolomeo e Giuseppe Lagumina, *Codice diplomatico dei giudei di Sicilia*, pt. I, vol. 2: 523, n. 826.

3. The Hebrew text of Obadiah's letter can now be consulted in M. E. Artom and A. David, "R. Ovadià Yare mi-Bertinoro ve-Igherotav me-Eretz Israel [R. Obadiah Yare of Bertinoro and His Letters from the Holy Land]," in *Jews in Italy: Studies Dedicated to the Memory of U. Cassuto* (Jerusalem, 1988), 54–108 of the Hebrew section.

4. Lagumina, *Codice diplomatico*, I: 78–80, n. 52.

5. Lagumina, *Codice diplomatico*, I: 201–203, n. 151.

6. For an example of a Jew exempted from the *giudaica* tax, see Lagumina, *Codice diplomatico*, II: 98–100, n. 530.

7. *The Book of the Moneylender and the Borrower*, chap. 2, 3–5; Léon Poliakov, *Les banchieri juifs*, 313–314.

8. *The Book of the Moneylender and the Borrower*, chap. 2, 6–8; Léon Poliakov, *Les banchieri juifs*, 314.

9. Paolo Uccello, Predella of the Miracle of the Profaned Host, Galleria Nazionale, Urbino.

10. Attilio Milano, "I capitoli di Daniel da Pisa e la Comunità di Roma," *Rassegna mensile di Israel* 10 (1935–1936), 324–338, 409–426.

CHAPTER III
THE PROBLEM OF SOCIOCULTURAL IDENTITY

1. Josef Colon, *Responsa* (Venice, 1519), no. 88.

2. Epistle of Messer Leon to the Jews of Florence, published by Simḥa Assaf, Mighinzey Beit ha-Sefarim bi-Yerushalayim [From the collections of the National Library of Jerusalem], in *Minḥa Le-David, Sefer ha-Yovel le-David Yellin [Minḥa Le-David: Volume in Honor of David Yellin]* (Jerusalem, 1935), 227.

3. Diane Owen-Hughes, "Distinguishing Signs: Ear-Rings, Jews and Franciscan Rhetoric in the Italian Renaissance City," *Past and Present* 112 (1986), 3–59.

4. Attilio Milano, "La pragmatica degli ebrei romani del secolo XVII," *Rassegna Mensile di Israel* 7 (1932), 178.

5. The complete text of the Forlì ordinances is available, along with an English translation, in Louis Finkelstein, *Jewish Self-Government in the Middle Ages* (New York, 1964), 281–295.

6. Isaiah Sonne, "Avney Binyan: Documents in the History of the Jews in Italy, no. 2, *Verona 1539–1653*," in *Kobetz 'al Yad* 3 (1939), 162.

7. All of the cases mentioned here are taken from the above-cited collection by S. Simonsohn, *The Jews in the Duchy of Milan*.

8. All of the examples mentioned are taken from the chapter entitled "Manners and Morals" in Cecil Roth's *The Jews in the Renaissance*, 44–63.

9. Ibid.

10. The correspondence was published by Renata Segre, "Il mondo ebraico nel carteggio di Carlo Borromeo," *Michael* 1 (1972), 163–260. The quotation is from p. 255.

11. David B. Ruderman, "A Jewish Apologetic Treatise from the Sixteenth Century," *Hebrew Union College Annual* 50 (1979), 276.

12. See the accusation, more rhetorically polemical than well-founded, leveled against the present writer in a recent essay by Ariel Toaff, "La storia degli ebrei in Italia nel tardo Medioevo. Un problema di fonti?" in *La storia degli ebrei nell'Italia medievale: tra filologia e metodologia*, ed. Maria Giuseppina Muzzarelli and Giacomo Todeschini (Bologna, Istituto per i Beni Artistici, Culturali e Naturali della Regione Emilia-Romagna, 1990), 42 and n. 15. And compare, in the same volume, the essay by Sofia Boesch Gajano, who seems instead quite ready to abandon the stereotyped positions of much "committed" historiography in favor of the at times contradictory richness of the overall picture. See Sofia Boesch Gajano, "Presenze ebraiche nell'Italia medievale. Identità, stereotipi, intrecci," in *La storia degli ebrei*, 13–18.

13. Ariel Toaff, "La storia degli ebrei," 39. My italics.

CHAPTER IV
EDUCATION AND THE RABBINICAL IDEAL

1. This letter was published by David Frankel, "Shelosha mikhtavim le-toledoth R. Yitzhak Yehoshua de Lattes [Three Letters Referring to the Life of R. Yitzhak Yehoshua de Lattes]," *'Alim le-Bibliografia ve-Toledoth Israel* III/2 (1937–1938), 24.

2. *The Autobiography of a Seventeenth-Century Venetian Rabbi: Leon Modena's "Life of Judah,"* trans. and ed. Marc R. Cohen (Princeton, 1988), 83.

3. The text is taken from Simḥa Assaf, *Mekorot le-Toledoth ha-Ḥinnukh be-Israel* (Tel Aviv, 1930), 2: 114.

4. The complete text of the ordinances has been published by Robert Bonfil, "Kavvim lidemutham ha-ḥevratith ve-ha-ruḥanith shel yehudey ezor Venezia be-

reshith ha-mea ha-shesh 'esre [Aspects of the Social and Spiritual Life of the Jews in the Region of Venice at the Beginning of the Sixteenth Century]," *Zion* 41 (1976), 68–96.

5. Samuel Archivolti, *Ma'yan Gannim* (Venice, 1553), letters XX and XXI.

6. The author of the letter is Joseph d'Arles, private tutor of the Rieti family in Siena. The text is cited from the partial edition of Simḥa Assaf, *Mekorot le-Toledoth ha-Ḥinnukh be-Israel*, 4: 20 sqq.

7. Elijah Capsali, *Seder Eliyahu Zuta*, ed. Aryeh Shmuelevitz, Shlomo Simonsohn, and Meir Benayahu (Jerusalem, 1977), 2: 246.

8. Ibid.

9. Elia Levita, *Sefer Tishbi*, Isna 1541, under the heading "Ḥaver," pp. 107–108.

10. See above, note 4.

11. The document, preserved in the archives of the Jewish Community of Rome, has been partially published by Robert Bonfil, *Ha-Rabbanut be-Italia bi-Tekufat ha-Renaissance* (Jerusalem, 1979), 247, doc. no. 33. See *Rabbis and Jewish Communities in Renaissance Italy* (Oxford, 1990), 64, 184–185. The document in question is not included in the English translation.

12. Shlomo Simonsohn, *History of the Jews in the Duchy of Mantua* (Jerusalem, 1972), 576.

CHAPTER V
JEWISH CULTURE, THE HEBRAISTS,
AND THE ROLE OF THE KABBALAH

1. The inventory, which dates back to 1385, has been published by Robert Bonfil, "Reshimath Sefarim 'Ivriim me-Imola, sof ha-meah ha-arba-esre [An Inventory of Jewish Books from Imola from the End of the 14th Century]," in *Scritti in memoria di Umberto Nahon*, ed. R. Bonfil and D. Carpi (Jerusalem, 1978), 47–62 of the section in Hebrew.

2. Zipora Baruchson, "Ha-sifriyot ha-peratiyot shel yehudey tzefon Italia be-sheley ha-Renaissance [Private Libraries of Northern Italian Jews at the Close of the Renaissance]," Ph.D. diss., Bar Ilan University, 1985.

3. David di Messer Leon, *Kevod Ḥakhamim* (Berlin, 1899 [reprinted Jerusalem, 1970]), 65.

4. Robert Bonfil, *Ha-Rabbanut be-Italia bi-tequfat ha-Renaissance*, doc. 5, p. 222.

5. MS 968, Bibliothèque Nationale, Paris, f. 74. Cited by David Geffen, "Insights into the Life of Elijah Medigo Based on His Published and Unpublished Works," *Proceedings of the American Academy for Jewish Research* 41–42 (1973–1974), 76.

6. Isaac Abravanel, *Yeshu'oth Meshiḥo*, pt. II, chap. 2 of the Koenigsberg edition, f. 39b.

7. Messer Leon, *Nofet Tzufim*, 1: 14, and Robert Bonfil, *Introduction* to the photostatic edition of the *editio princeps* (Mantua, 1475) [reprinted Jerusalem, 1981, 50].

8. Michel Foucault, "What Is an Author," in *Language, Counter-Memory, Practice: Selected Essays and Interviews*, ed. Donald F. Bouchard (Ithaca, N.Y., 1977), 113–138.

9. David B. Ruderman, "The Italian Renaissance and Jewish Thought," in *Renaissance Humanism: Foundations and Forms*, ed. A. Rabil, Jr. (Philadelphia, 1988), 1: 389.

10. David B. Ruderman, *The World of a Renaissance Jew: The Life and Thought of Abraham ben Mordecai Farissol* (Cincinnati, 1981), 77.

11. Judah ben Yeḥiel, called Messer Leon, *Nofet Tzufim*, 1: 13.

12. Judah ben Yeḥiel, *Nofet Tzufim*, 2: 4, 13, 18; 4: 68.

13. Heinrich Graetz, *Geschichte der Juden* (Leipzig, 1890), 8: 243.

14. A good translation of this correspondence into English is available in the introduction by Isaac Rabinowitz to Judah Messer Leon, *The Book of the Honeycomb's Flow: Sepher Nopeht Suphim, A Critical Edition and Translation by Isaac Rabinowitz* (Ithaca and London, 1983), xxxii–xlii.

15. Documents supporting this affirmation have been published recently by Joanna Weinberg, "Azariah dei Rossi: Towards a Reappraisal of the Last Years of His Life," *Annali della Scuola Normale Superiore di Pisa* Ser. 3, 8, 2 (1978), 493–511.

16. Samuel Archivolti, *Ma'yan Gannim*.

17. Todros ha-Kohen, later known as Lodovico Carretto, published in Paris in 1554 a book with the title *Epistola Ludouici Carreti ad Iudaeos*, in which he set out his arguments and invited his brethren to follow him on his new path.

18. The relevant passages from this letter by Dato to Rabbi Ezra da Fano are given in English in Robert Bonfil, *Rabbis and Jewish Communities in Renaissance Italy* (Oxford, 1990), 295–297.

1. Elijah Capsali, *Seder Eliyahu Zuta*, 244.

2. Isaac Abravanel, *Commentary* to 1 Samuel 8:4 and Deuteronomy 17:4.

3. Johannan Alemanno, *Heshek Shelomo* and *Ḥai ha-Olamim*.

4. Epistle of Messer Leon to the Jews of Florence, 227.

5. Leone Modena, *Responsa Zikney Yehudah*, ed. S. Simonsohn (Jerusalem, 1955), 43, n. 26.

6. *Pinkes Kahal Verona* [*Minutes Book of the Jewish Community of Verona*], ed. Yacob Boksenboim, 3 vols. (Tel Aviv, 1989–1990).

7. All these texts are collected in Louis Finkelstein, *Jewish Self-Government in the Middle Ages*.

8. All these texts are gathered in Isaiah Sonne, "Ha-wa'ad ha-kelali be-Italia av le-wa'ad arba' aratzot be-Polania [The Regional Synod in Italy, Prototype of the Synod of the Four Countries in Poland]," *Ha-Tekufah* 32–33 (1948), 617–689.

9. Elia Levita, *Sefer Tishbi*, Isna 1541, 201.

10. See above, note 6.

11. *Pinkes Va'ad KK Padova* [*Minutes Book of the Council of the Jewish Community of Padua*], ed. with intro. and notes by Daniel Carpi, 2 vols. (Jerusalem, 1973–1979).

12. This broadsheet, composed in Hebrew, is reproduced from the only extant copy, preserved by the Jewish Community of Mantua, in Robert Bonfil, *Ha-Rabbanut be-Italia*, 46.

13. Ronald Weissman, *Ritual Brotherhood in Renaissance Florence* (New York, 1982), ix.

14. The complete text of the ordinances is published by Robert Bonfil, *Ha-Rabbanut be-Italia*, chap. 3, n. 2.

15. For the complete text of the ordinances of the 1554 Synod of Ferrara, see Louis Finkelstein, *Jewish Self-Government in the Middle Ages*.

16. Summa Theologica, Secunda Secundae, X, 11.

17. *Codex Theodosianus* II, 1, 10; *Codex Justinianus* I, 9, 8.

18. Condotta of Francesco II Duke of Milan, cited above in chap. 1, art. 6.

19. The complete text of the ducal rescript and of the Levi brothers' petition is published by Robert Bonfil, *Ha-Rabbanut be-Italia*, pt. II, documents 57 and 60, pp. 278, 280 sqq.

CHAPTER VII
TIME AND SPACE

1. Leone Modena, *Historia de' riti hebraici*, pt. I, chap. 10, 15–19.

CHAPTER VIII
SOUNDS AND SILENCE

1. *Iggerot Melammedim* [*Letters by Jewish Teachers in Renaissance Italy*], ed. Yacob Boksenboim (Tel Aviv, 1985), 92.

2. Eliezer Naḥman Foa, *Sermons*, 4. MS vols. in the archive of the Community of Mantua, I, f. 3.

3. Simone Luzzatto, *Discorso circa il stato de gl'hebrei et in particolare dimoranti nell'inclita città di Venetia* (Venice, 1638), f. 85v.

CHAPTER IX
COLORS, TASTES, AND ODORS

1. The text was published by Robert Bonfil, "Bittuyim le-yihud am Israel be-Italia bi-tekufat ha-Renaissance [Expressions Stressing the Uniqueness of the Jewish People in Renaissance Italy]," *Sinai* 76 (1975), 36–46.

CHAPTER X
THE DAYS OF LIFE

1. Leone Modena, *Historia de' riti hebraici*, pt. IV, chap. 8, 101–106.

2. For Montaigne's description, see Emanuel Rodocanachi, *Le Saint Siège*, 95 and 311–314.

3. Leone Modena, *Historia de' riti hebraici*.

4. David B. Ruderman, *The World of a Renaissance Jew* (Cincinnati, 1981), 28.

1. Philippe Ariès, *L'homme devant la mort* (Paris, 1977). English translation by Helen Weaver, *The Hour of Our Death* (New York, 1981).

2. Leone Modena, *Historia de' riti hebraici*, 116–120.

3. Elijah Capsali, *Seder Eliyahu Zuta*, 253–255.

4. Elijah Capsali, *Seder Eliyahu Zuta*, 256.

5. The MS sermon is preserved in the Bodleian Library, Oxford University, n. 988, ff. 309a–315a.

6. Robert Bonfil, *Rabbis and Jewish Communities*, 40.

7. Vespasiano da Bisticci, *Vite di uomini illustri del secolo XV*, II.

8. A number of examples are found in Ariel Toaff, *Il vino e la carne* (Bologna, 1989), 57–67.

9. Several examples are provided by Carla Boccato, "Testamenti di israeliti nel fondo del notaio veneziano Pietro Bracchi seniore," *Rassegna mensile di Israel* 42 (1976), 281–295. See also, by the same author, "Ebrei e testamenti nei fondi dei notai veneziani del secolo XVII," *Memorie storiche forogiuliesi* 68 (1988), 157–163.

10. Ariel Toaff, *Il vino e la carne*, 69–70, 291.

11. Azriel Diena, *Responsa*, ed. Y. Boksenboim (Tel Aviv, 1977), 1: 245.

12. Nello Pavoncello, "Epigrafe ebraica nel Palazzo Affaiti in Cremona," *Annali dell'Istituto Orientale di Napoli* 41 (1981), 308–309.

13. Ariel Toaff, *Il vino e la carne*, 54. Toaff records various examples of the "topographical separation in death" in which he too sees "in some sense emphasized the different condition of the Christian citizens and the Jews."

BIBLIOGRAPHICAL
REFERENCES

THE ONLY WORK entirely devoted to our topic is that of Moses Avigdor Shulvass, *The Jews in the World of the Renaissance*, Leiden-Chicago, 1973 (the translation of a work published in Hebrew in New York in 1955). Absolutely noteworthy is Cecil Roth's *The Jews in the Renaissance*, Philadelphia, 1959 [reprinted 1977], which, however, is concerned only with cultural history. Roth, however, devotes to Renaissance Italy a good part of his *The History of the Jews of Italy*, Philadelphia, 1946 (103–288). So likewise do Salo W. Baron in *A Social and Religious History of the Jews*, 18 vols., 2d rev. ed., New York, 1952–1980; see especially vol. 10, 1965, chap. 46, 220–296, 398–432, vol. 13, 1969, chap. 57, 159–205, 389–414, and vol. 14, 1969, chap. 60, 71–146, 322-359; and Attilio Milano, *Storia degli Ebrei in Italia*, Turin, 1963 (109–211). It is also worth recalling the important chapter devoted to our period in volume 4 of Zinberg's classic work, available today in both Hebrew and English: Israel Zinberg, *A History of Jewish Literature*, ed. and trans. B. Martin, Cincinnati, 1974. We should also add the sources translated and presented in English by Louis Finkelstein, *Jewish Self-Government in the Middle Ages*, New York, 1924 [reprinted 1964]; and the illustrative materials collected by Thérèse and Mendel Metzger, *Jewish Life in the Middle Ages*, New York, 1982, much of which concerns precisely the Jews of Italy.

Though there are few works of synthesis, monographs dedicated to specific places or topics are fairly numerous and their number has tended to grow in the past few decades. We will cite, among others, the following works: Adolf Berliner, *Geschichte der Juden in Rom von der aeltesten Zeiten bis zur Gegenwart (2050 Jahre)*, Frankfurt, 1893; Hermann Vogelstein and Paul Rieger, *Geschichte der Juden in Rom*, Berlin, 1895–1896; Umberto Cassuto, *Gli ebrei a Firenze nell'età del Rinascimento*, Florence, 1918 [reprinted 1965]; Cecil Roth, *History of the Jews in Venice*, Philadelphia, 1930; Vittore

Colorni, *Legge ebraica e leggi locali*, Milan, 1945; Léon Poliakov, *Les banchieri juifs et le Saint Siège du XIIIᵉ au XVIIᵉ siècle*, Paris, 1965 [English trans. by Miriam Kochan: *Jewish Bankers and the Holy See From the Thirteenth to the Seventeenth Century*, London, 1977]; Shlomo Simonsohn, *History of the Jews in the Duchy of Mantua*, Jerusalem, 1977 [English trans. of the work originally published in Hebrew in Jerusalem in 1962–1964]; Ariel Toaff, *Gli Ebrei a Perugia*, Perugia, 1975; Ariel Toaff, *The Jews in Medieval Assisi (1305–1487)*, Florence, 1979; Ariel Toaff, *Il vino e la carne*, Bologna, 1989; Maria Giuseppina Muzzarelli, *Ebrei e città d'Italia in età di transizione: Il caso di Cesena dal XIV al XVI secolo*, Bologna, 1984; Brian Pullan, *Rich and Poor in Renaissance Venice: The Social Institutions of a Catholic State to 1620*, Oxford, England, and Cambridge, Mass., 1971; Brian Pullan, *The Jews of Europe and the Inquisition of Venice, 1550–1670*, Oxford, 1983; Kenneth R. Stow, *Catholic Thought and Papal Jewry Policy, 1555–1593*, New York, 1977; David B. Ruderman, *The World of a Renaissance Jew: The Life and Thought of Abraham ben Mordecai Farissol*, Cincinnati, 1981; David B. Ruderman, *Kabbalah, Magic, and Science: The Cultural Universe of a Sixteenth-Century Jewish Physician*, Cambridge, Mass., 1988; David B. Ruderman, *A Valley of Vision: The Heavenly Journey of Abraham ben Hananiah Yagel*, Baltimore, 1990; Robert Bonfil, *Ha-Rabbanut be-Italia bi-Tekufat ha-Renaissance* [The Rabbinate in Italy in the Renaissance], Jerusalem, 1979 [English edition: *Rabbis and Jewish Communities in Renaissance Italy*, Oxford, 1990]; Giacomo Todeschini, *La ricchezza degli Ebrei: Merci e denaro nella riflessione ebraica e nella definizione cristiana dell'usura alla fine del Medioevo*, Spoleto, 1989. It goes without saying that most of these works contain abundant bibliographies.

Current interest in our subject is also confirmed by the ever-growing number of dissertations on topics concerning the Jews of Italy, produced especially in the various universities of Israel, Italy, and the United States.

It would be impossible to list here all the articles, rich in data and suggestions, devoted to particular aspects of local history. Nevertheless, we will make a few exceptions. We will mention first of all some of the latest collections devoted entirely or almost entirely to the history of the Jews in Italy: vol. 54, no. 3 ["Ebrei d'Italia"] of the periodical *Quaderni storici*; vol. 2 ["Aspetti e problemi della presenza ebraica nell'Italia centro-settentrionale — secoli XIV e XV"] of the series *Quaderni dell'Istituto di Scienze Storiche dell'Università di Roma*, Rome, 1983; the first volume ["Itinerari ebraico-cristiani: società, cultura, mito"] of the series published by the University of Rome: "La Sapienza," *Collana del Dipartimento di Studi storici dal Medioevo all'età moderna*, Rome, 1987; the various proceedings of conferences dedicated to topics concerning Jews, in particular those of the Associazione Italiana per lo Studio del Giudaismo [Italian Association for the Study of Judaism], the latest of which is *Manoscritti, frammenti e libri ebraici nell'Italia dei secoli XV–XVII. Atti del VII Congresso internazionale dell'AISG, S. Miniato, 7–8–9 novembre 1988*, Rome, 1991; of *Italia Judaica* [organized by the Commissione mista per gli Scambi Culturali tra Italia e Israele], vol. 2 of which is dedicated to the precise period that concerns us (Rome, 1987); of the Fondazione Giorgio Cini of Venice, which recently published *Ebrei e Venezia — secoli XIV–XVIII*, ed. Gaetano Cozzi, Milan, 1987; *'Ovadiah Yare da Bertinoro e la presenza ebraica in Romagna nel Quattrocento*, ed. Giulio Busi, Turin, 1989; *La storia degli ebrei nell'Italia medievale: tra filologia e metodologia*, ed. Maria Giuseppina Muzzarelli and Giacomo Todeschini (Bologna, Istituto per i Beni Artistici, Culturali e Naturali della Regione Emilia-Romagna, 1990; David B. Ruderman, ed., *Preachers of the Italian Ghetto*, Berkeley, Los Angeles, Oxford, 1992; and finally the periodical *Italia, Studi e ricerche sulla storia, la cultura e la letteratura degli ebrei d'Italia*, published at the Hebrew University of Jerusalem by Robert Bonfil and Giuseppe B. Sermoneta, the most recent number of which came out in 1992. We should also mention the studies of Jewish intellectual history in the period that interests us published in the two volumes dedicated to the history of Jewish thought edited for the Center for Jewish Studies at Harvard University: *Jewish Thought in the Sixteenth Century*, ed. Bernard D. Cooperman, Cambridge, Mass., 1983, and *Jewish Thought in the Seventeenth Century*, ed. Isadore Twershy and Bernard Septimus, Cambridge, Mass., 1987. Twenty among the most recent essays were recently collected in a volume edited by David B. Ruderman, *Essential Papers on Jewish Culture in Renaissance and Baroque Italy*, New York, 1992.

It seems incumbent upon us to cite a number of essays that came to our attention recently during the composition of the present work: in the first place those collected by Michele Luzzati in *La casa dell'ebreo*, Pisa, 1983; as well as the following: Benjamin Ravid, "From Geographical Realia to Historiographical Symbol: The Odyssey of the Word *Ghetto*," in David B. Ruderman, ed., *Essential Papers on Jewish Culture in Renaissance and Baroque Italy*, New York, 1992, 373–385; Benjamin Ravid, "From Yellow to Red: On the Distinguishing Head-Covering of the Jews of Venice," in *The Frank Talmage Memorial Volume*, II, ed. Barry Walfish [*Jewish History*, vol. 6, nos. 1–2], Haifa, 1992, 179–210; Benjamin Ravid, *Economics and Toleration in Seventeenth-Century Venice: The Background and Context of the Discorso of Simone Luzzatto*, Jerusalem, 1979; Benjamin Ravid, "The Socioeconomic Background of the Expulsion and Readmission of the Venetian Jews, 1571–1573," in *Essays in Modern Jewish History: A Tribute to Ben Halpern*, ed. F. Malino and P. C. Albert, Rutherford, Madison, Teaneck, 1982, 27–54; David B. Ruderman, "The Founding of a Gemilut Hasadim Society in Ferrara in 1515," *Association for Jewish Studies Review* I (1976), 233–267; David B. Ruderman, "An Exemplary Sermon from the Classroom of a Jewish Teacher in Renaissance Italy," *Italia* I (1978), 7–38; Ariel Toaff, "Nuova luce sui marrani di Ancona," *Studi sull'ebraismo italiano in memoria di Cecil Roth*, ed. Elio Toaff, Rome, 1974, 261–280; Ariel Toaff, "Gli ebrei romani e il commercio del denaro nei comuni dell'Italia centrale alla fine del Duecento," *Italia Judaica* I (1983), 183–198; Gabriella Ferri Piccaluga, "Iconografia francescana in Valcamonica," *Atti del Convegno di Studi "Il Francescanesimo in Valcamonica" — 17–19 dicembre 1982*, Brescia, 1983, 253–282; Diane Owen Hughes, "Distinguishing Signs: Ear-Rings, Jews and Franciscan Rhetoric in the Italian Renaissance City," *Past and Present* 112 (1986), 3–59; Elliott Horowitz, "The Way We Were: Jewish Life in the Middle Ages," *Jewish History* I (1986), 75-90; Elliott Horowitz, "The Eve of the Circumcision: A Chapter in the History of Jewish Nightlife," *Journal of Social History* 23 (1989), 45–70; Elliott Horowitz, "Coffee-Houses and the Nocturnal Rituals of Early Modern Jewry," *AJS Review* 14 (1989), 17–46.

Finally, so as to allow the reader to obtain a more extended view of what has been presented in this volume in condensed form, we will mention in detail some of our own contributions: "Bittuyim le-yihud am Israel be-Italia bi-tekufat ha-Renaissance [Expressions of Jewish Particularism in the Italian Renaissance]," *Sinai* 76 (1975), 36–46; "Ahat miderashotav ha-Italkiyot shel Rabbi Mordechai Dato [A Sermon in Italian of Rabbi Mordechai Dato]," *Italia* I (1976), 1–32; "Torah ha-Nefesh ve-ha-Kedusha be-Mishnat Rabbi Ovadiah Sforno [The Doctrine of the Soul and of Sainthood in the Philosophy of Rabbi Ovadiah Sforno]," *Eshel Beer Sheva* I (1976), 200–257; "Kavvim li-demutam ha-hevratit va-ha-ruhanit shel yehudey ezor Venezia be-reshit ha-mea ha-shesh-esre [Some Features of the Social and Spiritual Profile of the Jews of the Veneto Region at the Beginning of the XVI Century]," *Zion* 41 (1976), 68–96; "Introduction" [in Hebrew] to the anastatic reproduction of the *editio princeps* of the *Nufet Tzufim* (Mantua, 1475) of Jehudah also known as Messer Leon, Jerusalem, 1981, 7–69; "Hityashevuth Yehudim nodedim be-Italia be-shaley yemei ha-benayim [The Settlement of Nomadic Jews in Italy in the Late Middle Ages]," in *Haghira ve-hityashvuth be-Israel u-va-ammim* [*Emigration and Settlement among the People of Israel and Other Peoples*], Jerusalem, 1982, 139–153; "Some Reflections on the Place of Azariah de Rossi's *Meor Enayim* in the Cultural Milieu of Italian Renaissance Jewry," in *Jewish Thought in the Sixteenth Century*, ed. Bernard D. Cooperman, Cambridge, Mass., 1983, 23–48; "The Historian's Perception of the Jews in the Italian Renaissance: Towards a Reappraisal," *Revue des Etudes Juives* 134 (1984), 59–82; "Una 'Enciclopedia' di sapere sociale: L'epistolario ebraico quattrocentesco di Josef Sark," *Rivista di storia della filosofia* (1985), 113–130; "La sinagoga in Italia come luogo di riunione e di preghiera," in *Il Centenario del Tempio Israelitico di Firenze. Atti del Convegno . . . 24 ottobre 1982*, Firenze, 1985, 36–44; "Riflessioni sulla storiografia ebraica in Italia nel Cinquecento," *Italia Judaica* II (1986), 55–66; "Halakha, Kabbala and Society: Some Insights into Rabbi Menahem Azariah da Fano's Inner World," in *Jewish Thought in the Seventeenth Century*, Cambridge, Mass., 1987, 39–61; "Cultura e mistica a Venezia nel Cinquecento," in *Ebrei a Venezia* (1987), 469–508; "Change in Cultural Patterns of Jewish Society in Crisis: The Case of Italian Jewry at the Close of the Sixteenth Century," *Jewish History* 3 (1988), 11–30; "Società ebraica e società cristiana:

riflessioni sul significato e sui limiti di una convergenza," in *Ebrei e cristiani nell'Italia medioevale e moderna: conversioni, scambi, contrasti. Atti del VI Congresso Internazionale dell'AISG, San Miniato, 4–6 November 1986*, Rome, 1988, 231–260; "How Golden Was the Age of the Renaissance in Jewish Historiography?" in *History and Theory: Essays in Jewish Historiography*, ed. Ada Rapoport-Albert, in memoriam Arnaldo Momigliano (Beiheft 27), 1988, 78–102; "La presenza ebraica in Romagna nel Quattrocento. Appunti per un profilo socio-culturale," in *'Ovadyah Yare da Bertinoro e la presenza ebraica in Romagna nel Quattrocento cit.*, ed. Giulio Busi, Turin, 1989, 3–20; "Le biblioteche degli ebrei d'Italia nell'epoca del Rinascimento," in *Manoscritti, frammenti e libri ebraici nell'Italia dei secoli XV–XVI*, Rome, 1981, 137–150; "Accademie rabbiniche e presenza ebraica nelle università," in *Le Università dell'Europa*, vol. II: *Dal rinascimento alle riforme religiose*, a cura di Gian Paolo Brizzi, Milan, 1991, 133–151; "Preaching as Mediation between Elite and Popular Cultures: The Case of Judah del Bene," in *Preachers of the Italian Ghetto*, Berkeley, Los Angeles, Oxford, 67–88; "The Book of Honeycomb's Flow by Judah Messer Leon: The Rhetoric Dimension of Jewish Humanism in Fifteenth-Century Italy," in *The Frank Talmage Memorial Volume*, Haifa, 1992, 21–33.

Very recently we have begun to see the fruits of a number of far-reaching projects, two of which are conducted under the auspices of the University of Tel Aviv: *Fontes ad Res Judaicas Spectantes: A Documentary History of the Jews of Italy*, edited by Shlomo Simonsohn, of which there have appeared the four volumes dedicated to the Jews of the Duchy of Milan (*The Jews in the Duchy of Milan*, edited with an introduction and notes by Shlomo Simonsohn, Jerusalem, 1982–1990) and the three dedicated to the Jews of Piedmont (*The Jews in Piedmont*, edited with an introduction and notes by Renata Segre, Jerusalem, 1986–1988) and most recently the eight dedicated to the documents of the Holy See (Shlomo Simonsohn, *The Apostolic See and the Jews*, Toronto, 1988–1991); exemplary editions by Jacob Boksenboim of a large number of volumes of *responsa* and Hebrew epistolography bearing on the topics dealt with in our history have been published, in particular: the two volumes of the *Responsa of Rabbi Azriel Diena*, Tel Aviv, 1977–1979; *Responsa Mattanoth Ba-adam*, Tel Aviv, 1983;

"Parashiot" — Some Controversial Affairs of Renaissance Italian Jews, Tel Aviv, 1986; *Iggherot Beth Carmi* [Letters of the Carmi Family, Cremona 1570–1577], Tel Aviv, 1983; *Iggherot Rabbi Yehudah Aryeh Mi-Modena* [Letters of Rabbi Leon Modena], Tel Aviv, 1984; *Iggherot Melammedim* [Letters of Jewish Teachers], Tel Aviv, 1985. We would also like to remember here the project of Pier Cesare Ioly Zorattini, *Processi del S. Uffizio di Venezia contro ebrei e giudaizzanti,* of which vol. 8 (1587–1598) recently appeared (Florence, 1990); and last, the collections of documents edited by Cesare Colafemmina, *Documenti per la storia degli Ebrei in Puglia nell'Archivio di Stato di Napoli,* Bari, 1990; as well as those edited by Anna Esposito and Diego Quaglioni, *Processi contro gli Ebrei di Trento (1475–1478),* vol. 1: *I processi del 1475* (Padua, 1990).

We conclude this brief summary by pointing out that the interested reader will find the following bibliographical compendiums extremely useful: Attilio Milano, *Biblioteca historica italo-judaica,* Florence, 1954; Attilio Milano, *Supplemento per gli anni 1954–1963,* Florence, 1964; Attilio Milano, "Supplemento per gli anni 1964–1966," *Rassegna mensile di Israel* 32 (1966), appendix; *Biblioteca Italo-Ebraica: Bibliografia per la storia degli Ebrei in Italia, 1964–1973,* compiled by Aldo Luzzatto and Moshe Moldavi, edited by Daniele Carpi, Rome, 1982; Aldo Luzzatto, *Biblioteca Italo-Ebraica: Bibliografia per la storia degli Ebrei in Italia, 1974–1985,* Rome, 1989. With the aid of these works, in addition to the bibliographical references contained in the present volume, the reader will have a reliable guide in the relatively easy task of tracking down studies concerning the topics that interest him/her particularly.

INDEX

Abelard, 4
Aboab, Samuel, 276
Abraham, son of Elia, 147
Abravanel, Isaac, 164, 181
Acculturation, 2–3, 6–7, 102, 105, 208
Acqui, 72
Adam Hashuv, 200
Adolescence, 131, 255
Adultery, 111, 115
Adulthood, 256
Agone e Testaccio. *See* Taxation and taxes
Agriculture, 4
Alemanno, Johannan, 158, 164, 168, 173–174, 181
Alessandro de Imola, 41
Al-Farabi, 161
Alfassi, Isaac (Talmudic compendium of), 130–131
Alfonso (king of Naples), 40
Alienation, xi, 1, 122, 156, 157, 285
Alsace, 20
Ambivalence of Jewish condition, 120–124
Amelia, 23, 24
Amsterdam, 62
Amulets, 247
Anau (family). *See* Min ha-Anawim
Ancona, 56, 61, 63, 66, 77, 229
    march of, 188–189
    conversos of, 66–67
    embargo on, 66
Anna of Rome, 114
Anselmo del Banco, 43
Anticlericalism, 13
Anti-Jewish feeling and anti-Semitism, 21–22, 65, 91, 102, 285. *See also* Hatred for Jews; Stereotypes

Antiquity, classical, 5, 162, 173
Apostolic Chamber, 30–31
Aramaic translation of Pentateuch. *See* Targum
Arba 'ah Turim. See Jacob ben Asher
Arbitration. *See* Law and justice
Architecture, 4
Archivolti, Samuel, 133, 169, 201
Aries, Philippe, 265
Aristeas, letter of, 164
Aristotle, 159, 161, 166
    Aristotelian texts and tradition, 159, 163, 164
    Poetics, 164
    Rhetorica ad Alexandrum, 165
Arithmetic. *See* Education and teaching
Ark. *See* Synagogue (ark)
Aron. *See* Synagogue (ark)
Artillery, 76
Art of war, 4
Arukh, 95
Assimilation, 2–3, 6–9, 101–104, 109, 111, 119, 135, 167–168, 177, 285
Astronomy and astrology, 4, 247
Augustine, 49
    Augustinian notion of the need for Jews, 45–46
Augustinians. *See* Friars
Austerity, 105, 108–110, 243
Authority, 159, 161, 166, 173, 270
Autonomy. *See* Communities and self-government
Averroës and Averroism, 60, 159, 161–164, 166, 173
    Averroistic mysticism, 162

memorizing, 131
music, 135
preceptors and tutors, 55, 126, 134, 136,
139, 186, 195, 199, 236
public, 135–137, 196
recreation, 134
ritual slaughtering, 130, 132
sport, 134
study of Torah, 131, 268
teaching to Christians, 174
writing, 130
Yeshivah (pl. Yeshivot), 126, 135–137,
197, 220, 274
Yeshivah (Paduan), 135, 143, 197, 267,
274
Yeshivot, heads of, 202, 268
Egidio da Viterbo, 173
Egypt, 40
Elia Levita, 137, 175, 190
Eliano, Vittorio, 118
Elijah (prophet), chair of, 252–253
Elijah ben Asher Halevi. See Elia Levita
Emancipation, 6, 212
Emancipation of children. See Fathers and
children
Emanuel Philibert, 61
England, 119
Epistolography. See Literary production
Erasmus of Rotterdam, 173
Estates, 83
Este, 71, 263
house of, 10, 11
Excommunication, 24, 58, 141, 199–200,
203–204, 208, 210, 212, 260
Expulsion and expulsions, 20, 22, 24, 26,
49, 56, 57, 59, 60, 63, 71–73, 84

Fair, 54
Family, 255–264
names, 256
Fano, da (family), 260
Fano, Menahem Azariah da, 140, 171, 184,
231, 257, 278
Farissol, Abraham, 165, 250
Fashion, 104–105, 111, 120, 243

Fathers and children, emancipation of, 255,
257
authority, 255–257
Fathers of the church, 175
Feltre, 20
Ferdinand (king of Naples), 56
Ferrara, 10, 56, 63, 71, 74, 75, 77, 188, 201,
207 -208, 229, 235, 262, 276, 282
Festivities. See Religion (ritual)
Ficino, Marsilio, 4, 161, 168, 183
Finale (Emilia), 72
Finzi, Abraham Raphael, 210
Fiscal exemptions. See Privileges
Flavius Mithridates, 174
Florence, 5, 11, 21, 25, 26, 31, 51–52, 56,
57, 71, 77, 164, 169, 174, 176, 181–
185, 188
myth of, 180
Foligno, 22, 23
Food and eating habits, 245–246
Forli, 108, 188, 262
Fortunato da Perugia, 24
Foscarini, Sebastian, 41
Foucault, Michel, 72, 159, 228
France, 39, 119
Franceschini, Alessandro, 118
Francesco da Bologna, 52
Francesco II (duke of Milan), 206
Frederick II (emperor), 8, 80
French Revolution, 72
Friars and anti-Jewish preaching, 21–29,
32–33, 49, 52, 91, 93
Augustinians, 47–48
Dominicans, 47
Franciscans, 23, 29, 33, 47–48, 50, 52,
106
Funerals. See Death

Gambling, 67, 115, 234
Games and pastimes, 6
General assemblies. See Communities
Genoa, 11, 21, 56
Geographical discoveries, 229
Gersonides, 149, 183–184

Designer:	Seventeenth Street Studios
Compositor:	Wilsted & Taylor
Text:	12.5/16 Centaur
Display:	Centaur and Arrighi
Printer:	Edwards Brothers, Inc.
Binder:	Edwards Brothers, Inc.